400 Affordable

P9-CAL-950

HOME PLANS

TABLE OF CONTENTS

CRE🏠TIVE
HOMEOWNER®

COPYRIGHT © 2002
CREATIVE HOMEOWNER®
A Division of Federal Marketing Corp.
Upper Saddle River, NJ

Library of Congress
Catalogue Card No.: 98-85180
ISBN: 1-58011-022-3

Creative Homeowner
A Division of
Federal Marketing Corp.
24 Park Way,
Upper Saddle River, NJ 07458

Manufactured in the
United States of America

Current Printing (last digit)
10 9 8 7 6 5 4 3

Cover Photography by
John Ehrenclou

Graceful Arches

Photography by John Ehrenclou

A tiled threshold provides a distinctive entrance into this spacious home. There's room for gracious living everywhere, from the comfortable living room with a wood-burning fireplace and tiled hearth, to the elegant dining room with a vaulted-ceiling, to the outside deck. Plan your meals in a kitchen that has all the right ingredients: a central work island, pantry, planning desk, and breakfast area. A decorative ceiling will delight your eye in the master suite, which includes a full bath and bow window. The photographed home may have been modified to suit individual tastes.

plan info

Main Floor	1,850 sq. ft.
Basement	1,850 sq. ft.
Garage	503 sq. ft.
Bedrooms	Three
Baths	2(full)
Foundation	Basement

Escape after a long hard day in your whirlpool bathtub.

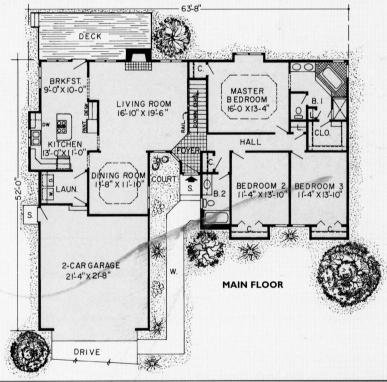

63'-8"

DECK

BRKFST.
9'-0" X 10'-0"

LIVING ROOM
16'-10" X 19'-6"

C.

MASTER
BEDROOM
16'-0 X 13'-4"

B.1

CLO.

DW

PANT. DESK

KITCHEN
13'-0" X 11'-0"

DOWN 15 RISE.

RAIL

HALL

52'-0"

LAUN.

W D

DINING ROOM
11'-8" X 11'-10"

COURT.

FOYER

S.

C.

B.2

BEDROOM 2
11'-4" X 13'-10"

BEDROOM 3
11'-4" X 13'-10"

S.

C.

C.

2-CAR GARAGE
21'-4" X 21'-8"

W.

MAIN FLOOR

DRIVE

The essence of this unique elevation is captured by the bedroom window design.

2 6 7 4 0

total living area: **1,512 sq. ft.**

Ranch Design

Photography supplied by The Garlinghouse Company

S loping cathedral ceilings are found throughout the entirety of this home. A kitchen holds the central spot in the floor plan. It is partially open to a Great hall room with a firebox and deck access on one side. The daylight room is lit by ceiling glass and full length windows on the other side. The daylight room leads out onto a unique double deck. Bedrooms lie to the outside of the plan. Two smaller bedrooms at the rear share a full bath. The more secluded master bedroom at the front has its own full bath and access to a private deck. The photographed home may have been modified to suit individual tastes.

plan info

Main Floor	1,512 sq. ft.
Garage	478 sq. ft.
Bedrooms	Three
Baths	2(full)
Foundation	Basement or Crawlspace

The daylight room is an ideal place to spend quality time with the family as you look out into your spacious backyard.

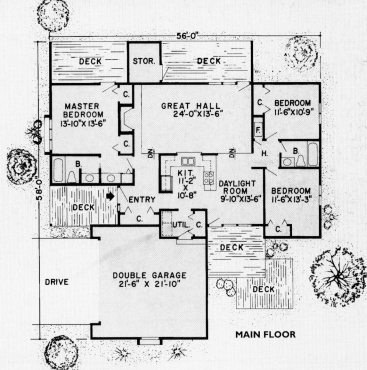

MAIN FLOOR

Wrap around counter makes plenty of counter space for food preparation.

plan no. **price code** C   total living area: **1,778** sq. ft.

1 0 3 9 4

Master Suite Crowns Plan

Photography by John Ehrenclou

The master bedroom suite occupies the entire second level of this passive solar design. The living room rises two stories in the front, as does the foyer, and can be opened to the master suite to aid in air circulation. Skylights in the sloping ceilings of the kitchen and master bath give abundant light to these areas. Angled walls, both inside and out, lend a unique appeal. An air-lock entry, 2x6 exterior studs, 6-inch concrete floor, and generous use of insulation help make this an energy efficient design.

plan info

First Floor	1,306 sq. ft.
Second Floor	472 sq. ft.
Garage	576 sq. ft.
Bedrooms	Three
Baths	2(full)
Foundation	Basement, Slab or Crawlspace

Sunlight beams down on the living room from windows up above.

FIRST FLOOR

68'-0"

UP

PATIO

DECK

BRM.

UTIL.

HW

S.

C.

BEDROOM
12'-10"X11'-4"

D. W.

F

S.

B.

DOUBLE GARAGE
23'-8" X 23'-4"

P.

S.

KITCHEN
11'-6" X
11'-8"

PLANTER

HALL

C.

L

C.

34'-10"

DINING ROOM
11'-6"X10'-0"

AIR-LOCK ENTRY

LIVING ROOM
13'-0"X20'-3"

BEDROOM
11'-6"X13'-0"

DRIVEWAY

W.

PORCH

WOOD STOVE

FIRST FLOOR

SECOND FLOOR

20'-2"

DOWN

L

B.

DRESSING AREA

C.

C.

32'-10"

SITTING AREA

MASTER
BEDROOM SUITE
19'-2"X15'-7"

OPEN TO ENTRY

OPEN TO LIVING ROOM

SECOND FLOOR

Spacious kitchen opens to the dining room and adds luminosity to area. Plenty of counter space for preparing dinner for family or friends.

26112

Contemporary Design

Photography by Beth Singer

Wood adds its warmth to the contemporary features of this solar design. Generous use of Southern glass doors and windows, an air-lock entry, skylights and a living room fireplace reduce energy needs. R-26 insulation is used for floors and sloping ceilings. Decking rims the front of the home and gives access through sliding glass doors to a bedroom/den area and living room. The dining room lies up several steps from the living room and is separated from it by a half-wall. The dining room flows into the kitchen through an eating bar. A second floor landing balcony overlooks the living room. Two bedrooms, one with its own private deck, and a full bath, finish the second level. The photographed home may have been modified to suit individual tastes.

plan info

First Floor	911 sq. ft.
Second Floor	576 sq. ft.
Basement	911 sq. ft.
Bedrooms	Three
Baths	1(full), 1(half)
Foundation	Basement

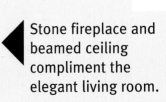

Stone fireplace and beamed ceiling compliment the elegant living room.

FIRST FLOOR

Vest.

Entry

Kitchen

Cl

Lav.

up

Bedroom/Den
12'-0"x12'-0"

Dining
13'-0"x10'-0"

dn

34'

Deck

Living
20'-0"x16'-0"

Deck

32'

SECOND FLOOR

Cl

Bath

Cl   Cl

Bedroom
12'-0"x12'-0"

Bedroom
13'-0"x14'-0"

dn

Balcony

Deck

Open to Living

Skylights

32'

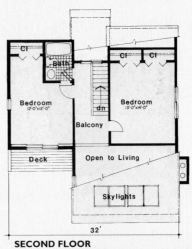

The back deck, which gives access to the back yard is perfect for entertaining guests or relaxing on the weekends.

2099

One-Floor Living

Photography by John Ehrenclou

Y ou'll find an appealing quality of open space in every room of this unique one-level home. Angular windows and recessed ceilings separate the two dining rooms from the adjoining island kitchen without compromising the airy feeling. A window-wall flanks the fireplace in the soaring, skylit living room uniting the interior spaces with the outdoor deck. The sunny atmosphere continues in the master suite, with its bump-out window and double-vanity bath, and in the two bedrooms off the foyer. The photographed home may have been modified to suit individual tastes.

plan info

First Floor	2,020 sq. ft.
Basement	2,020 sq. ft.
Garage	534 sq. ft.
Bedrooms	**Three**
Baths	**2(full), 1(half)**
Foundation	**Basement**

Kitchen adjacent to the breakfast room for early morning convenience.

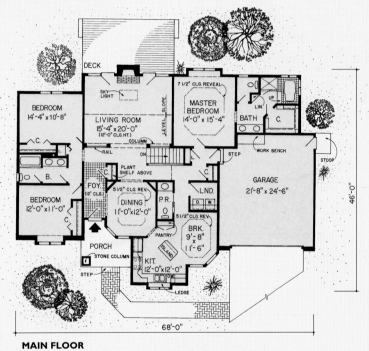

MAIN FLOOR

68'-0"

46'-0"

DECK

SKY LIGHT

BEDROOM
14'-4" x 10'-8"

LIVING ROOM
15'-4" x 20'-0"
(12'-0" CLG.HT.)

7 1/2" CLG. REVEAL

MASTER BEDROOM
14'-0" x 15'-4"

BATH

LIN.

UP

C.

COLUMN

RAIL

C.

B.

FOY.
(12' CLG.)

PLANT SHELF ABOVE

5 1/2" CLG. REV.

C.

DN

STEP

WORK BENCH

STOOP

GARAGE
21'-8" x 24'-6"

BEDROOM
12'-0" x 11'-0"

DINING
11'-0"x12'-0"

P.R.

L.ND.

D. W.

C.

PANTRY

BRK.
9'-8"
x
11'-6"

5 1/2" CLG. REV.

PORCH

STONE COLUMN

ISLAND

KIT.
12'-0"x12'-0"

STEP

LEDGE

Ceiling fans and lighting add to the look of the living room.

plan no. **price code** **C** **total living area: 1,898 sq. ft.**

92647

Warm and Inviting

Photography by Donna & Rob Kolb
Exposures Unlimited

The stone and siding exterior with a covered porch and a boxed window combine to create a warm and an inviting home. Family activities will center around the sunken Great room, a wood-burning fireplace and an entertainment center, and can be easily expanded to the outdoors. A pass through is featured at the kitchen sink and an expanded counter space is handy for serving quick meals. Steps away is the dining room which adds formality to those special occasions. Split stairs trimmed with wood rails lead to the second floor. A master suite, featuring an ultra bath and a sloped ceiling, and two additional bedrooms are included on the second floor. No materials list is available for this plan. The photographed home may have been modified to suit individual tastes.

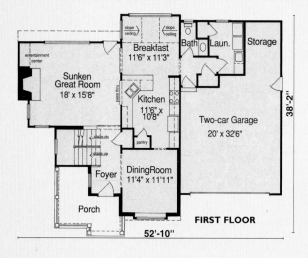

FIRST FLOOR

entertainment center

Sunken Great Room 18' x 15'8"

Breakfast 11'6" x 11'3"

Bath Laun. Storage

Kitchen 11'6" x 10'8"

Two-car Garage 20' x 32'6"

pantry

Foyer

DiningRoom 11'4" x 11'11"

Porch

52'-10"

38'-2"

SECOND FLOOR

Bath

walk-in closet

Master Bedroom 18' x 12'

Bedroom 11'6" x 10'8"

Hall

Bath

Bonus Room 20' x 12'

Bedroom 11'6"x 10'10"

plan info

First Floor	**1,065 sq. ft.**
Second Floor	**833 sq. ft.**
Bonus	**254 sq. ft.**
Basement	**995 sq. ft.**
Garage	**652 sq. ft.**
Bedrooms	**Three**
Baths	**2(full), 1(half)**
Foundation	**Basement**

C price code

plan no.

9 4 9 0 2

Inviting Covered Porch

Photography by Rob Lowe

From the welcoming covered porch into the tiled entry this home attracts attention. There are an abundance of windows naturally illuminating the home. Ten foot ceilings top the Great room which is further accented by a handsome fireplace. A work island/snack bar, pantry, and desk enhance the spacious kitchen/dinette area. A beautiful arched window under a volume ceiling adds elegance to bedroom two. The pampering features of the master suite are the dressing area with a double vanity, comparmented stall and shower, plus a whirlpool under a window. The secondary bedrooms have easy access to the full hall bath. The photographed home may have been modified to suit individual tastes. Alternate foundation options available at an additional charge. Please call 1.800.235.5700 for more information.

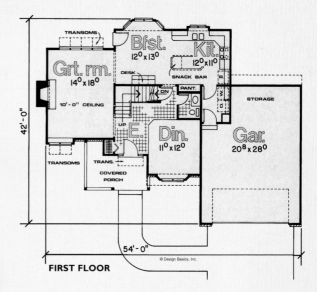

FIRST FLOOR

© Design Basics, Inc.

plan info

First Floor	944 sq. ft.
Second Floor	987 sq. ft.
Basement	944 sq. ft.
Garage	557 sq. ft.
Bedrooms	Four
Baths	2(full), 1(half)
Foundation	Basement

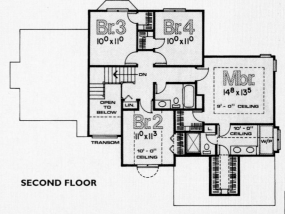

SECOND FLOOR

plan no.

9
9
4
3
1

price code E

total living area: 2,277 sq. ft.

Striking First Impression

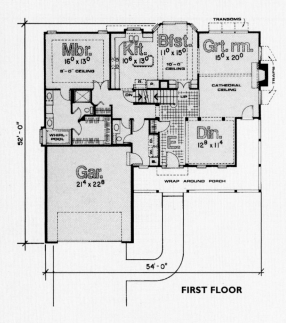

FIRST FLOOR

52' - 0"

54' - 0"

Mbr. 16⁰ x 13⁰ 8'-0" CEILING

Kit. 10⁶ x 13⁰

Bfst. 11⁰ x 15⁰ 10'-0" CEILING

Grt. rm. 15⁰ x 20⁰

TRANSOMS

CATHEDRAL CEILING

WHIRL-POOL

Din. 12⁸ x 11⁴

Gar. 21⁴ x 22⁸

WRAP AROUND PORCH

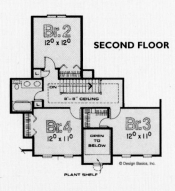

SECOND FLOOR

Br. 2 12⁰ x 12⁰

8'-8" CEILING

Br. 4 12⁰ x 11⁰

Br. 3 12⁰ x 11⁰

OPEN TO BELOW

PLANT SHELF

© Design Basics, Inc.

The wrap-around covered porch and windows of this elevation combine to create a striking appearance, sure to attract attention from the curb. The entry offers a tremendous open view of the dining and Great room. The fireplace centers on the cathedral ceiling which soars to over sixteen feet high in the Great room. The French doors to the dinette add a formal touch to the area. The kitchen features such amenities as a lazy Susan, a large food preparation island, and an ample pantry. Double doors access the master bedroom which is further enhanced by a decorative boxed ceiling. The master bath has a large whirlpool, a separate shower, a makeup vanity, and a walk-in closet. A walk-in closet is also featured in the third bedroom. Alternate foundation options available at an additional charge. Please call 1.800.235.5700 for more information. The photographed home may have been modified to suit individual tastes.

plan info

First Floor	**1,570 sq. ft.**
Second Floor	**707 sq. ft.**
Basement	**1,570 sq. ft.**
Garage	**504 sq. ft.**
Bedrooms	**Four**
Baths	**2(full), 1(half)**
Foundation	**Basement**

total living area: 2,031 sq. ft.

D price code   plan no.

Friendly Colonial

Photography Supplied by Homes for Living

Casual living is the theme of this elegant Farmhouse Colonial. A beautiful circular stair ascends from the central foyer, flanked by the formal living and dining rooms. The informal family room, accessible from the foyer, captures the Early American style with exposed beams, wood paneling, and a brick fireplace wall. A separate dinette opens to an efficient kitchen. Four bedrooms and a two-basin family bath, arranged around the central hall, occupy the second floor. The photographed home may have been modified to suit individual tastes.

plan info

First Floor	**1,099 sq. ft.**
Second Floor	**932 sq. ft.**
Basement	**1,023 sq. ft.**
Garage	**476 sq. ft.**
Bedrooms	**Four**
Baths	**2(full), 1(half)**
Foundation	**Basement**

56' - 8"

PATIO

service entry

sl. gl. dr.   cl.

exposed beams

DINETTE
10' x 8'

cook-top   s   dw ov   closet   d.

FAMILY RM
16' x 11'-4"

KITCHEN
11'-4" x 10'

dn.   MUD RM   w.   STORAGE

ref.

heat-circulating fireplace

LAV.

34' - 2"

dn.

railing
open
abv.

DINING RM
14' x 11'

TWO CAR GARAGE
20' x 20'

LIVING RM
19'-6" x 12'-8"

up

cl.   FOYER

cl.

PORCH

FIRST FLOOR

SECOND FLOOR

2x6 studs for added insulation

BED RM
11'-4" x 10'-4"   cl.

BED RM
12'-8" x 11'-4"

W.I.C.   BATH

cl.

railing   H.   planter

dn.

lin.

MASTER BED RM
16' x 11'

BED RM
12'-8" x 10'-8"

railing
open

BATH

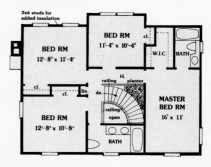

plan no. price code **B**   total living area: **1,683** sq. ft.

93298

Inviting Front Porch

Photography by John Ehrenclou

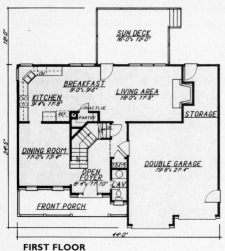

FIRST FLOOR

Tⁱhis home's inviting front porch and detailed gables create an impressive facade. The open foyer features an angled staircase, a half bath, and a coat closet. The informal family living area is to the rear of the home. The efficient kitchen opens to the breakfast area which flows into the expansive living area. A fireplace and access to the rear deck highlight the living area. The formal dining room has direct access to the kitchen. The second floor includes a master bedroom with a large walk-in closet and a compartmented master bath. The secondary bedrooms share a compartmented, double vanity bath. There is a convenient second floor laundry center. The photographed home may have been modified to suit individual tastes.

SECOND FLOOR

plan info

First Floor	797 sq. ft.
Second Floor	886 sq. ft.
Basement	797 sq. ft.
Garage	414 sq. ft.
Bedrooms	Three
Baths	2(full), 1(half)
Foundation	Basement,Slab or Crawlspace

total living area: 1,583 sq. ft.

B price code

Traditional Victorian

Photography by John Ehrenclou

This convenient, one-level plan is perfect for the modern family with a taste for classic design. Traditional Victorian touches in this three-bedroom beauty include a romantic, railed porch and an intriguing breakfast tower just off the kitchen. You will love the step-saving arrangement of the kitchen between the breakfast and formal dining rooms. Enjoy the wide-open living room with sliders out to a rear deck, and the handsome master suite with its skylit, compartmentalized bath. Notice the convenient laundry location in the bedroom hall. The photographed home may have been modified to suit individual tastes.

MAIN FLOOR

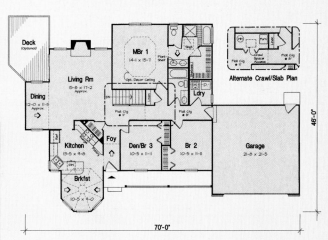

plan info

Main Area	**1,583 sq. ft.**
Basement	**1573 sq. ft.**
Garage	**484 sq. ft.**
Bedrooms	**Three**
Baths	**2(full)**
Foundation	**Basement, Slab or Crawlspace**

99840

Beauty all Around

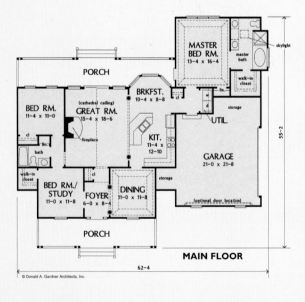

PORCH

BED RM.
11-4 x 11-0

GREAT RM.
(cathedral ceiling)
15-4 x 18-6

fireplace

BRKFST.
10-4 x 8-8

KIT.
11-4 x
12-10

MASTER
BED RM.
13-4 x 16-4

master
bath

skylight

walk-in
closet

UTIL.

storage

GARAGE
21-0 x 21-8

bath

walk-in
closet

BED RM./
STUDY
11-0 x 11-8

FOYER
6-0 x 8-4

DINING
11-0 x 11-8

storage

(optional door location)

PORCH

MAIN FLOOR

62-4

55-2

© Donald A. Gardner Architects, Inc.

This country home is as beautiful from the back as it is from the front. Porches front and back, gables, and dormers provide special charm. The central Great room has a cathedral ceiling, fireplace, and a clerestory window which brings in lots of natural light. Columns divide the open Great room from the kitchen and breakfast bay. A tray ceiling and columns dress up the formal dining room. The master suite with tray ceiling and back porch access is privately-located in the rear. The skylit master bath features a whirlpool tub, a shower, dual vanity, and a spacious walk-in closet. The front bedroom with walk-in closet doubles as a study. A garage with ample storage completes the plan. Alternate foundation options available at an additional charge. Please call 1.800.235.5700 for more information. The photographed home may have been modified to suit individual tastes.

plan info

Main Floor	1,632 sq. ft.
Garage/storage	561 sq. ft.
Bedrooms	Three
Baths	2(full)
Foundation	Crawlspace

total living area: 1,685 sq. ft.   Welcoming Entry

B price code

plan no. 94924

The entry of this home views the formal dining room, accented with boxed window, and the Great room beyond. The open kitchen/dinette area features a pantry, desk, and a snack bar counter. The elegant master suite includes a formal ceiling detail and a window seat. A skylight above the whirlpool tub provides natural illumination. Alternate foundation options available at an additional charge. Please call 1.800.235.5700 for more information.

FIRST FLOOR

SECOND FLOOR

© Design Basics, Inc.

plan info	
First Flr.	1,297 sq. ft.
Second Flr.	388 sq. ft.
Basement	1,297 sq. ft.
Garage	466 sq. ft.
Bedrooms	Three
Baths	2(full), 1(half)
Foundation	Basement

---

total living area: 2,388 sq. ft.   Double Gables

E price code

plan no. 92692

Split stairs decorated with rich wood rails lead to the second floor. The master bedroom suite pampers the homeowner with its spaciousness, dual vanity, whirlpool tub and shower stall. Family activities will center around the kitchen/breakfast bay and family room with fireplace.

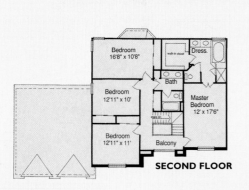

SECOND FLOOR

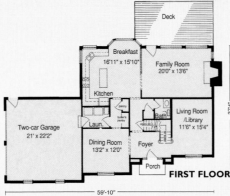

FIRST FLOOR

plan info	
First Flr.	1,207 sq. ft.
Second Flr.	1,181 sq. ft.
Basement	1,207 sq. ft.
Garage	484 sq. ft.
Bedrooms	Four
Baths	2(full), 1(half)
Foundation	Basement

price code **A**

total living area: **1,307 sq. ft.**

Detailed Charmer

Photography by John Ehrenclou

W alk past the charming front porch, in through the foyer and you'll be struck by the exciting, spacious living room. Complete with high sloping ceilings and a beautiful fireplace flanked by large windows. The large master bedroom shows off a full wall of closet space, its own private bath, and an extraordinary decorative ceiling. Just down the hall are two more bedrooms and another full bath. Take advantage of the accessibility off the foyer and turn one of these rooms into a private den or office space. The dining room provides a feast for your eyes with its decorative ceiling details, and a full slider out to the deck. Along with great counter space, the kitchen includes a double sink, and an attractive bump-out window. The adjacent laundry room, optional expanded pantry, and a two-car garage make this Ranch a charmer. The photographed home may have been modified to suit individual tastes.

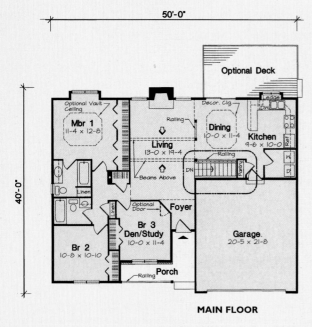

MAIN FLOOR

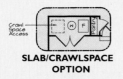

SLAB/CRAWLSPACE OPTION

plan info

Main Floor	**1,307 sq. ft.**
Basement	**1,298 sq. ft.**
Garage	**462 sq. ft.**
Bedrooms	**Three**
Baths	**2(full)**
Foundation	**Basement, Slab or Crawlspace**

total living area: 1,312 sq. ft.

 **A** price code

Extra Touch of Style

Y ou don't have to sacrifice style when buying a smaller home. Notice the palladian window with a fan light above at the front of the home. The entrance porch includes a turned post entry. Once inside, the living room is topped by an impressive vaulted ceiling. A fireplace accents the room. A decorative ceiling enhances both the master bedroom and the dining room. Efficiently designed, the kitchen includes a peninsula counter and serves the dining room with ease. A private bath and double closet highlight the master suite. Two additional bedrooms are served by a full hall bath.

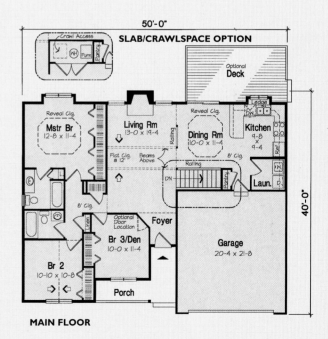

MAIN FLOOR

plan info

First Floor	**1,312 sq. ft.**
Basement	**1,293 sq. ft.**
Garage	**459 sq. ft.**
Bedrooms	**Three**
Baths	**2(full)**
Foundation	**Basement, Slab or Crawlspace**

Multiple Gables

An enchanting one level home with grand openings between rooms creates a spacious effect. The functional kitchen provides an abundance of counter space. Additional room for quick meals or serving an oversized crowd is provided at the breakfast bar. Double hung windows and angles add light and dimension to the dining area. The bright and cheery Great room with a sloped ceiling and a wood burning fireplace opens to the dining area and the foyer, making this three bedroom ranch look and feel much larger than its actual size.

MAIN FLOOR

Porch

Dining Area 11'6" x 14'2"

Kitchen 18' x 10'10"

Great Room 16'6" x 17'

Master Bedroom 14' x 11'9"

Bath

Two-car Garage 20' x 22'

Laun.

Foyer

Bath

Hall

Bath

Porch

Bedroom 10'6" x 10'6"

Bedroom 11' x 10'6"

60'

47'

plan info

Main Floor	1,508 sq. ft.
Basement	1,439 sq. ft.
Garage	440 sq. ft.
Bedrooms	Three
Baths	2(full)
Foundation	Basement

total living area: 2,101 sq. ft.

D price code

plan no.

92610

Luxury Plan

A n octagonal master bedroom with a vaulted ceiling, a sunken Great room with a balcony above, and an exterior with an exciting roof line provide this home with all the luxurious ammenities in a moderate size. The first floor master bedroom targets this home for the empty-nester market. The elegant exterior has a rich solid look that is very important to the discriminating buyer. The kitchen features a center island and a breakfast nook. The sunken Great room has a cozy fireplace. Elegant and luxurious in a moderate size, this home has what your looking for.

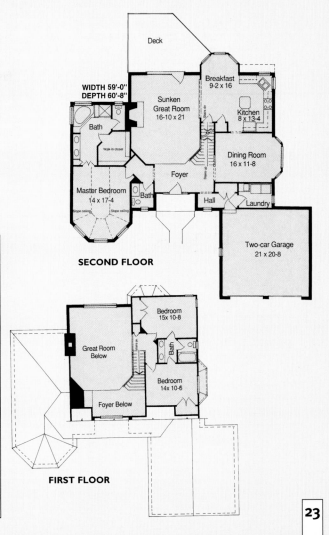

WIDTH 59'-0"
DEPTH 60'-8"

SECOND FLOOR

FIRST FLOOR

plan info

First Floor	**1,626 sq. ft.**
Second Floor	**475 sq. ft.**
Basement	**1,512 sq. ft.**
Garage	**438 sq. ft.**
Bedrooms	**Three**
Baths	**2(full), 1(half)**
Foundation	**Basement**

Perfect Compact Ranch

T his Ranch home features a large sunken Great room, centralized with a cozy fireplace. The master bedroom has an unforgettable bathroom with a super skylight. The huge three-car plus garage can include a work area for the family carpenter. In the center of this home, a kitchen includes an eating nook for family gatherings. The porch at the rear of the house has easy access from the dining room. One other bedroom and a den, which can easily be converted to a bedroom, are on the opposite side of the house from the master bedroom.

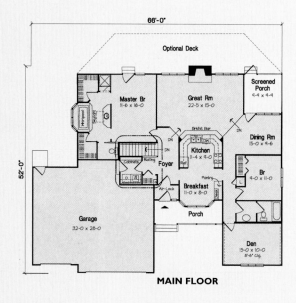

MAIN FLOOR

CRAWLSPACE/SLAB OPTION

plan info

First Floor	1,738 sq. ft.
Basement	1,083 sq. ft.
Garage	796 sq. ft.
Bedrooms	Two
Baths	2(full)
Foundation	Basement, Slab or Crawlspace

A price code

Neat and Tidy

This compact house has plenty of closets and storage areas where you can stow away the gear you usually need on vacation. The utility room is also larger than most, and opens directly outside, so there's no reason for anyone to track in snow or mud. Sliding glass doors lead from the two-story living room and dining room out to a paved patio. Tucked into a corner, the kitchen is both out of the way and convenient. A handsome stone fireplace adds a functional and a decorative element to both the interior and the exterior of the home. A downstairs bedroom will sleep either children or guests. Beyond the railed loft, a master suite with a full bath and a walk-in closet provides the owner of this home with every comfort. This plan is available with a basement or crawl-space foundation. Please specify when ordering.

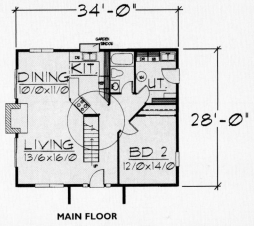

MAIN FLOOR

plan info

Main Floor	952 sq. ft.
Upper Floor	297 sq. ft.
Bedrooms	Two
Baths	2(full)
Foundation	Basement or Crawlspace

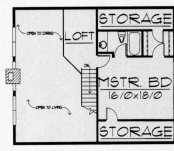

UPPER FLOOR

OPTIONAL BASEMENT PLAN

2 0 1 6 4

Easy Living

Here's a pretty, one-level home designed for carefree living. The central foyer divides active and quiet areas. Step back to a fireplaced living room with dramatic, towering ceilings and a panoramic view of the backyard. The adjoining dining room features a sloping ceiling crowned by a plant shelf, and sliders to an outdoor deck. Just across the counter, a handy, U-shaped kitchen features abundant cabinets, a window over the sink overlooking the deck, and a walk-in pantry. You'll find three bedrooms tucked off the foyer. Front bedrooms share a handy full bath, but the master suite boasts its own private bath with both shower and tub, a room-sized walk-in closet, and a bump-out window that adds light and space.

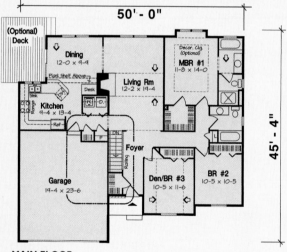

MAIN FLOOR

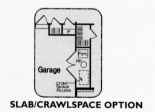

SLAB/CRAWLSPACE OPTION

plan info

Main Floor	1,456 sq. ft.
Basement	1,448 sq. ft.
Garage	452 sq. ft.
Bedrooms	Three
Baths	2(full)
Foundation	Basement, Slab or Crawlspace

total living area: 1,560 sq. ft.

B price code

plan no.

34602

Cozy Country Trimmings

A wrap-around porch and dormer windows lend an old-fashioned country feeling to this home. Yet inside, a floor plan designed for today's lifestyle unfolds. A Great room enhanced by a large hearth fireplace and a vaulted ceiling gives a cozy welcome to guests. It is separated by the breakfast bar from the kitchen/dining area. An island extends the work space in this efficiently laid out area. The dining area has direct access to the rear yard. The first floor master suite also includes a vaulted ceiling and is highlighted by a private, double vanity bath. Two additional bedrooms on the second floor share a full double vanity bath in the hall.

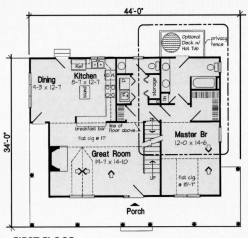

FIRST FLOOR

plan info

First Floor	1,061 sq. ft.
Second Floor	499 sq. ft.
Bedrooms	Three
Baths	2(full), 1(half)
Foundation	Basement, Slab or Crawlspace

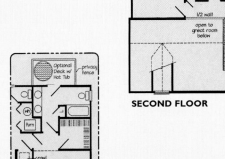

ALTERNATE FOUNDATION

SECOND FLOOR

plan no.

24701

price code **B**

total living area: **1,625 sq. ft.**

Single Level Convenience

This home features a well designed floor plan, offering convenience and style. The roomy living room includes a two-sided fireplace shared with the dining room. An efficient U-shaped kitchen, equipped with a peninsula counter/breakfast bar, is open to the dining room. An entrance from the garage into the kitchen eliminates tracked in dirt and affords step-saving convenience when unloading groceries. The private master suite includes a whirlpool tub, a double vanity, and a step-in shower. A large walk-in closet adds ample storage space to the suite. The secondary bedroom and the den/guest room share use of the full hall bath.

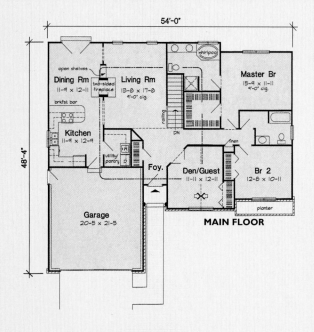

MAIN FLOOR

ALTERNATE FOUNDATION

plan info

Main Floor	**1,625 sq. ft.**
Basement	**1,625 sq. ft.**
Garage	**455 sq. ft.**
Bedrooms	**Three**
Baths	**2(full)**
Foundation	**Basement, Slab, or Crawlspace**

total living area: 1,452 sq. ft.
Country Charmer

E price code

plan no. 96418

This compact three bedroom country charmer doesn't scrimp on details with its open, contemporary interior punctuated by elegant columns. Dormers above the covered porch light the foyer which leads to the dramatic Great room with cathedral ceiling and fireplace. Tray ceilings add interest to the bedroom/study, dining room, and master bedroom. The luxurious master suite features a walk-in closet and a bath with double vanity, separate shower, and whirlpool tub. Alternate foundation options available at an additional charge. Please call 1.800.235.5700 for more information.

MAIN FLOOR

© Donald A. Gardner Architects, Inc.

plan info	
Main Flr.	1,452 sq. ft.
Garage/storage	427 sq. ft.
Bedrooms	Three
Baths	2(full)
Foundation	Crawlspace

total living area: 1,688 sq. ft.
Sloped-Ceiling

B price code

plan no. 10548

The fireplace and sloped-ceiling in the family room offer something a bit out of the ordinary in this small home. The master bedroom is complete with a full bath and a dressing area. A bump-out bay window is shown in the spacious breakfast room, and a bay window with a window seat has been designed in the master bedroom. The screened porch off of the breakfast room is an inviting feature for meals outside.

MAIN FLOOR

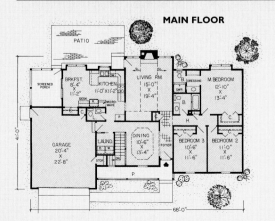

plan info	
Main Flr.	1,688 sq. ft.
Basement	1,688 sq. ft.
Screened Porch	120 sq. ft.
Garage	489 sq. ft.
Bedrooms	Three
Baths	2(full), 1(half)
Foundation	Basement

Dramatic Ranch

The exterior of this ranch home is all wood with interesting lines. More than an ordinary ranch home, it has an expansive feeling to drive up to. The large living area has a stone fireplace and decorative beams. The kitchen and dining room lead to an outside deck. The laundry room has a large pantry, and is off the eating area. The master bedroom has a wonderful bathroom with a huge walk-in closet. In the front of the house, there are two additional bedrooms with a bathroom. This house offers one floor living and has nice big rooms.

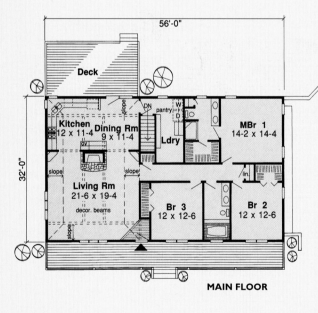

MAIN FLOOR

plan info

Main Floor	1,792 sq. ft.
Basement	818 sq. ft.
Garage	857 sq. ft.
Bedrooms	Three
Baths	2(full)
Foundation	Basement

total living area: 1,386 sq. ft.

Sunny Dormer

 E price code

plan no. 99812

© Donald A. Gardner Architects, Inc.

DECK

DINING 9-10 x 11-0 (cathedral ceiling)

GREAT RM. 15-10 x 16-10 (cathedral ceiling)

fireplace

MASTER BED RM. 12-4 x 13-6 (cathedral ceiling)

walk-in closet

master bath

KIT. 9-10 x 11-8

FOYER 9-6 x 5-6

bath

storage

up

PORCH

BED RM. 11-0 x 11-0

BED RM. 11-0 x 11-0 (cathedral ceiling)

GARAGE 22-0 x 20-8

MAIN FLOOR

10-0

48-0

54-10

© Donald A. Gardner Architects, Inc.

down

skylights

attic storage

BONUS RM. 12-0 x 20-8 (cathedral ceiling)

BONUS

This cozy home is full of today's comforts yet cost-effective to construct. The open Great room, dining room, and kitchen feature a cathedral ceiling that emphasizes a sense of spaciousness. The front bedroom is expanded by a cathedral ceiling that shows off a double window with a curved top. The master suite is highlighted by a cathedral ceiling in the bedroom and includes a private bath. Alternate foundation options available at an additional charge. Please call 1.800.235.5700 for more information.

plan info

First Flr.	1,386 sq. ft.
Garage	517 sq. ft.
Bonus room	314 sq. ft.
Bedrooms	Three
Baths	2(full)
Foundation	Crawlspace

---

total living area: 1,372 sq. ft.

Open Floor Plan

E price code

plan no. 99830

© Donald A. Gardner Architects, Inc.

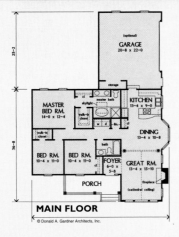

(optional) **GARAGE** 20-8 x 22-0

storage

skylight

master bath

MASTER BED RM. 14-0 x 12-4

walk-in closet

KITCHEN 13-4 x 9-0

DINING 13-4 x 10-8

walk-in closet

bath

BED RM. 10-4 x 11-0

BED RM. 10-4 x 11-0

FOYER 6-0 x 5-8

GREAT RM. 13-4 x 15-10 (cathedral ceiling)

fireplace

PORCH

MAIN FLOOR

25-2

36-8

© Donald A. Gardner Architects, Inc.

The Great room's cathedral ceiling, combined with the openness of the adjoining dining room and kitchen, create spaciousness beyond this plan's modest square footage. The dining room is enlarged by a bay window while a palladian window allows ample light into the Great room. The master suite features ample closet space and a skylit bath which boasts a dual vanity, and a separate tub and shower. Alternate foundation options available at an additional charge. Please call 1.800.235.5700 for more information.

plan info

Main Flr.	1,372 sq. ft.
Garage/storage	537 sq. ft.
Bedrooms	Three
Baths	2(full)
Foundation	Crawlspace

Casually Elegant

© Donald A. Gardner Architects, Inc.

This country classic offers a casually elegant exterior with arched windows, dormers, and charming front and back porches with columns. Inside, the open, casual mood is continued in the central Great room which features a cathedral ceiling, a fireplace, and a clerestory window that splashes the room with natural light. Other special touches include a breakfast bay and interior columns. The master suite with cathedral ceiling is privately located and features a skylit bath with a whirlpool tub, a shower, and a double vanity. Two additional bedrooms share a bath, and a garage with storage completes the plan. Alternate foundation options available at an additional charge. Please call 1.800.235.5700 for more information.

MASTER BED RM.
13-4 x 13-4
(cathedral ceiling)

master bath

PORCH

arched window above door

(cathedral ceiling)

BRKFST.
9-6 x 9-8

UTIL.

walk-in closet

lin.

stor.

BED RM.
11-4 x 10-0

GREAT RM.
15-4 x 17-8

fireplace

cl

lin.

bath

KITCHEN
11-8 x 11-2

GARAGE
20-0 x 20-4

51-6

BED RM.
11-4 x 11-8

FOYER
5-4 x 11-8

DINING
12-0 x 11-8

cl

MAIN FLOOR

PORCH

60-10

© Donald A. Gardner Architects, Inc.

plan info

Main Floor	1,561 sq. ft.
Garage & storage	346 sq. ft.
Bedrooms	**Three**
Baths	**2(full)**
Foundation	**Crawlspace**

© Donald A. Gardner Architects, Inc.

B. NATHAN

■ *Total living area 1,515 sq. ft.* ■ *Price Code F* ■

No. 99835

■ This plan features:

— Three bedrooms

— Two full baths

■ Working at the Kitchen island focuses your view to the Great Room with its vaulted ceiling and a fireplace

■ Clerestory dormers emanate light into the Great Room

■ Both the Dining Room and Master Suite are enhanced by tray ceilings

■ This home comes with a crawlspace foundation.

■ Alternate foundation options available at an additional charge. Please call 1.800.235.5700 for more information.

Main floor — 1,515 sq. ft.
Bonus — 288 sq. ft.
Garage — 476 sq. ft.

MAIN FLOOR

BONUS

Yesteryear Flavor

Total living area 2,356 sq. ft. ■ Price Code E

Workshop
14-5 x 14-5

CRAWLSPACE/SLAB OPTION

Br 4
11-1 x 9-7

Br 3
10-6 x 12-5

DN

OPTIONAL SECOND FLOOR

Family
Dining
8-10 x 14-1

Kit.
10-0
x
14-1

desk

OPTIONAL KITCHEN

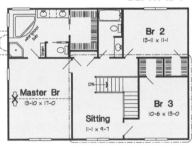

Master Br
13-10 x 17-0

Sitting
11-1 x 9-7

Br 2
13-11 x 11-1

Br 3
10-6 x 13-0

DN

WIDTH 68'-8.5"
DEPTH 42'-0"

SECOND FLOOR

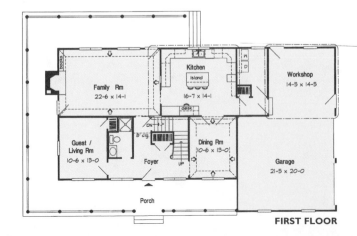

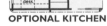

Family Rm
22-6 x 14-1

Kitchen
island
16-7 x 14-1

desk

DN

Workshop
14-5 x 14-5

Guest /
Living Rm
10-6 x 13-0

Foyer

Dining Rm
10-6 x 13-0

Garage
21-5 x 20-0

UP

Porch

FIRST FLOOR

No. 24404

■ This plan features:

— Three or four bedrooms

— Three full baths

■ Wrap-around Porch leads to Foyer
with a landing staircase

■ Formal Living Room doubles as a
Guest Room

■ Huge Family Room highlighted
by a decorative ceiling, cozy
fireplace, and book shelves

■ Country-size Kitchen with island
snackbar, built-in desk and nearby
Dining Room, Laundry/Workshop
and Garage access

■ Master Bedroom with a large
walk-in closet and a whirlpool tub

■ An optional basement, slab or
crawlspace foundation — please
specify when ordering.

First floor — 1,236 sq. ft.
Second floor — 1,120 sq. ft.

■ *Total living area 1,345 sq. ft.* ■ *Price Code A* ■

No. 91342

■ This plan features:

— Three bedrooms

— Two full baths

■ A handicapped Master Bath plan is available

■ Vaulted Great Room, Dining Room and Kitchen Areas

■ A Kitchen accented with angles and an abundance of cabinets for storage

■ A Master Bedroom with an ample sized wardrobe, large covered private Deck, and private Bath

■ An optional slab or crawlspace foundation — please specify when ordering.

Main floor — 1,345 sq. ft.

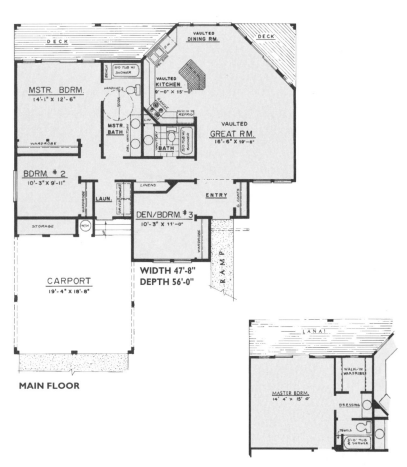

DECK

VAULTED DINING RM.

DECK

MSTR. BDRM.
14'-1" X 12'-6"

VAULTED KITCHEN
9'-0" X 15'-0"

MSTR. BATH

REFRIG.

VAULTED GREAT RM.
16'-6" X 19'-6"

BATH

BDRM. # 2
10'-3" X 9'-11"

LAUN.

LINENS

ENTRY

DEN/BDRM. # 3
10'-3" X 11'-0"

STORAGE

WIDTH 47'-8"
DEPTH 56'-0"

CARPORT
19'-4" X 18'-8"

RAMP

MAIN FLOOR

LANAI

WALK-IN WARDROBE

MASTER BDRM.
14' 4" X 15' 0"

DRESSING

TOWELS

ALTERNATE BATH

Your Classic Hideaway

■ *Total living area 1,773 sq. ft.* ■ *Price Code C* ■

No. 90423

■ **This plan features:**

— Three bedrooms

— Two full baths

■ A lovely fireplace in the Living Room which is both cozy and a source of heat for the core area

■ An efficient Country Kitchen, connecting the large Dining and Living Rooms

■ A lavish Master Suite enhanced by a step-up sunken tub, more than ample closet space, and separate shower

■ A screened Porch and Patio area for outdoor living

■ An optional basement, slab or crawlspace foundation — please specify when ordering.

Main floor — 1,773 sq. ft.
Screened porch — 240 sq. ft.

MAIN FLOOR

GARAGE
21-0x21-0

SCR. PORCH
12-0x20-4

PATIO
16-0x10-0

DINING
12-0x13-4

KITCHEN
10x13

UTILITY

BEDROOM
11-0x13-4

M. BATH

M. BEDROOM
12-0x18-0

LIVING ROOM
15-6x17-8

CLOSET

DRESSING

LINEN

BEDROOM
12-0x11-4

BATH

COATS

FOYER

PORCH
26-0x6-0

88'-8"

43'-8"

Bay Windows and a Terrific Front Porch

■ *Total living area 1,778 sq. ft.* ■ *Price Code B* ■

No. 93261

■ **This plan features:**

— Three bedrooms

— Two full baths

■ A Country front Porch

■ An expansive Living Area that includes a fireplace

■ A Master Suite with a private Master Bath and a walk-in closet, as well as a bay window view of the front yard

■ An efficient Kitchen that serves the sunny Breakfast Area and the Dining Room with equal ease

■ A built-in Pantry and a desk add to the conveniences in the Breakfast Area

■ Two additional Bedrooms that share the full hall Bath

■ This home comes with a basement foundation.

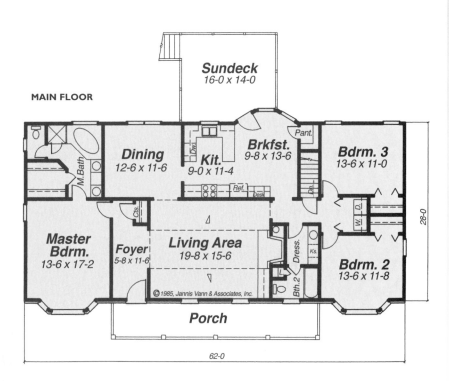

Main floor — 1,778 sq. ft.
Basement — 1,008 sq. ft.
Garage — 728 sq. ft.

Traditional Ranch has Many Modern Features

■ *Total living area 2,301 sq. ft.* ■ *Price Code E* ■

LOFT

MAIN FLOOR

No. 90444

■ **This plan features:**

— Three bedrooms

— Three full baths

■ A vaulted-ceiling Great Room with skylights and a fireplace

■ A double L-shaped Kitchen with an eating bar opening to a bayed Breakfast Room

■ A Master Suite with a walk-in closet, corner garden tub, separate vanities and a linen closet

■ Two additional Bedrooms each with a walk-in closet and built-in desk, sharing a full hall Bath

■ A loft that overlooks the Great Room which includes a vaulted ceiling and open rail balcony

■ An optional basement or crawlspace foundation — please specify when ordering.

Main floor — 1,996 sq. ft.
Loft — 305 sq. ft.

© Donald A. Gardner Architects, Inc.

B. NATHAN.

■ *Total living area 1,864 sq. ft.* ■ *Price Code F* ■

No. 96468

■ This plan features:

— Three bedrooms

— Two full baths

■ Sunlit Foyer flows easily into the generous Great Room

■ Great Room crowned in a cathedral ceiling and accented by a fireplace

■ Accent columns define the open Kitchen and Breakfast Bay

■ Master Bedroom topped by a tray ceiling and highlighted by a well-appointed Master Bath

■ This home comes with a crawlspace foundation.

■ Alternate foundation options available at an additional charge, call 1-800-235-5700 for more information.

Main floor—1,864 sq. ft.
Bonus room—319 sq. ft.
Garage—503 sq. ft.

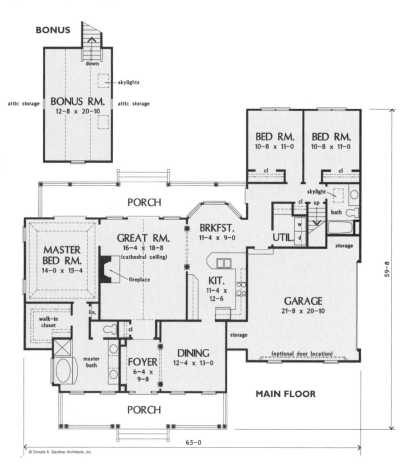

© Donald A. Gardner Architects, Inc.

Tandem Garage

Total living area 1,761 sq. ft. ■ *Price Code C* ■

WIDTH 67'-8'
DEPTH 42'-8"

MASTER BEDROOM
13'8"x16'4"

LIVING ROOM
15'6"x18'4"

NOOK
10'x11'9"

KITCHEN
10'6"x11'9"

11'x20'

FOYER

DINING ROOM
11'6"x12'4"

BEDROOM #2
12'4"x11'9"

BEDROOM #3
13'x10'9"

3 CAR GARAGE
22'x22'

MAIN FLOOR

No. 93133

■ **This plan features:**

— Three bedrooms

— Two full baths

■ Open Foyer leads into spacious Living highlighted by a wall of windows

■ Country-size Kitchen with efficient, U-shaped counter, work island, eating Nook with backyard access, and nearby Laundry/ Garage entry

■ French doors open to pampering Master Bedroom with window alcove, walk-in closet and double vanity Bath

■ This home comes with a basement foundation.

Main floor — 1,761 sq. ft.
Garage — 658 sq. ft.
Basement — 1,761 sq. ft.

■ *Total living area 2,022 sq. ft.* ■ *Price Code D* ■

No. 92629

■ **This plan features:**

— Four bedrooms

— Two full and one half bath

■ Corner fireplace and atrium door highlight Great Room

■ Hub Kitchen with walk-in Pantry and peninsula counter easily accesses glass Breakfast Bay, backyard, Great Room, Dining Room, Laundry and Garage

■ Master Bedroom wing crowned by tray ceiling offers plush Bath and walk-in closet

■ Three additional Bedrooms with decorative windows and large closets share a full Bath

■ This home comes with a basement foundation.

First floor — 1,401 sq. ft.
Second floor — 621 sq. ft.
Basement — 1,269 sq. ft.
Garage — 478 sq. ft.

European Style

■ *Total living area 2,727 sq. ft.* ■ *Price Code F* ■

No. 92501

■ **This plan features:**

— Four bedrooms

— Three full and one half baths

■ Central Foyer between spacious Living and Dining Rooms with arched windows

■ Hub Kitchen with extended counter and nearby Utility/Garage entry, easily serves Breakfast Area and Dining Room

■ Spacious Den with a hearth fireplace between built-ins and sliding glass doors to Porch

■ Master Bedroom wing with decorative ceiling, plush Bath with two walk-in closets

■ Three additional Bedrooms with ample closets and private access to a full Bath

■ An optional slab or crawlspace foundation — please specify when ordering.

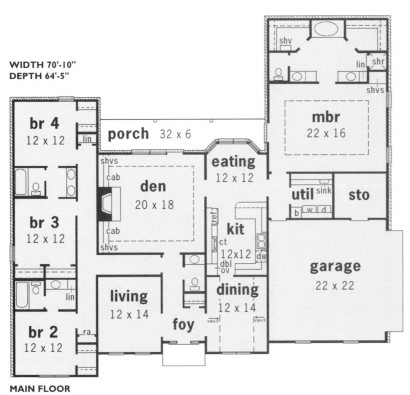

WIDTH 70'-10"
DEPTH 64'-5"

MAIN FLOOR

Main floor — 2,727 sq. ft.
Garage — 569 sq. ft.

© Donald A. Gardner Architects, Inc.

■ Total living area 1,977 sq. ft. ■ Price Code G ■

No. 99803

■ This plan features:

— Three bedrooms

— Two full baths

■ Private Master Bedroom has a walk-in closet and a skylit Bath

■ Two additional Bedrooms, one with a possible use as a Study, share a full Bath

■ From the Foyer columns lead into the Great Room with a cathedral ceiling and a fireplace

■ The Kitchen is conveniently located between the Dining Room and the skylit Breakfast Area

■ This home comes with a crawlspace foundation.

■ Alternate foundation options available at an additional charge. Please call 1.800.235.5700 for more information.

Main floor — 1,977 sq. ft.
Bonus room — 430 sq. ft.
Garage & storage — 610 sq. ft.

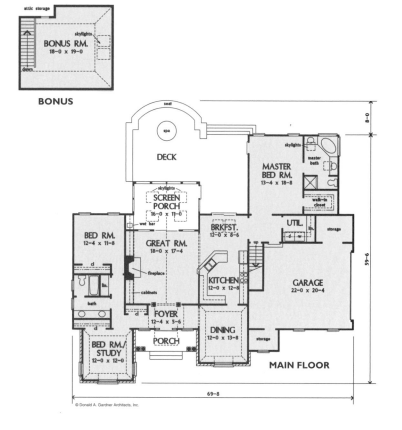

Classic Country Farmhouse

© Donald A. Gardner Architects, Inc.

Total living area 1,663 sq. ft. ■ *Price Code F* ■

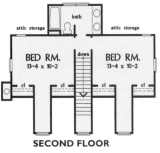

attic storage | bath | attic storage

BED RM.
13-4 x 10-2

down

BED RM.
13-4 x 10-2

cl | cl | cl | cl

SECOND FLOOR

First floor — 1,145 sq. ft.
Second floor — 518 sq. ft.
Bonus room — 380 sq. ft.
Garage & storage — 509 sq. ft.

No. 99800

■ **This plan features:**

— Three bedrooms

— Two full and one half baths

■ Covered Porch gives classic
Country farmhouse look, and
includes multiple dormers and a
Bonus Room

■ Large Great Room with fireplace
opens to the Dining/Breakfast/
Kitchen space, which leads to a
spacious Deck with optional spa

■ First floor Master Suite offers
privacy and luxury with a
separate shower, whirlpool tub
and a double vanity

■ This home comes with a
crawlspace foundation.

■ Alternate foundation options
available at an additional charge.
Please call 1.800.235.5700 for
more information.

attic storage

skylights

down

BONUS RM.
24-8 x 14-4

attic storage

BONUS

seat

spa

DECK

storage

GARAGE
21-0 x 21-8

up

BRKFST.
10-10 x 7-6

DINING
12-4 x 11-6

KITCHEN
13-2 x 8-2

pd.
rm.

d
w

UTIL

walk-in
closet

master
bath

GREAT RM.
13-4 x 19-4

fireplace

up

MASTER
BED RM.
13-4 X 13-0

PORCH

56-6

59-4

© Donald A. Gardner Architects, Inc.

FIRST FLOOR

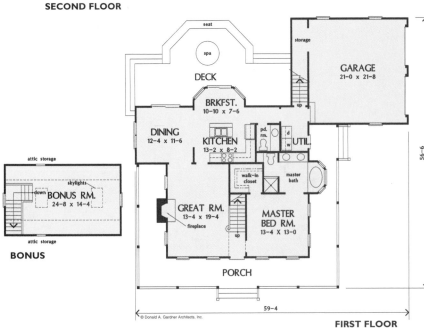

© Donald A. Gardner Architects, Inc.

■ *Total living area 2,301 sq. ft.* ■ *Price Code G* ■

No. 96404

■ This plan features:

— Three bedrooms

— Two full and one half baths

■ Two-story Foyer with palladian, clerestory window and balcony overlooking Great Room

■ Great Room with cozy fireplace provides perfect gathering place

■ Privately located Master Bedroom accesses Porch

■ This home comes with a crawlspace foundation.

■ Alternate foundation options available at an additional charge, call 1-800-235-5700 for more information.

First floor — 1,632 sq. ft.
Second floor — 669 sq. ft.
Bonus room — 528 sq. ft.
Garage & storage — 707 sq. ft.

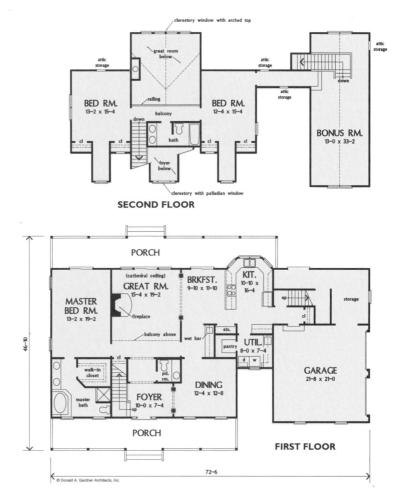

SECOND FLOOR

FIRST FLOOR

© Donald A. Gardner Architects, Inc.

Country Style Charm

■ *Total living area 1,857 sq. ft.* ■ *Price Code C* ■

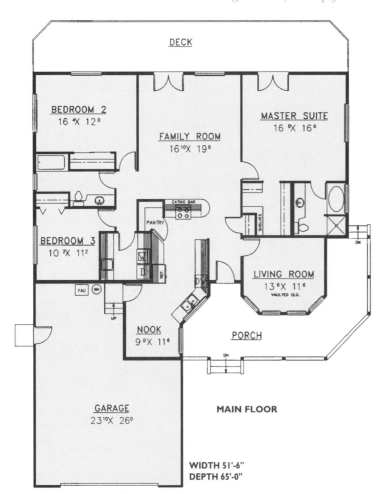

DECK

BEDROOM 2
16⁴X 12⁰

FAMILY ROOM
16¹⁰X 19⁶

MASTER SUITE
16⁵X 16⁶

EATING BAR

PANTRY

BEDROOM 3
10²X 11²

SHELVES

LIVING ROOM
13⁶X 11⁶
VAULTED CLG.

REF.

FAU

DN

NOOK
9⁰X 11⁶

PORCH

DN

UP

GARAGE
23¹⁰X 26⁰

MAIN FLOOR

WIDTH 51'-6"
DEPTH 65'-0"

No. 91731

■ This plan features:

— Three bedrooms

— Two full baths

■ Brick accents, front facing gable, and railed wraparound covered Porch

■ A built-in range and oven in an L-shaped Kitchen

■ A Nook with Garage access for convenient unloading of groceries and other supplies

■ A bay window wrapping around the front of the formal Living Room

■ A Master Suite with French doors opening to the Deck

■ This home comes with a crawlspace foundation.

Main floor — 1,857 sq. ft.
Garage — 681 sq. ft.

The Great Outdoors

© Donald A. Gardner Architects, Inc.

■ *Total living area 2,563 sq. ft.* ■ *Price Code H* ■

No. 99843

■ **This plan features:**

— Four bedrooms

— Two full and one half baths

■ Bay windows and a long, skylit, screened Porch make this four Bedroom Country-style home a haven for outdoor enthusiasts

■ Foyer is open to take advantage of the light from the central dormer with palladian window

■ Contemporary Kitchen is open to the Great Room

■ This home comes with a crawlspace foundation.

■ Alternate foundation options available at an additional charge. Please call 1.800.235.5700 for more information.

First floor — 1,907 sq. ft.
Second floor — 656 sq. ft.
Bonus room — 467 sq. ft.
Garage & storage — 580 sq. ft.

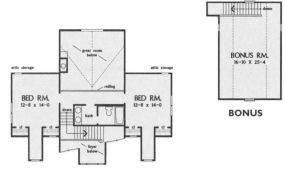

SECOND FLOOR

BONUS RM.
16-10 X 25-4

BONUS

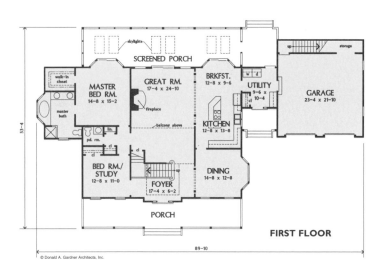

FIRST FLOOR

© Donald A. Gardner Architects, Inc.

Formal Balance

■ *Total living area 1,476 sq. ft.* ■ *Price Code A* ■

No. 90689

■ This plan features:

— Three bedrooms

— Two full baths

■ A cathedral ceiling in the Living Room with a heat-circulating fireplace as the focal point

■ A bow window in the Dining Room that adds elegance as well as natural light

■ A well-equipped Kitchen that serves both the Dinette and the formal Dining Room efficiently

■ A Master Bedroom with three closets and a private Master Bath with sliding glass doors to the Master Deck with a hot tub

■ An optional basement or slab foundation — please specify when ordering.

Main floor — 1,476 sq. ft.
Basement — 1,361 sq. ft.
Garage — 548 sq. ft.

75'-9"

DECK

fence · opt. hot tub · MASTER DECK

bow window

sl. gl. dr. · sl. gl. dr.

storage, bicycles etc. · pantry · MUD RM · laundry · w. · d. · dw · s. · range · DINETTE 8' x 8' · KITCHEN 11'-4" x 8'-8" · DINING RM 12'-6"x 10'-1" · BATH · MASTER BED RM 15' x 11'-4" · cl.

BATH · cl.

dn. · ref. · columns · cl.

dn.

alt. heater slab version · HALL · lin. · cl. · cl.

cathedral ceiling · cl.

TWO CAR GARAGE · LIVING RM 22' x 14' · cl. · BED RM 12' x 10'-8" · BED RM 12'-4" x 10'-8"

heat-circulating fireplace · FOYER · cl.

2x6 studs for added insulation

34'-6"

MAIN FLOOR · ENTRANCE PORCH

wood columns

Multiple Porches Provide Added Interest

■ *Total living area 3,149 sq. ft.* ■ *Price Code H* ■

No. 94622

■ **This plan features:**

— Four bedrooms

— Three full and one half baths

■ Great Room with large fireplace and French doors to Porch and Deck

■ Country-size Kitchen with cooktop work island, walk-in Pantry and Breakfast Area with Porch access

■ Pampering Master Bedroom offers a decorative ceiling, Sitting Area, Porch and Deck access, a huge walk-in closet and lavish Bath

■ Three second floor Bedrooms with walk-in closets have private access to a full Bath

■ An optional slab or pier/post foundation — please specify when ordering.

First floor — 2,033 sq. ft.
Second floor — 1,116 sq. ft.

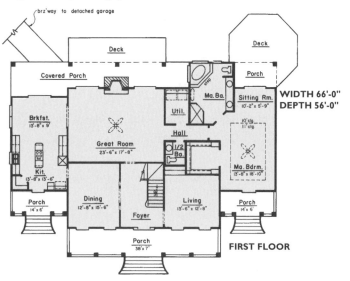

WIDTH 66'-0"
DEPTH 56'-0"

FIRST FLOOR

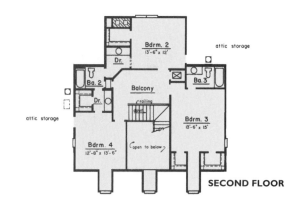

SECOND FLOOR

A Touch of Old World Charm

Total living area 2,320 sq. ft. ■ *Price Code D* ■

Bedroom 10'8" x 13'5"

Bedroom 10'9" x 10'

Great Room Below

slope ceiling

Hall

linen | linen

Bath

Balcony

book/shelves

desk

stairs dn

Bedroom 11' x 11'2"

Porch

slope ceiling

slope ceiling

SECOND FLOOR

FIRST FLOOR

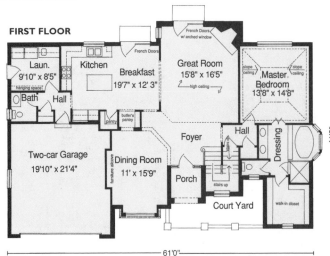

Laun. 9'10" x 8'5"

Kitchen

Breakfast 19'7" x 12' 3"

French Doors w/ arched window

French Doors

Great Room 15'8" x 16'5"

high ceiling

slope ceiling

Master Bedroom 13'8" x 14'8"

slope ceiling

hanging space

Bath

Hall

butler's pantry

pantry

Foyer

Hall

Dressing

Two-car Garage 19'10" x 21'4"

furniture alcove

Dining Room 11' x 15'9"

Porch

stairs up

Court Yard

walk-in closet

41'8"

61'0"

No. 92646

■ **This plan features:**

— Four bedrooms

— Two full and one half baths

■ Authentic balustrade railings and front courtyard greet one and all

■ High ceiling in Great Room tops corner fireplace and French doors

■ Formal Dining Room enhanced by a decorative window and furniture alcove

■ Country Kitchen with work island, two Pantries, Breakfast Area with French door to rear yard, and Laundry and Garage entry

■ Master Bedroom wing offers a sloped ceiling, and a plush Bath

■ This home comes with a basement foundation.

First floor — 1,595 sq. ft.
Second floor — 725 sq. ft.
Basement — 1,471 sq. ft.
Garage — 409 sq. ft.

Country Style Home With Corner Porch

© Donald A. Gardner Architects, Inc.

■ *Total living area 1,815 sq. ft.* ■ *Price Code F* ■

No. 99804

■ This plan features:

— Three bedrooms

— Two full baths

■ Dining Room has four floor-to-ceiling windows that overlook front Porch

■ Great Room topped by a cathedral ceiling and enhanced by a fireplace

■ Utility Room located near Kitchen and Breakfast Nook

■ Master Bedroom has a walk in closet and private Bath

■ This home comes with a crawlspace foundation.

■ Alternate foundation options available at an additional charge. Please call 1.800.235.5700 for more information.

Main floor — 1,815 sq. ft.
Garage — 522 sq. ft.
Bonus — 336 sq. ft.

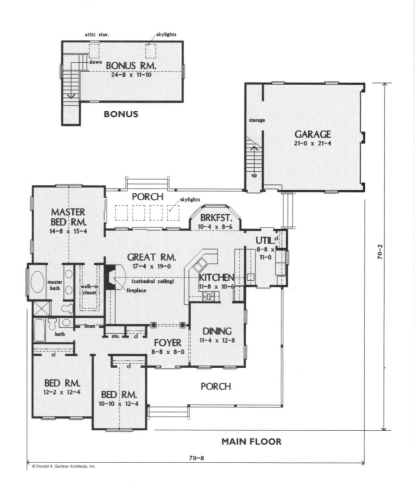

© Donald A. Gardner Architects, Inc.

Lovely Second Home

■ *Total living area 1,096 sq. ft.* ■ *Price Code A* ■

No. 91002

■ This plan features:

— Two bedrooms

— One full and one three-quarter baths

■ Fireplace warms both entryway and Living Room

■ Dining and Living Rooms opening onto the Deck, which surrounds the house on three sides

■ This home comes with a crawlspace foundation.

Main floor — 808 sq. ft.
Upper floor — 288 sq. ft.

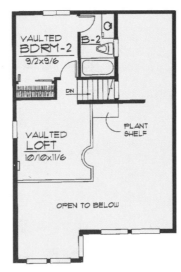

UPPER FLOOR

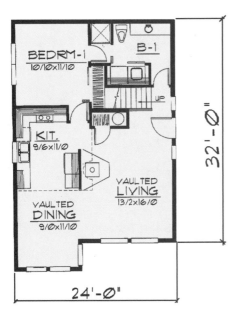

MAIN FLOOR

■ *Total living area 1,735 sq. ft.* ■ *Price Code B* ■

No. 93269

■ This plan features:

— Three bedrooms

— Two full and one half baths

■ A Living Room enhanced by a large fireplace

■ A formal Dining Room that is open to the Living Room

■ An efficient Kitchen that includes ample counter and cabinet space as well as double sinks and pass-thru window

■ Breakfast Area with vaulted ceiling and a door to the Sundeck

■ First floor Master Suite with separate tub & shower stall, plus a walk-in closet

■ This home comes with a basement foundation.

First floor — 1,045 sq. ft.
Second floor — 690 sq. ft.
Basement — 465 sq. ft.
Garage — 580 sq. ft.

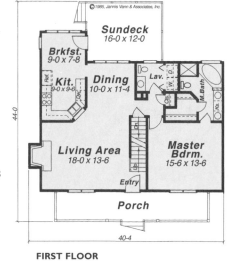

© 1985, Jannis Vann & Associates, Inc.

Sundeck 16-0 x 12-0

Brkfst. 9-0 x 7-8

Kit. 9-0 x 9-6

Dining 10-0 x 11-4

Lav.

W. D.

M.Bath

44-0

Living Area 18-0 x 13-6

Master Bdrm. 15-6 x 13-6

Entry

Porch

40-4

FIRST FLOOR

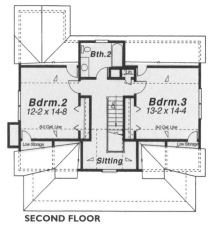

Bth.2

Bdrm.2 12-2 x 14-8

Bdrm.3 13-2 x 14-4

Low Storage

8-0 Cell. Line

8-0 Cell. Line

Low Storage

Sitting

SECOND FLOOR

53

Delightful, Compact Home

■ *Total living area 1,146 sq. ft.* ■ *Price Code A* ■

MAIN FLOOR

44'-0"

28'-0"

Br 2
10 x 12-8

Br 3
10 x 9-4

PANTRY

Kit
10 x 11

Dining
9 x 11

linen

MBr 1
13-4 x 12

slope · slope

Living Rm
19 x 12-4

DN

Deck

CRAWLSPACE/SLAB OPTION

W

D

No. 34003

■ **This plan features:**

— Three bedrooms

— Two full baths

■ A fireplaced Living Room brightened by a wonderful picture window

■ A counter island featuring double sinks separating the Kitchen and Dining Areas

■ A Master Bedroom that includes a private Master Bath and double closets

■ Two additional Bedrooms with ample closet space that share a full Bath

■ An optional basement, slab or crawlspace foundation — please specify when ordering.

Main floor — 1,146 sq. ft.

Tradition Combined with Contemporary

■ *Total living area 1,289 sq. ft.* ■ *Price Code A* ■

No. 99327

■ **This plan features:**

— Three bedrooms

— Two full baths

■ A vaulted ceiling in the Entry

■ A formal Living Room with a fireplace and a half-round transom

■ A Dining Room with sliders to the Deck and easy access to the Kitchen

■ A first floor Master Suite with corner windows, a closet and private Bath access

■ This home comes with a basement foundation.

First floor — 858 sq. ft.
Second floor — 431 sq. ft.
Basement — 858 sq. ft.
Garage — 400 sq. ft.

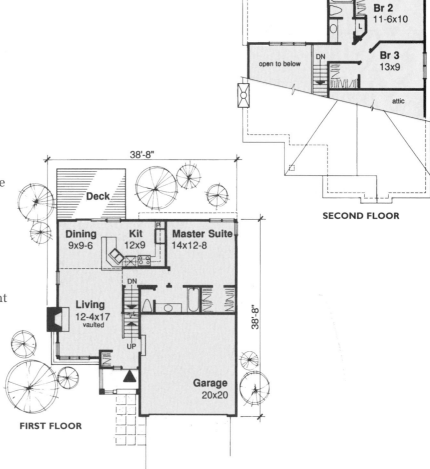

SECOND FLOOR

Br 2
11-6x10

open to below

DN

Br 3
13x9

attic

FIRST FLOOR

38'-8"

Deck

Dining
9x9-6

Kit
12x9

Master Suite
14x12-8

DN

Living
12-4x17
vaulted

UP

38'-8"

Garage
20x20

Appealing Farmhouse Design

© Donald A. Gardner Architects, Inc.

■ *Total living area 1,792 sq. ft.* ■ *Price Code F* ■

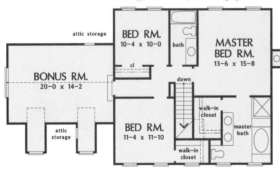

SECOND FLOOR

First floor — 959 sq. ft.
Second floor — 833 sq. ft.
Bonus room — 344 sq. ft.
Garage & storage — 500 sq. ft.

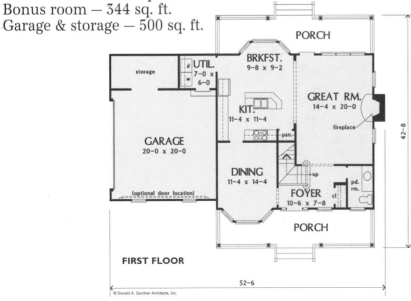

FIRST FLOOR

© Donald A. Gardner Architects, Inc.

No. 99836

■ **This plan features:**

— Three bedrooms

— Two full and one half baths

■ Comfortable farmhouse features an easy to build floor plan with all the extras

■ Active families will enjoy the Great Room which is open to the Kitchen and Breakfast Bay, as well as expanded living space provided by the full back Porch

■ For narrower lot restrictions, the Garage can be modified to open in front

■ Master Bedroom has a private Bath with a garden tub and separate shower

■ This home comes with a crawlspace foundation.

■ Alternate foundation options available at an additional charge. Please call 1.800.235.5700 for more information.

Carefree Convenience

■ Total living area 1,600 sq. ft. ■ Price Code B ■

No. 10674

■ **This plan features:**

— Three bedrooms

— Two full baths

■ A galley Kitchen, centrally-located between the Dining, Breakfast and Living Room Areas

■ A huge Family Room which exits onto the Patio

■ A Master Suite with double closets and vanity

■ This home comes with a slab foundation.

Main floor — 1,600 sq. ft.
Garage — 465 sq. ft.

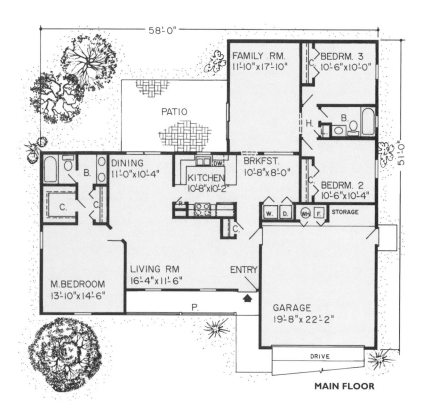

MAIN FLOOR

Country Porch Topped by Dormer

■ *Total living area 1,470 sq. ft.* ■ *Price Code A* ■

No. 24706

■ **This plan features:**

— Three bedrooms

— Two full baths

■ Front Porch leads into tiled Entry and spacious Living Room with focal point fireplace

■ Side entrance leads into Utility Room and central Foyer with a landing staircase

■ Kitchen with cooktop island, and a bright Breakfast Area

■ Second floor Master Bedroom offers dormer window, vaulted ceiling, walk-in closet and double vanity Bath

■ An optional basement, slab or crawlspace foundation — please specify when ordering.

First floor — 1,035 sq. ft.
Second floor — 435 sq. ft.
Basement — 1,018 sq. ft.

SECOND FLOOR

Master Br
14-3 × 12-11

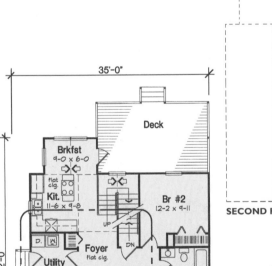

35'-0"

42'-0"

Deck

Brkfst
9-0 × 6-0

Kit.
11-6 × 9-8

flat clg.

Br #2
12-2 × 9-11

Foyer
flat clg.

Utility

Living Rm
18-11 × 12-11

Br #3
12-2 × 9-3

Porch

FIRST FLOOR

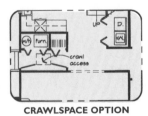

crawl access

CRAWLSPACE OPTION

■ *Total living area 2,464 sq. ft.* ■ *Price Code E* ■

No. 93209

■ **This plan features:**

— Four bedrooms

— Two full and one half baths

■ A wrap-around Porch adding a cozy touch to this classic style

■ A two-story Foyer area opens to the formal Dining and Living Rooms

■ A large Family Room accentuated by columns and a fireplace

■ A sunny Breakfast Area with direct access to the Sun Deck

■ A convenient Kitchen situated between the formal Dining Room and informal Breakfast Area has a Laundry Center and a Pantry

■ A private Deck highlights the Master Suite which includes a luxurious Bath

■ This home comes with a basement foundation.

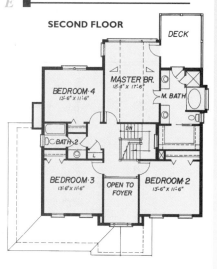

First floor — 1,250 sq. ft.
Second floor — 1,166 sq. ft.
Finished stairs — 48 sq. ft.
Basement — 448 sq. ft.
Garage — 706 sq. ft.

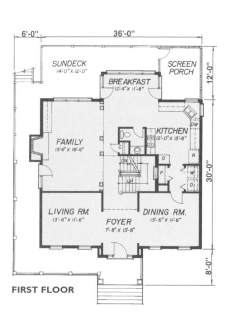

Ten Foot Entry

■ *Total living area 1,604 sq. ft.* ■ *Price Code B* ■

No. 94986

■ **This plan features:**

— Three bedrooms

— Two full baths

■ Large volume Great Room highlighted by a fireplace flanked by windows

■ See-through wetbar enhancing the Breakfast Area and the Dining Room

■ Fully equipped Kitchen with a planning desk and a Pantry

■ Roomy Master Suite has a skylighted Dressing/Bath Area, plant shelf, a double vanity and a whirlpool tub

■ This home comes with a basement foundation.

Main floor — 1,604 sq. ft.
Garage — 466 sq. ft.

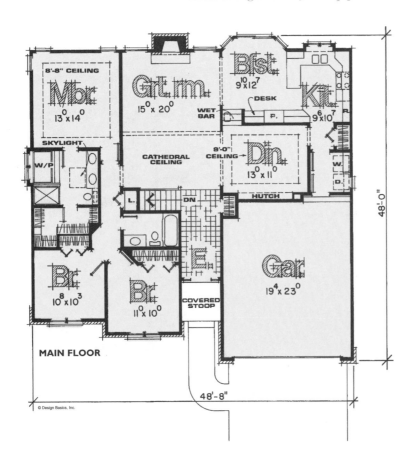

Total living area 1,987 sq. ft. ■ *Price Code C*

No. 92544

■ This plan features:

— Four bedrooms

— Two full and one half baths

■ Front and back Porches expand the living space and provide inviting access to the open layout

■ Spacious Den with a fireplace flanked by built-in shelves and double access to the rear Porch

■ Formal Dining Room with an arched window

■ Efficient, U-shaped Kitchen with a snackbar counter, a bright Breakfast Area and an adjoining Laundry and Garage

■ Secluded Master Bedroom Suite

■ Three additional Bedrooms with walk-in closets, share one and a half Baths

■ An optional slab or crawl space foundation available — please specify when ordering.

Main floor — 1,987 sq. ft.
Garage/Storage — 515 sq. ft.

Luxuriant Living

© Donald A. Gardner Architects, Inc.

■ *Total living area 2,869 sq. ft.* ■ *Price Code H* ■

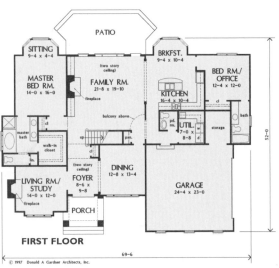

PATIO

SITTING
9-4 x 4-4

MASTER
BED RM.
14-0 x 16-0

FAMILY RM.
21-8 x 19-10
(two story ceiling)
fireplace

BRKFST.
9-4 x 10-4

KITCHEN
16-4 x 10-4

BED RM./
OFFICE
12-4 x 12-0

master bath

balcony above

UTIL.
7-0 x 8-8

storage

walk-in closet

up

DINING
12-8 x 13-4

FOYER
8-6 x 9-8

GARAGE
24-4 x 23-0

LIVING RM./
STUDY
14-0 x 12-0
fireplace

PORCH

FIRST FLOOR

© 1997 Donald A Gardner Architects, Inc.

69-6

52-0

First floor — 2,249 sq. ft.
Second floor — 620 sq. ft.
Bonus — 308 sq. ft.
Garage — 642 sq. ft.

family room below

BED RM.
14-0 x 14-8

railing

balcony

bath

walk-in closet

down

attic storage

down

BED RM.
12-8 x 13-4

foyer below

walk-in closet shelf

BONUS RM.
14-4 x 17-0

attic storage

SECOND FLOOR

No. 99825

■ **This plan features:**

— Four bedrooms

— Three full and one half baths

■ French doors, windows and a high gabled Foyer make a dramatic entrance

■ Living Room features a box bay window and a fireplace

■ Dining Room is illuminated by a bank of windows

■ Family Room has a two-story ceiling, a fireplace and access to the rear Patio

■ The Master Suite features a private Bath and a Sitting Area

■ This home comes with a crawlspace foundation.

■ Alternate foundation options available at an additional charge. Please call 1.800.235.5700 for more information.

Welcoming Wrap-Around Country Porch

■ *Total living area 2,083 sq. ft.* ■ *Price Code D* ■

No. 24245

■ **This plan features:**

— Three bedrooms

— Two full and one half baths

■ Formal areas flanking the Entry Hall

■ A Living Room that includes a wonderful fireplace

■ A Mudroom entry that will help keep the tracked-in dirt under control

■ An expansive Family Room with direct access to the rear Deck

■ A Master Suite highlighted by a walk-in closet and a private Master Bath

■ An optional basement, slab or crawlspace foundation — please specify when ordering.

First floor — 1,113 sq. ft.
Second floor — 970 sq. ft.
Garage — 480 sq. ft.
Basement — 1,113 sq. ft.

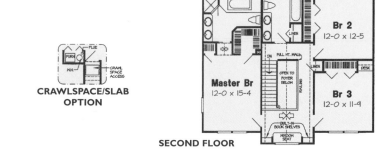

CRAWLSPACE/SLAB OPTION

SECOND FLOOR

Master Br 12-0 x 15-4

Br 2 12-0 x 12-5

Br 3 12-0 x 11-9

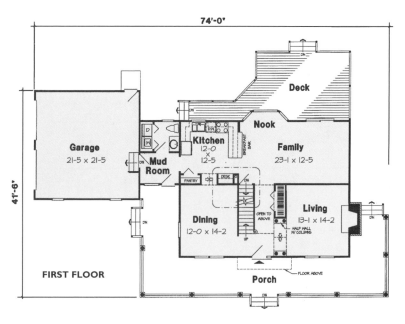

74'-0"

41'-6"

FIRST FLOOR

Garage 21-5 x 21-5

Mud Room

Kitchen 12-0 x 12-5

Nook

Deck

Family 23-1 x 12-5

Dining 12-0 x 14-2

Living 13-1 x 14-2

Porch

Large Front Porch Adds a Country Touch

■ *Total living area 1,415 sq. ft.* ■ *Price Code A* ■

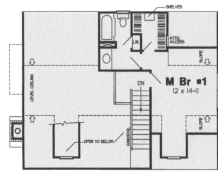

SECOND FLOOR

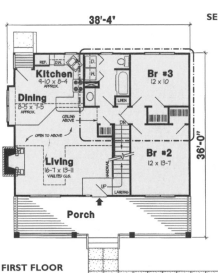

FIRST FLOOR

38'-4'

36'-0"

Kitchen 9-10 x 8-4 APPROX.

Dining 8-5 x 7-5 APPROX.

Br #3 12 x 10

Br #2 12 x 13-7

Living 16-7 x 13-11 VAULTED CLG.

Porch

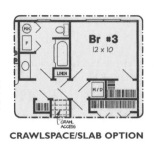

Br #3 12 x 10

CRAWLSPACE/SLAB OPTION

No. 34601

■ **This plan features:**

— Three bedrooms

— Two full baths

■ A Country-styled front Porch

■ Vaulted ceiling in the Living Room which includes a fireplace

■ An efficient Kitchen with double sinks and peninsula counter that may double as an eating bar

■ Two first floor Bedrooms with ample closet space

■ A second floor Master Suite with sloped ceiling, walk-in closet and private Master Bath

■ An optional basement, slab or crawlspace foundation — please specify when ordering.

First floor — 1,007 sq. ft.
Second floor — 408 sq. ft.
Basement — 1,007 sq. ft.

Windows Add Warmth To All Living Areas

■ Total living area 1,672 sq. ft. ■ Price Code B ■

No. 34011

■ **This plan features:**

- Three bedrooms

- Two full baths

■ A Master Suite with huge his and her walk-in closets and private Bath

■ A second and third Bedroom with ample closet space

■ A Kitchen equipped with an island counter, and flowing easily into the Dining and Family Rooms

■ A Laundry Room conveniently located near all three Bedrooms

■ An optional Garage

■ An optional basement, slab or crawlspace foundation — please specify when ordering.

Main floor — 1,672 sq. ft.
Garage — 566 sq. ft.

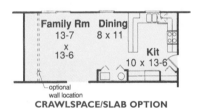

CRAWLSPACE/SLAB OPTION

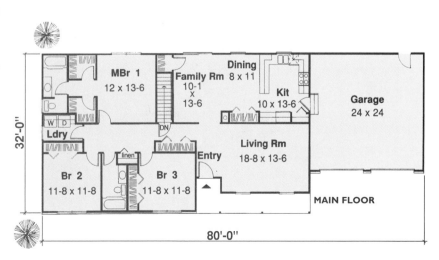

Sophisticated Southern Styling

■ *Total living area 2,858 sq. ft.* ■ *Price Code G* ■

First floor — 2,256 sq. ft.
Second floor — 602 sq. ft.
Bonus — 264 sq. ft.
Garage — 484 sq. ft.

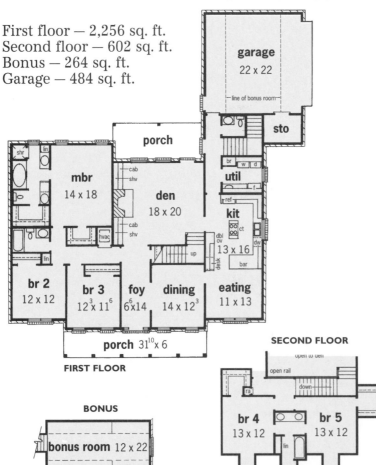

No. 92576

■ **This plan features:**

— Five bedrooms

— Three full and one half baths

■ Covered front and rear Porches expanding the living space to the outdoors

■ A Den with a large fireplace and built-in cabinets and shelves

■ A cooktop island, built-in desk, and eating bar complete the Kitchen

■ The Master Suite has two walk-in closets and a luxurious Bath

■ Four additional Bedrooms, two or the First level and two on the Second level, all have easy access to a full Bath

■ An optional slab or Crawlspace foundation — please specify when ordering.

Total living area 1,351 sq. ft. ■ Price Code A

No. 90356

■ This plan features:

- Three bedrooms

- Two full and one half baths

■ A vaulted ceiling Living Room with a balcony above, and a fireplace

■ An efficient, well-equipped Kitchen with stovetop island and easy flow of traffic into the Dining Room

■ A Deck accessible from the Living Room

■ A luxurious Master Suite with a bay window seat, walk-in closet, Dressing Area and a private shower

■ Two additional Bedrooms that share a full hall Bath

■ This home comes with a basement foundation.

First floor — 674 sq. ft.
Second floor — 677 sq. ft.

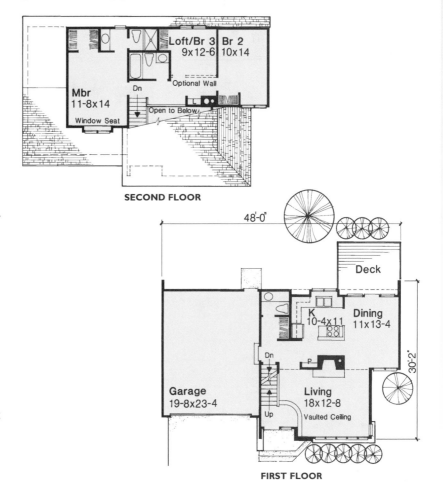

SECOND FLOOR

FIRST FLOOR

Country Influence

Total living area 1,554 sq. ft. ■ Price Code B

First floor — 806 sq. ft.
Second floor — 748 sq. ft.
Garage — 467 sq. ft.

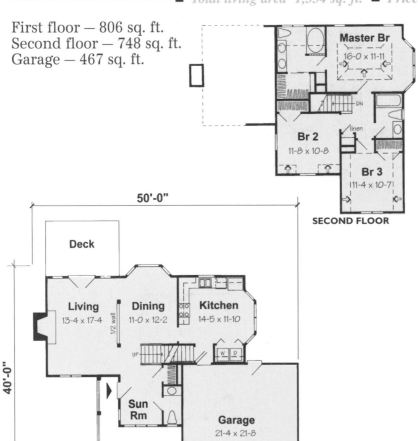

Master Br
16-0 x 11-11

Br 2
11-8 x 10-8

linen

Br 3
11-4 x 10-7

SECOND FLOOR

Deck

Living
13-4 x 17-4

½ wall

Dining
11-0 x 12-2

Kitchen
14-5 x 11-10

UP

W D

50'-0"

40'-0"

Sun Rm

Garage
21-4 x 21-8

FIRST FLOOR

No. 24654

■ **This plan features:**

— Three bedrooms

— Two full and one half baths

■ Front Porch enters into unique Sun Room with half Bath and coat closet

■ Open Living Room enhanced by palladium window, focal point fireplace and atrium door to Deck

■ Bay window brightens formal Dining Room which is conveniently located between the Living Room and Kitchen

■ Efficient L-shaped Kitchen with bay windowed Eating Area, Laundry closet and Garage access

■ Plush Master Bedroom is crowned by a tray ceiling and offers a private Bath with double vanity

■ An optional basement, slab or crawlspace foundation — please specify when ordering.

■ *Total living area 2,455 sq. ft.* ■ *Price Code E* ■

No. 98518

This plan features:

– Three bedrooms

– Two full and one half baths

■ Serve guests dinner in the bayed Dining Room and then gather in the Living Room which features a cathedral ceiling

■ The Family Room which is accented by a fireplace

■ The Master Bedroom has a Sitting Area, walk-in closet, and a private Bath

■ There is a bonus room upstairs for future expansion

■ An optional basement or slab foundation — please specify when ordering

First floor — 1,447 sq. ft.
Second floor — 1,008 sq. ft.
Garage — 756 sq. ft.

WIDTH 65'-0'
DEPTH 37'-11"

Covered Porch on Farm Style Traditional

■ *Total living area 1,763 sq. ft.* ■ *Price Code C* ■

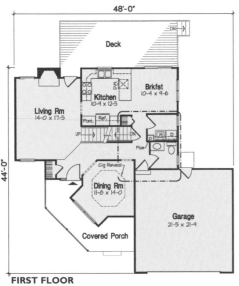

FIRST FLOOR

SECOND FLOOR

No. 34901

■ **This plan features:**

— Three bedrooms

— Two full and one half baths

■ A Dining Room with bay window and elevated ceiling

■ A Living Room complete with gas-light fireplace

■ A two-car Garage

■ Ample storage space throughout the home

■ An optional basement, slab or crawlspace foundation — please specify when ordering.

First floor — 909 sq. ft.
Second floor — 854 sq. ft.
Basement — 899 sq. ft.
Garage — 491 sq. ft.

■ *Total living area 3,335 sq. ft.* ■ *Price Code I* ■

No. 92219

■ This plan features:

- Four bedrooms

- Two full, one three-quarter and one half baths

■ Entry hall with a graceful landing staircase, flanked by formal areas

■ Fireplaces highlight the Living Room/Parlor and Dining Room

■ Kitchen with an island cooktop, built-in Pantry and Breakfast Area

■ Cathedral ceiling crowns Family Room and is accented by a fireplace

■ Lavish Master Bedroom wing with plenty of storage space

■ An optional basement, slab or crawlspace foundation — please specify when ordering.

First floor — 2,432 sq. ft.
Second floor — 903 sq. ft.
Basement — 2,432 sq. ft.
Garage — 742 sq. ft.

An Extraordinary Home

■ *Total living area 2,082 sq. ft.* ■ • *Price Code D* ■

Bedroom
11'1" x 13'3"

Bedroom
11'5" x 12'0"

linen

Bath

bookshelves
computer desk

wood rail

Balcony | Foyer Below

wood rail

Bonus
Room
11'0" x 22'0"

SECOND FLOOR

Master Bedroom
13'6" x 15'1"

Triple French Doors
w/ arched window above

Great Room
17'4" x 21'2"

Dining
Room
10'10" x 14'0"

12' high ceiling

Bath

pass thru

hanging space

Bath

Kitchen
12'4" x 11'6"

walk-in closet

Laun

Foyer

50'4"

Two-car Garage
22'9" x 22'0"

wood rail

pantry

Breakfast
11' x 9'4"

FIRST FLOOR

60'

No. 92642

■ **This plan features:**

— Three bedrooms

— Two full and one half baths

■ A grand Foyer into the formal Dining Room with a volume ceiling

■ A roomy, well-equipped Kitchen that includes a pass-through

■ Large windows in the Breakfast Area flood the room with natural light

■ A private Master Bedroom with a luxurious, compartmented Bath

■ Split stairs, graced with wood railings, lead to the second floor

■ This home comes with a basement foundation.

First floor — 1,524 sq. ft.
Second floor — 558 sq. ft.
Basement — 1,460 sq. ft.

Country Farmhouse

Total living area 1,898 sq. ft. ■ Price Code F ■

No. 99852

■ **This plan features:**

– Three bedrooms

– Two full and one half baths

■ Ready, set, grow with this lovely Country home enhanced by wrap-around Porch and rear Deck

■ Palladian window in clerestory dormer bathes two-story Foyer in natural light

■ Private Master Bedroom offers everything: walk-in closet, whirlpool tub, shower and double vanity

■ This home comes with a crawlspace foundation.

■ Alternate foundation options available at an additional charge. Please call 1.800.235.5700 for more information.

First floor — 1,356 sq. ft.
Second floor — 542 sq. ft.
Bonus room — 393 sq. ft.
Garage & storage — 543 sq. ft.

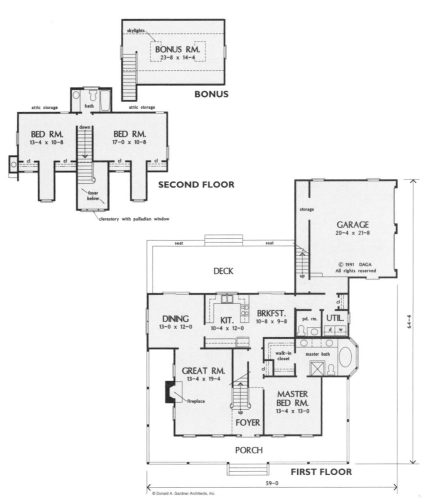

Beckoning Country Porch

■ Total living area 1,560 sq. ft. ■ Price Code B ■

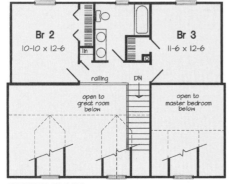

SECOND FLOOR

Br 2
10-10 x 12-6

Br 3
11-6 x 12-6

railing

DN

open to
great room
below

open to
master bedroom
below

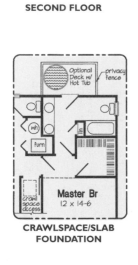

CRAWLSPACE/SLAB FOUNDATION

Optional
Deck w/
Hot Tub

privacy
fence

Master Br
12 x 14-6

crawl
space
access

furn

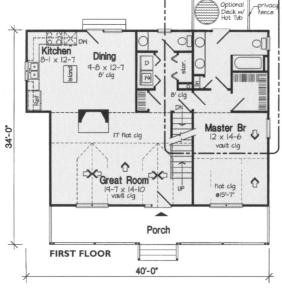

FIRST FLOOR

Kitchen
8-1 x 12-7

Dining
9-8 x 12-7
8' clg

island

Ref

DW

Optional
Deck w/
Hot Tub

privacy
fence

stor.

D

W

8' clg

DN

Master Br
12 x 14-6
vault clg

17' flat clg

Great Room
19-7 x 14-10
vault clg

UP

flat clg
@15'-7"

Porch

34'-0"

40'-0"

No. 34603

■ **This plan features:**

— Three bedrooms

— Two full and one half baths

■ Country style exterior with dormer windows

■ Vaulted ceiling and central fireplace in the Great Room

■ L-shaped Kitchen/Dining Room with work island and atrium door to backyard

■ First floor Master Suite with vaulted ceiling, walk-in closet, private Bath and optional private Deck with hot tub

■ Two additional Bedrooms on the second floor with easy access to full Bath

■ An optional basement, slab or crawlspace foundation — please specify when ordering.

First floor — 1,061 sq. ft.
Second floor — 499 sq. ft.
Basement — 1,061 sq. ft.

Elegant Window Treatment

■ *Total living area 1,492 sq. ft.* ■ *Price Code A* ■

No. 34150

This plan features:

- Two bedrooms (optional third)

- Two full baths

- An arched window that floods the front room with light

- A homey, well-lit Office or Den

- Compact, efficient use of space

- The Kitchen has easy access to the Dining Room

- A fireplaced Living Room with a sloping ceiling and a window wall

- The Master Bedroom sports a private Master Bath and a roomy walk-in closet

- An optional basement, slab or crawlspace foundation — please specify when ordering.

Main floor — 1,492 sq. ft.
Basement — 1,486 sq. ft.
Garage — 462 sq. ft.

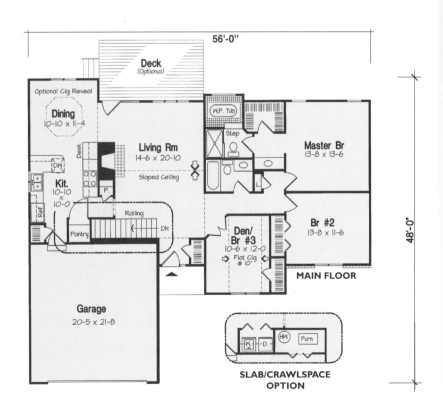

Home Builders on a Budget

© Donald A. Gardner Architects, Inc.

■ *Total living area 1,498 sq. ft.* ■ *Price Code E* ■

spa

DECK

MASTER BED RM.
13-4 x 13-8

master bath

skylights

BRKFST.
11-4 x 7-4

fireplace

GREAT RM.
15-4 x 16-10
(cathedral ceiling)

BED RM.
11-4 x 11-4

cl

bath

cl

FOYER
8-2 x 6-2

cl

KITCHEN
11-4 x 10-0

w
d

walk-in closet

storage

GARAGE
20-0 x 19-8

50-8

BED RM./STUDY
11-4 x 10-4

cl

PORCH

DINING RM.
11-4 x 11-4

MAIN FLOOR

59-8

© Donald A. Gardner Architects, Inc.

No. 99860

■ This plan features:

— Three bedrooms

— Two full baths

■ Down-sized Country plan for home builder on a budget

■ Columns punctuate open, one-level floor plan and connect Foyer with clerestory window dormers

■ Front Porch and large, rear Deck extend living space outdoors

■ Private Master Bath features garden tub, double vanity, separate shower and skylights

■ This home comes with a crawlspace foundation.

■ Alternate foundation options available at an additional charge. Please call 1.800.235.5700 for more information.

Main floor — 1,498 sq. ft.
Garage & storage — 427 sq. ft.

Cathedral Ceiling Enlarges Great Room

© Donald A. Gardner Architects, Inc.

■ Total living area 1,699 sq. ft. ■ Price Code F ■

No. 99811

This plan features:

Three bedrooms

Two full baths

Two dormers add volume to the Foyer

Great Room is topped by a cathedral ceiling

Accent columns define the Foyer, Great Room, Kitchen, and Breakfast Area

Private Master Suite crowned in a tray ceiling and highlighted by a skylit Bath

This home comes with a crawlspace foundation.

Alternate foundation options available at an additional charge. Please call 1.800.235.5700 for more information.

Main floor — 1,699 sq. ft.

Garage — 498 sq. ft.

Bonus — 336 sq. ft.

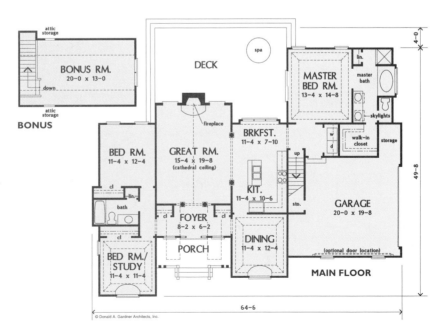

Easy One Floor Living

■ *Total living area 1,671 sq. ft.* ■ *Price Code B* ■

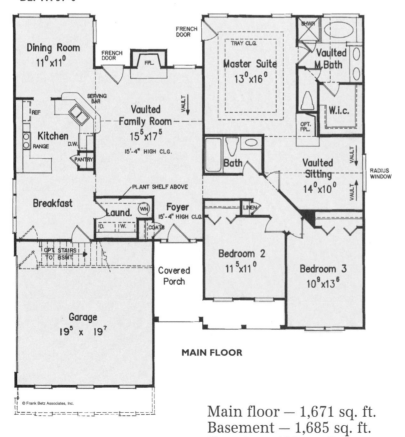

WIDTH 50'-0"
DEPTH 51'-0"

Dining Room
11⁰ x 11⁰

FRENCH DOOR

FRENCH DOOR

FPL.

SERVING BAR

REF

Kitchen
RANGE   D.W.

PANTRY

Vaulted
Family Room
15⁵ x 17⁵
15'-4" HIGH CLG.

VAULT

Master Suite
13⁰ x 16⁰

TRAY CLG.

SH-WH

Vaulted M. Bath

W.i.c.

OPT. FPL.

VAULT

Bath

Vaulted
Sitting
14⁰ x 10⁰

VAULT

VAULT

RADIUS WINDOW

Breakfast

PLANT SHELF ABOVE

Laund.   WH

ID.   I.W.

COATS

Foyer
15'-4" HIGH CLG.

LINEN

OPT. STAIRS TO BSMT.

Covered
Porch

Bedroom 2
11⁵ x 11⁰

Bedroom 3
10⁹ x 13⁶

Garage
19⁵ x 19⁷

© Frank Betz Associates, Inc.

MAIN FLOOR

Main floor — 1,671 sq. ft.
Basement — 1,685 sq. ft.
Garage — 400 sq. ft.

No. 98423

■ **This plan features:**

— Three bedrooms

— Two full baths

■ A spacious Family Room topped by a vaulted ceiling and highlighted by a large fireplace and a French door to the rear yard

■ A serving bar open to the Family Room and the Dining Room, a Pantry and a peninsula counter adding more efficiency to the Kitchen

■ A crowning tray ceiling over the Master Bedroom and a vaulted ceiling over the Master Bath

■ A vaulted ceiling over the cozy Sitting Room in the Master Suite

■ Two additional Bedrooms, roomy in size, sharing the full Bath in the hall

■ An optional basement, crawl space or slab foundation — please specify when ordering

Gazebo Porch Creates Old-Fashioned Feel

■ *Total living area 1,452 sq. ft.* ■ *Price Code A* ■

No. 24718

This plan features:

- Three bedrooms

- Two full baths

- An old-fashioned welcome is created by the covered Porch

- The Breakfast Area overlooks the Porch and is separated from the Kitchen by an extended counter

- The Dining Room and the Great Room are highlighted by a two sided fireplace

- The roomy Master Suite is enhanced by a whirlpool Bath with double vanity and a walk-in closet

- Each of the two secondary Bedrooms feature a walk-in closet

- An optional slab or crawlspace foundation — please specify when ordering.

Main floor — 1,452 sq. ft.
Garage — 584 sq. ft.

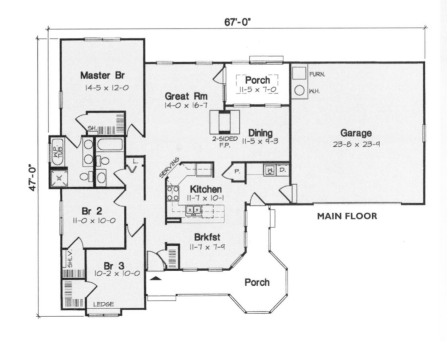

Country Brick

■ Total living area 2,443 sq. ft. ■ Price Code E ■

SECOND FLOOR

FIRST FLOOR

No. 92653

■ **This plan features:**

— Three or four bedrooms

— Two full and one half baths

■ Friendly front porch leads into a gracious open Foyer

■ Secluded Library offers a quiet space with built-in shelves

■ Great Room with a focal point fireplace topped by sloped ceiling

■ Kitchen with island snack bar, bright Breakfast Area, Pantry and nearby Laundry/Garage Entry

■ Master Bedroom offers a deluxe Bath and spacious walk-in closet

■ This home comes with a basement foundation.

First floor — 1,710 sq. ft.
Second floor — 733 sq. ft.
Bonus — 181 sq. ft.
Basement — 1,697 sq. ft.
Garage — 499 sq. ft.

■ Total living area 1,670 sq. ft. ■ Price Code B ■

No. 90409

■ **This plan features:**

— Three bedrooms

— Two full baths

■ A massive fireplace separating Living and Dining Rooms

■ An isolated Master Suite with a walk-in closet and handy compartmentalized Bath

■ A galley-type Kitchen between the Breakfast Room and Dining Room

■ An optional basement, slab or crawlspace foundation — please specify when ordering.

Main floor — 1,670 sq. ft.

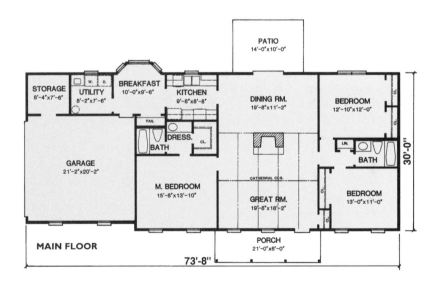

Carefree Living on One Level

■ *Total living area 1,588 sq. ft.* ■ *Price Code B* ■

No. 20089

■ **This plan features:**

— Three bedrooms

— Two full baths

■ A full basement and an oversized two-car Garage

■ A spacious Master Suite with a walk-in closet

■ A fireplaced Living Room, and an open Dining Room and Kitchen for convenience

■ This home comes with a basement foundation.

Main floor — 1,588 sq. ft.
Basement — 780 sq. ft.
Garage — 808 sq. ft.

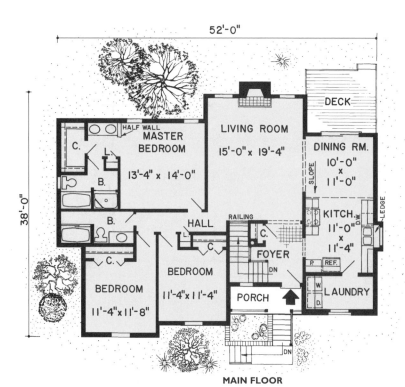

MAIN FLOOR

■ *Total living area 1,552 sq. ft.* ■ *Price Code B* ■

No. 90844

■ **This plan features:**

– Three bedrooms

– Two full and one half baths

■ A wrap-around Deck providing outdoor living space, ideal for a sloping lot

■ Two-and-a-half story glass wall and two separate atrium doors providing natural light for the Living/Dining Area

■ An efficient galley Kitchen with easy access to the Dining Area

■ A Master Bedroom suite with a half Bath and ample closet space

■ This home comes with a basement foundation.

■ A second floor Bedroom/Studio, with a private Deck, adjacent to a full hall Bath and a Loft area

First floor — 1,086 sq. ft.
Second floor — 466 sq. ft.
Basement — 1,080 sq. ft.

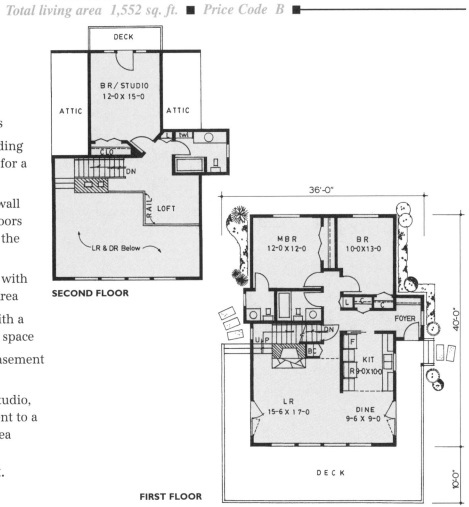

SECOND FLOOR

FIRST FLOOR

Traditional Ranch

■ *Total living area 2,275 sq. ft.* ■ *Price Code E* ■

DECK

BR.#2
14x11

BREAKFAST

MASTER
14x18

KITCHEN
10x10

FAMILY ROOM
16X18

Tray Clg.

BR.#3
13x12

Stairs Down

DINING
12x13

FOYER

LIVING
13x13

Tray Clg.

UTILITY

Cathedral

Cathedral

WORKSHOP

60'

MAIN FLOOR

62'

GARAGE
22x19

Drive

No. 92404

■ **This plan features:**

— Three bedrooms

— Two full baths

■ A tray ceiling in the Master Suite

■ A formal Living Room with a cathedral ceiling

■ A decorative tray ceiling in the elegant formal Dining Room

■ A spacious Family Room with a vaulted ceiling and a fireplace

■ A modern, well-appointed Kitchen with snack bar and bayed Breakfast Area

■ Two additional Bedrooms share a full hall Bath

■ This home comes with a basement foundation.

Main floor — 2,275 sq. ft.
Basement — 2,207 sq. ft.
Garage — 512 sq. ft.

Private Master Suite

■ *Total living area 1,293 sq. ft.* ■ *Price Code A* ■

No. 92523

This plan features:

- Three bedrooms
- Two full baths
- A spacious Den enhanced by a vaulted ceiling and fireplace
- A well-equipped Kitchen with windowed double sink
- A secluded Master Suite with decorative ceiling, private Master Bath and walk-in closet
- Two additional Bedrooms sharing hall Bath
- An optional Crawlspace or slab foundation — please specify when ordering

Main floor — 1,293 sq. ft.
Garage — 433 sq. ft.

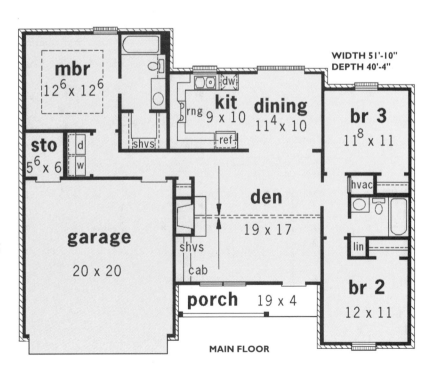

WIDTH 51'-10"
DEPTH 40'-4"

mbr 12⁶ x 12⁶

sto 5⁶ x 6

kit rng 9 x 10

dining 11⁴ x 10

br 3 11⁸ x 11

garage 20 x 20

den 19 x 17

br 2 12 x 11

porch 19 x 4

MAIN FLOOR

Timeless Appeal

■ Total living area 1,170 sq. ft. ■ Price Code A ■

No. 93075

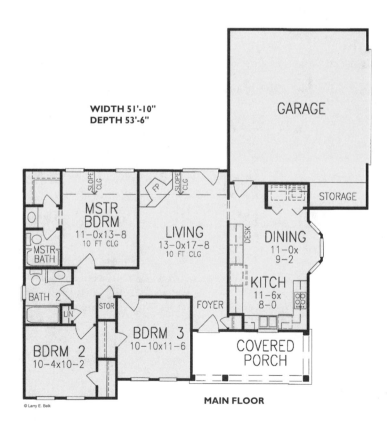

WIDTH 51'-10"
DEPTH 53'-6"

GARAGE

STORAGE

MSTR
BDRM
11–0x13–8
10 FT CLG

LIVING
13–0x17–8
10 FT CLG

DINING
11–0x
9–2

DESK

MSTR
BATH

BATH 2

KITCH
11–6x
8–0

LIN

STOR

FOYER

BDRM 2
10–4x10–2

BDRM 3
10–10x11–6

COVERED
PORCH

© Larry E. Belk

MAIN FLOOR

■ **This plan features:**

— Three bedrooms

— Two full baths

■ Ten-foot ceilings give the Living Room an open feel

■ Corner fireplace highlights the Living Room

■ Dining area enhanced by a sunny bay window

■ Master Bedroom features a private Bath

■ Garage is located on the rear and not visible from the front

■ An optional crawl space or slab foundation—please specify when ordering.

Main floor — 1,170 sq. ft.
Garage — 478 sq. ft.

Classic Warmth

■ *Total living area 1,838 sq. ft.* ■ *Price Code C* ■

No. 34878

■ This plan features:

— Three bedrooms

— Two full and one half baths

■ Clapboard and brick exterior

■ Cathedral ceilings gracing the Living and Dining rooms lending an airy quality

■ A Master Bedroom with private Master Bath and a walk-in closet

■ A spacious fireplaced Family Room

■ Sliders leading from both Dining and Family rooms to the rear Deck adding to living space

■ An optional basement, Crawlspace or slab foundation—please specify when ordering.

First floor — 1,088 sq. ft.
Second floor — 750 sq. ft.
Basement — 750 sq. ft.
Garage — 517 sq. ft.

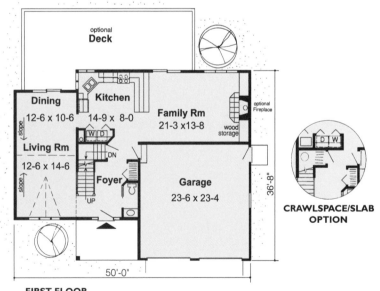

FIRST FLOOR

CRAWLSPACE/SLAB OPTION

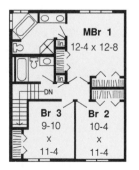

SECOND FLOOR

Country Styled Home

■ *Total living area 1,833 sq. ft.* ■ *Price Code C* ■

STORAGE

Storage

22 x 24

Garage

SECOND FLOOR

Br.#2
15 x 11
8' Ceiling

Br.#3
13 x 11
8' Ceiling

Attic Storage

Attic Storage

Stairs Down

Dining
13 x 11
9' Ceiling

Kitchen
12 x 11

Family Room
15 x 19
9' Ceiling

Open Above

Master
15 x 14
9' Ceiling

Foyer

Porch
39/6 x 8

FIRST FLOOR

**WIDTH 50'-8'
DEPTH 74'-0"**

No. 93432

■ **This plan features:**

— Three bedrooms

— Two full and one half baths

■ A country styled front Porch provides a warm welcome

■ The Family Room is highlighted by a fireplace and front windows

■ The Dining Room is separated from the U-shaped Kitchen by only an extended counter

■ The first floor Master Suite pampers the owners with a walk-in closet and a five-piece Bath

■ There are two additional Bedrooms with a convenient Bath in the hall

■ An optional slab or crawlspace foundation — please specify when ordering.

First floor — 1,288 sq. ft.
Second floor — 545 sq. ft.
Garage — 540 sq. ft.

Grand Four Bedroom Farmhouse

© Donald A. Gardner Architects, Inc.

■ *Total living area 2,561 sq. ft.* ■ *Price Code H* ■

No. 99891

■ **This plan features:**

— Four bedrooms

— Two full and one half baths

■ Double gables, wrap-around Porch and custom window details add appeal to farmhouse

■ Formal Living and Dining rooms connected by Foyer in front, while casual living areas expand rear

■ Efficient Kitchen with island cooktop and easy access to all eating areas

■ This home comes with a crawlspace foundation.

■ Alternate foundation options available at an additional charge. Please call 1.800.235.5700 for more information.

First floor — 1,357 sq. ft.
Second floor — 1,204 sq. ft.
Garage & storage — 546 sq. ft.

SECOND FLOOR

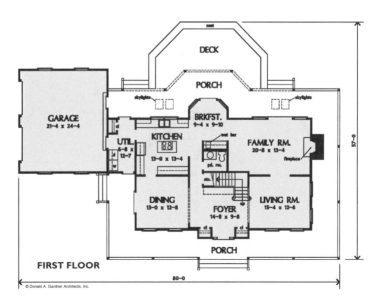

FIRST FLOOR

© Donald A. Gardner Architects, Inc.

Lots of Space in this Small Package

■ *Total living area 1,283 sq. ft.* ■ *Price Code A* ■

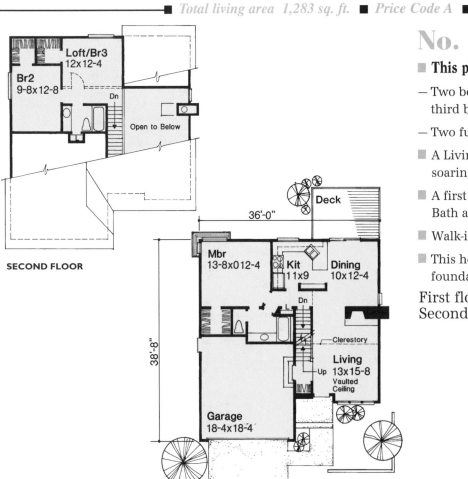

Loft/Br3
12x12-4

Br2
9-8x12-8

Dn

Open to Below

SECOND FLOOR

Deck

36'-0"

Mbr
13-8x012-4

Kit
11x9

Dining
10x12-4

Dn

38'-8"

Clerestory

Living
13x15-8
Vaulted
Ceiling

Up

Garage
18-4x18-4

FIRST FLOOR

No. 90378

■ **This plan features:**

— Two bedrooms with possible
third bedroom/loft

— Two full baths

■ A Living Room with dynamic,
soaring angles and a fireplace

■ A first floor Master Suite with full
Bath and walk in-closet

■ Walk-in closets in all Bedrooms

■ This home comes with a basement
foundation.

First floor — 878 sq. ft.
Second floor — 405 sq. ft.

Enhanced by a Columned Porch

■ *Total living area 1,754 sq. ft.* ■ *Price Code C* ■

No. 92531

■ **This plan features:**

– Three bedrooms

– Two full baths

■ A Great Room with a fireplace and decorative ceiling

■ A large efficient Kitchen with Breakfast Area

■ A Master Bedroom with a private master Bath and walk-in closet

■ A formal Dining Room conveniently located near the Kitchen

■ Two additional Bedrooms with walk-in closets and use of full hall Bath

■ An optional crawl space or slab foundation — please specify when ordering

Main floor — 1,754 sq. ft.
Garage — 552 sq. ft.

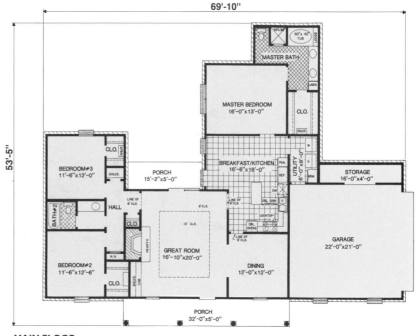

MAIN FLOOR

Style and Convenience

■ *Total living area 1,373 sq. ft.* ■ *Price Code A* ■

No. 98411

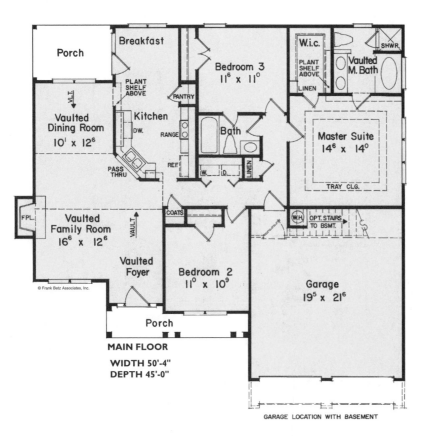

MAIN FLOOR

WIDTH 50'-4"
DEPTH 45'-0"

© Frank Betz Associates, Inc.

GARAGE LOCATION WITH BASEMENT

This plan features:

— Three bedrooms

— Two full baths

■ Large front windows, dormers and an old-fashioned Porch

■ A vaulted ceiling in the Foyer

■ A Formal Dining Room crowned in an elegant vaulted ceiling

■ An efficient Kitchen enhanced by a pantry, a pass through to the Family Room

■ A decorative tray ceiling, a five-piece private Bath and a walk-in closet in the Master Suite

■ An optional Basement or crawl space foundation — please specify when ordering

Main floor — 1,373 sq. ft.
Basement — 1,386 sq. ft.

■ *Total living area 2,733 sq. ft.* ■ *Price Code F* ■

No. 92538

■ This plan features:

— Four bedrooms

— Three full baths

■ A central Den with a large fireplace, built-in shelves and cabinets and a decorative ceiling

■ Columns defining the entrance to the formal Dining Room, adding a touch of elegance

■ An island Kitchen that has been well thought out and includes a walk-in Pantry

■ An informal Breakfast Room

■ A Master Bedroom with a decorative ceiling, a walk-in closet, and a luxurious Master Bath

■ Four additional Bedrooms, each with private access to a full Bath, two of which have walk-in closets

■ An optional crawl space or slab foundation — please specify when ordering.

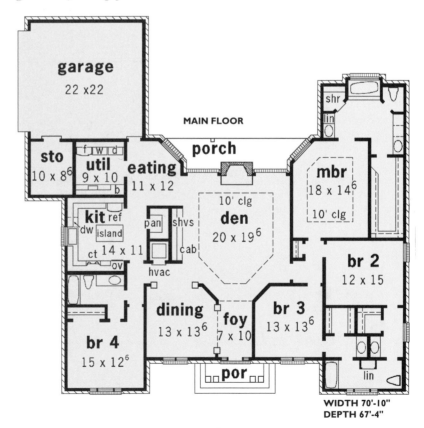

Main floor — 2,733 sq. ft.
Garage and storage — 569 sq. ft.

A Little Drama

■ *Total living area 1,768 sq. ft.* ■ *Price Code C* ■

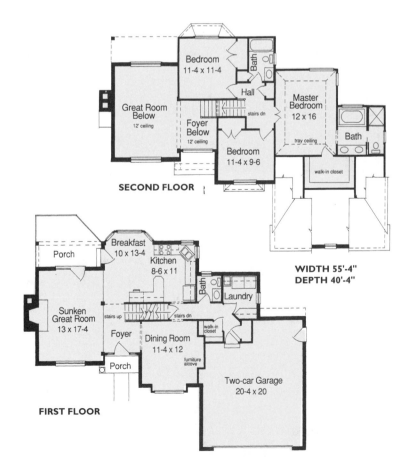

SECOND FLOOR

Bedroom
11-4 x 11-4

Bath

Hall

Great Room
Below
12' ceiling

Master
Bedroom
12 x 16

stairs dn

Foyer
Below
12' ceiling

tray ceiling

Bath

Bedroom
11-4 x 9-6

walk-in closet

WIDTH 55'-4"
DEPTH 40'-4"

FIRST FLOOR

Porch

Breakfast
10 x 13-4

Kitchen
8-6 x 11

Bath

Laundry

Sunken
Great Room
13 x 17-4

stairs up   stairs dn

walk-in
closet

Foyer

Dining Room
11-4 x 12

furniture
alcove

Porch

Two-car Garage
20-4 x 20

No. 92609

■ **This plan features:**

— Three bedrooms

— Two full and one half baths

■ A 12' high Entry with transom and sidelights, multiple gables and a box window

■ A sunken Great Room with a fireplace and access to a rear Porch

■ A Breakfast Bay and Kitchen flowing into each other and accessing a rear Porch

■ A Master Bedroom with a tray ceiling, walk-in closet and a private Master Bath

■ This home comes with a basement foundation.

First floor — 960 sq. ft.
Second floor — 808 sq. ft.
Basement — 922 sq. ft.
Garage — 413 sq. ft.

Private Master Suite

■ *Total living area 2,069 sq. ft.* ■ *Price Code D* ■

No. 96505

■ This plan features:

— Three bedrooms

— Two full and one half baths

■ Secluded Master Bedroom tucked into the rear left corner of the home with a five-piece Bath and two walk-in closets

■ Two additional Bedrooms at the opposite side of the home sharing the full Bath in the hall

■ Expansive Living Room highlighted by a corner fireplace and access to the rear Porch

■ Kitchen is sandwiched between the bright, bayed Nook and the formal Dining Room providing ease in serving

■ An optional slab or crawlspace foundation — please specify when ordering.

Main floor — 2,069 sq. ft.
Garage — 481 sq. ft.

WIDTH 70'-0"
DEPTH 58'-0"

CLOSET
BATH
MASTER SUITE
13×19
CLOSET
1/2 BATH
GARAGE
20×23
UTIL
KIT'N
12×14
NOOK
9×9
PORCH
LIVING RM
17×25
11'-0" CEILING
BEDRM
11×12
HALL
BATH
DINING
12×12
FOYER
STUDY
8×9
BEDRM
12×12
PORCH

MAIN FLOOR

An American Bungalow

■ Total living area 1,322 sq. ft. ■ Price Code A ■

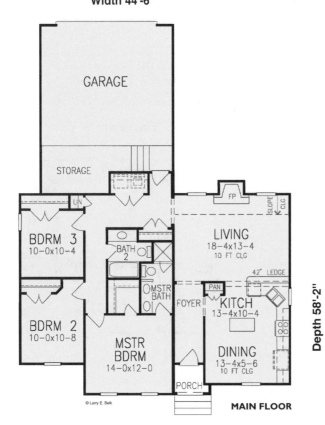

Width 44'-6"

GARAGE

STORAGE

BDRM 3
10-0x10-4

BATH
2

BDRM 2
10-0x10-8

LIN

MSTR
BATH

MSTR
BDRM
14-0x12-0

FOYER

PORCH

LIVING
18-4x13-4
10 FT CLG

FP

SLOPE CLG

42" LEDGE

PAN

KITCH
13-4x10-4

DINING
13-4x5-6
10 FT CLG

Depth 58'-2"

© Larry E. Belk

MAIN FLOOR

No. 93070

■ **This plan features:**

— Three bedrooms

— One full and one three-quarter bath

■ Simple and classic, the exterior is reminiscent of a less complicated time

■ This compact design has ten-foot ceilings adding a spacious feeling

■ The Kitchen flows into the Dining Area

■ The two-car Garage is tucked in the rear

■ The Master Suite with a private three-quarter Bath and a walk-in closet

■ An optional crawl space or slab foundation — please specify when ordering

Main floor — 1,322 sq. ft.
Garage — 528 sq. ft.

Updated Victorian

■ *Total living area 2,099 sq. ft.* ■ *Price Code D* ■

No. 91053

■ This plan features:

— Three bedrooms

— Two full and one half baths

■ A classic Victorian exterior design accented by a wonderful turret room and second floor covered Porch above a sweeping veranda

■ A spacious formal Living Room

■ An efficient, U-shaped Kitchen with a peninsula snackbar, opens to an eating Nook and Family Room for informal gatherings

■ An elegant Master Suite with a unique, octagon Sitting Area, a private Porch, an oversized, walk-in closet and private Bath with a double vanity and a window tub

■ This home comes with a crawlspace foundation.

First floor — 1,150 sq. ft.
Second floor — 949 sq. ft.
Garage — 484 sq. ft.

SECOND FLOOR

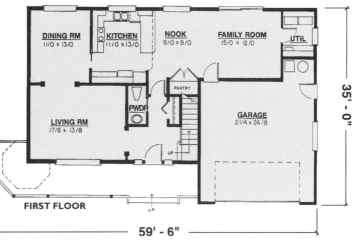

FIRST FLOOR

Casual Country Charmer

© Donald A. Gardner Architects, Inc.

B. NATHAN

■ *Total living area 1,770 sq. ft.* ■ *Price Code F* ■

BONUS

attic storage

down

BONUS RM.
13-6 x 24-0

PORCH

DINING
11-4 x 12-0

(dormers above)

PORCH

master bath

lin.

UTIL.
7-0 x
10-0

KIT.
13-0 x 12-0

walk-in
closet

walk-in
closet

pan.

fireplace

(cathedral ceiling)

MASTER
BED RM.
13-0 x 14-8

storage

GREAT RM.
17-8 x 20-4

57-4

shelves

cl

up

GARAGE
22-0 x 24-0

FOYER
8-0 x
9-3

BED RM.
11-4 x 11-8

cl

lin.

bath

cl

PORCH

BED RM.
11-0 x 11-0

MAIN FLOOR

54-0

© Donald A. Gardner Architects, Inc.

No. 96493

■ **This plan features:**

— Three bedrooms

— Two full baths

■ Columns and arches frame the front Porch

■ The open floor plan combines the Great room, Kitchen and Dining room

■ The Kitchen offers a convenient breakfast bar for meals on the run

■ The Master Suite features a private Bath oasis

■ This home comes with a crawlspace foundation.

■ Alternate foundation options available at an additional charge, call 1.800.235.5700 for more information.

Main floor — 1,770 sq. ft.
Bonus — 401 sq. ft.
Garage — 630 sq. ft.

A-Frame for Year-Round Living

■ *Total living area 1,702 sq. ft.* ■ *Price Code B* ■

No. 90930

■ This plan features:

— Three bedrooms

— One full and one three-quarter baths

■ A vaulted ceiling in the Living Room with a massive fireplace

■ A wrap-around Sun Deck that gives you a lot of outdoor living space

■ A luxurious Master Suite complete with a walk-in closet, full Bath and private Deck

■ Two additional Bedrooms that share a full hall Bath

■ This home comes with a basement foundation.

First floor — 1,238 sq. ft.
Second floor — 464 sq. ft.
Basement — 1,175 sq. ft.

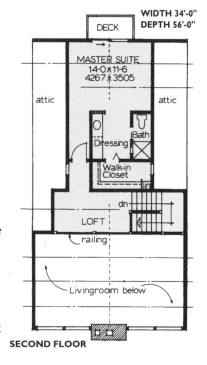

WIDTH 34'-0"
DEPTH 56'-0"

DECK

MASTER SUITE
14-0 x 11-6
4267 x 3505

attic   attic

Bath

Dressing

Walk-in Closet

dn

LOFT

railing

Livingroom below

SECOND FLOOR

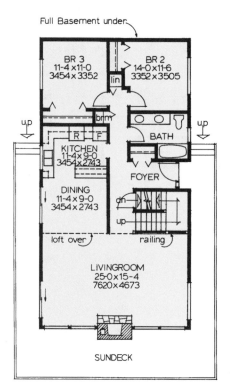

Full Basement under

BR 3
11-4 x 11-0
3454 x 3352

BR 2
14-0 x 11-6
3352 x 3505

lin

up   up

BATH

KITCHEN
11-4 x 9-0
3454 x 2743

FOYER

DINING
11-4 x 9-0
3454 x 2743

dn

up

loft over   railing

LIVINGROOM
25-0 x 15-4
7620 x 4673

SUNDECK

FIRST FLOOR

Compact Victorian Ideal for Narrow Lot

■ *Total living area 1,737 sq. ft.* ■ *Price Code B* ■

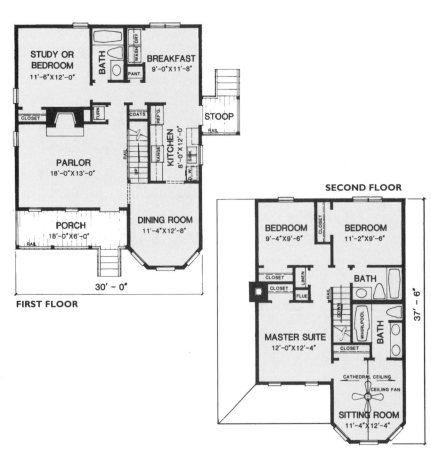

FIRST FLOOR

STUDY OR BEDROOM 11'-6"X12'-0"

BATH

BREAKFAST 9'-0"X11'-8"

WASH DRY

PANT.

CLOSET

FURN

COATS

REF'G

STOOP

RAIL

KITCHEN 8'-0"X12'-0"

RANGE

SINK

PARLOR 18'-0"X13'-0"

PORCH 18'-0"X6'-0"

DINING ROOM 11'-4"X12'-8"

30' - 0"

SECOND FLOOR

BEDROOM 9'-4"X9'-6"

CLOSET

BEDROOM 11'-2"X9'-6"

CLOSET

LINEN

CLOSET

BATH

FLUE

MASTER SUITE 12'-0"X12'-4"

WHIRLPOOL

BATH

CLOSET

37' - 6"

CATHEDRAL CEILING

CEILING FAN

SITTING ROOM 11'-4"X12'-4"

No. 90406

■ **This plan features:**

— Three bedrooms

— Three full baths

■ A large, front Parlor with a raised hearth fireplace

■ A Dining Room with a sunny bay window

■ An efficient galley Kitchen serving the formal Dining Room and informal Breakfast Room

■ A beautiful Master Suite with two closets, an oversized tub and double vanity, plus a private Sitting Room with a bayed window and vaulted ceiling

■ An optional basement, slab or crawlspace foundation — please specify when ordering.

First floor — 954 sq. ft.
Second floor — 783 sq. ft.

Spectacular Traditional

■ *Total living area 1,237 sq. ft.* ■ *Price Code A* ■

No. 92502

■ This plan features:

— Three bedrooms

— Two full baths

■ The use of gable roofs and the blend of stucco and brick to form a spectacular exterior

■ A high vaulted ceiling and a cozy fireplace, with built-in cabinets in the Den

■ An efficient, U-shaped Kitchen with an adjacent Dining Area

■ A Master Bedroom, with a raised ceiling, that includes a private Bath and a walk-in closet

■ Two family Bedrooms that share a full hall Bath

■ An optional crawlspace or slab foundation available — please specify when ordering.

Main floor — 1,237 sq. ft.
Garage — 436 sq. ft.

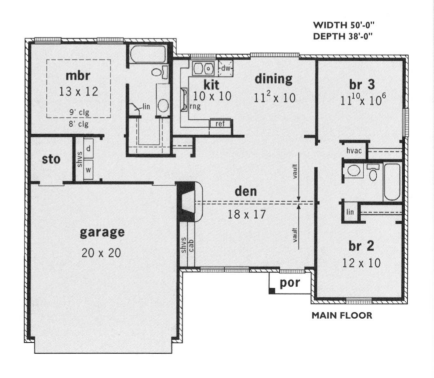

WIDTH 50'-0"
DEPTH 38'-0"

MAIN FLOOR

Classic Country Farmhouse

© Donald A. Gardner Architects, Inc.

■ *Total living area 1,832 sq. ft.* ■ *Price Code F* ■

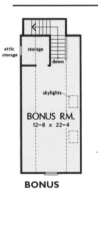

attic storage

storage

down

skylights

BONUS RM.
12-8 x 22-4

BONUS

PORCH

BED RM.
12-8 x 11-0

(cathedral ceiling)

BRKFST.
11-4 x 9-2

MASTER
BED RM.
14-0 x 16-4

skylight

master
bath

lin.

up

walk-in
closet

w d

UTIL. cl

storage

GREAT RM.
16-4 x 18-8

fireplace

KIT.
11-4 x 12-4

cl

lin.

bath

walk-in
closet

cl

BED RM./
STUDY
12-4 x 13-0

FOYER
6-4 x
9-8

vaulted
ceiling

DINING
12-4 x 13-0

GARAGE
21-8 x 22-4

storage

(optional door location)

PORCH

MAIN FLOOR

62-0

65-4

© Donald A. Gardner Architects, Inc.

No. 99808

■ **This plan features:**

— Three bedrooms

— Two full baths

■ Dormers, arched windows and multiple columns give this home country charm

■ Foyer, expanded by vaulted ceiling, accesses Dining Room, Bedroom/Study and Great Room

■ Expansive Great Room, with hearth fireplace topped by cathedral ceiling, opens to rear Porch and efficient Kitchen

■ Alternate foundation options available at an additional charge. Please call 1.800.235.5700 for more information.

■ This home comes with a crawlspace foundation.

Main floor — 1,832 sq. ft.
Bonus room — 425 sq. ft.
Garage & storage — 562 sq. ft.

Plush Master Bedroom Wing

■ *Total living area 1,849 sq. ft.* ■ *Price Code C* ■

No. 92705

■ **This plan features:**

— Three bedrooms

— Two full baths

■ A raised, tile Foyer with a decorative window leading into an expansive Living Room, accented by a tiled fireplace and framed by French doors

■ An efficient Kitchen with a walk-in Pantry and serving bar adjoining the Breakfast and Utility Areas

■ A private Master Bedroom, crowned by a stepped ceiling, offering an atrium door to outside, a huge, walk-in closet and a luxurious Bath

■ This home comes with a slab foundation.

Main floor — 1,849 sq. ft.
Garage — 437 sq. ft.

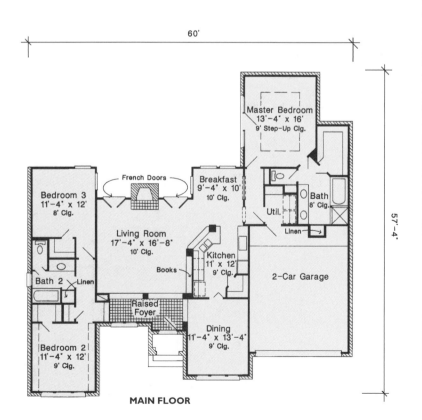

Delightful Home

■ *Total living area 1,853 sq. ft.* ■ *Price Code D* ■

No. 94248

■ **This plan features:**

— Three bedrooms

— Two full baths

■ Grand Room with a fireplace, vaulted ceiling and double French doors to the rear Deck

■ Kitchen has a large walk-in Pantry, island with a sink and dishwasher creating a perfect triangular workspace

■ Master Bedroom features a double door entry, private Bath and a Morning Kitchen

■ This home comes with a pier/post foundation.

First floor — 1,342 sq. ft.
Second floor — 511 sq. ft.

SECOND FLOOR

FIRST FLOOR

Symmetrical and Stately

■ *Total living area 2,387 sq. ft.* ■ *Price Code E* ■

No. 92546

■ **This plan features:**

— Four bedrooms

— Two full and one half baths

■ Dining Room accented by an arched window and pillars

■ Decorative ceiling crowns the Den which contains a hearth fireplace, built-in shelves and large double window

■ Kitchen with a peninsula serving counter and Breakfast Area, adjoining the Utility Room and Garage

■ Master Bedroom Suite with a decorative ceiling, two vanities and a large walk-in closet

■ Three additional Bedrooms with double closets share a full Bath

■ An optional slab or crawlspace foundation — please specify when ordering

Main floor — 2,387 sq. ft.
Garage — 505 sq. ft.

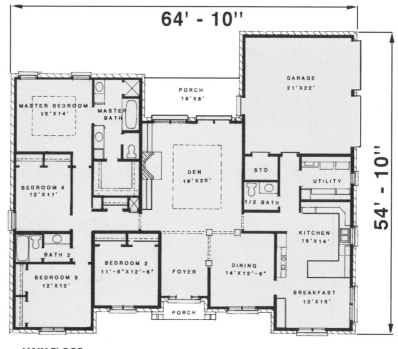

MAIN FLOOR

Essence of Style & Grace

■ *Total living area 2,902 sq. ft.* ■ *Price Code G* ■

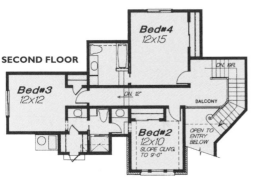

SECOND FLOOR

Bed#4
12x15

Bed#3
12x12

Bed#2
12x10
SLOPE CLNG.
TO 9'-0"

BALCONY

OPEN TO
ENTRY
BELOW

FIRST FLOOR

65'-0"

53'-4"

Patio

Brkfst
15x11

FamRm
17x15
CATH. CLNG.

Kit
12x11

Util
SLOPE CLNG. TO 9'

BUTLERS
PANTRY

LivRm
15x14
10'-0" CLNG. HT.

Gallery
10'-0" CLNG. HT.

FmlDin
11x13
10'-0" CLNG. HT.

Patio

MstrBed
14x16
VAULT
CLNG.

Ent
SLOPE
CLNG. TO
9'-0"

Study
10x12
VAULT
CLNG.

Por

3 Car Gar
30x26

No. 98524

■ **This plan features:**

— Four bedrooms

— Three full and one half baths

■ French doors introduce Study and columns define the Gallery and formal areas

■ The expansive Family Room with an inviting fireplace and a cathedral ceiling opens to the Kitchen

■ The Kitchen features a cooktop island, butler's Pantry, Breakfast Area and Patio access

■ The first floor Master Bedroom offers a private Patio, vaulted ceiling, twin vanities and a walk-in closet

■ An optional basement or slab foundation — please specify when ordering

First floor — 2,036 sq. ft.
Second floor — 866 sq. ft.
Garage — 720 sq. ft.

Covered Front and Rear Porches

■ *Total living area 1,660 sq. ft.* ■ *Price Code B* ■

No. 92560

■ **This plan features:**

— Three bedrooms

— Two full baths

■ Traditional country styling with front and rear covered Porches

■ Peninsula counter/eating bar in Kitchen for meals on the go

■ Formal Dining Room with built-in cabinet

■ Vaulted ceiling and cozy fireplace highlighting Den

■ Private Master Bedroom suite pampered by five-piece Bath

■ Two Bedrooms at the opposite of home sharing a full Bath

■ An optional slab or crawlspace foundation — please specify when ordering

Main floor — 1,660 sq. ft.
Garage — 544 sq. ft.

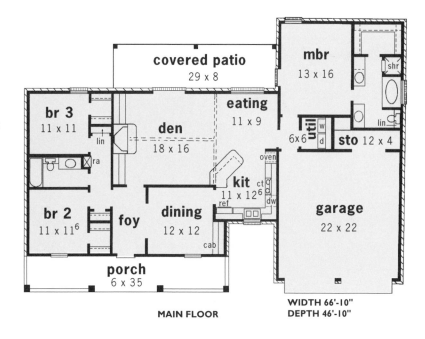

Eye-Catching Turret Adds to Master Suite

■ *Total living area 2,403 sq. ft.* ■ *Price Code E* ■

SECOND FLOOR

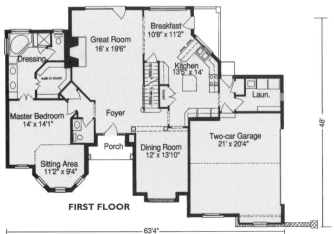

FIRST FLOOR

No. 92651

■ This plan features:

— Four bedrooms

— Three full and one half baths

■ Sheltered entry surrounded by glass leads into open Foyer and Great Room with high ceiling, hearth fireplace and atrium door to backyard

■ Columns frame entrance to Dining Room

■ Kitchen with built-in Pantry, work island and bright Breakfast Area

■ Master Bedroom wing with Sitting Area, walk-in closet and private Bath with corner window tub and double vanity

■ An optional basement or slab foundation — please specify when ordering.

First floor — 1,710 sq. ft.
Second floor — 693 sq. ft.
Basement — 1,620 sq. ft.
Garage — 467 sq. ft.

Dramatic Dormers

© Donald A. Gardner Architects, Inc.

B. NATHAN

■ *Total living area 1,685 sq. ft.* ■ *Price Code F* ■

No. 99810

■ **This plan features:**

– Three bedrooms

– Two full baths

■ A Foyer open to the dramatic dormer, defined by columns

■ A Dining Room augmented by a tray ceiling

■ A Great Room expanded into the open Kitchen and Breakfast Room

■ A privately located Master Suite, topped by a tray ceiling in the Bedroom

■ This home comes with a crawlspace foundation.

■ Alternate foundation options available at an additional charge. Please call 1.800.235.5700 for more information.

Main floor — 1,685 sq. ft.
Bonus area — 331 sq. ft.
Garage & storage — 536 sq. ft.

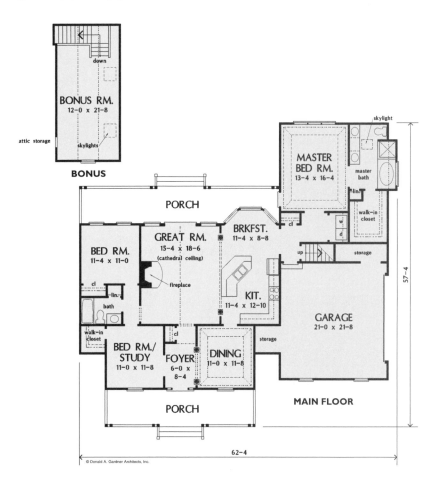

Quaint Starter Home

■ *Total living area 1,050 sq. ft.* ■ *Price Code A* ■

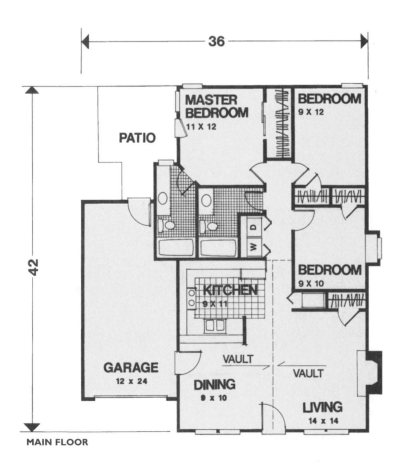

MAIN FLOOR

No. 92400

■ **This plan features:**

— Three bedrooms

— Two full baths

■ A vaulted ceiling giving an airy feeling to the Dining and Living Rooms

■ A streamlined Kitchen with a comfortable work area, a double sink and ample cabinet space

■ A cozy fireplace in the Living Room

■ A Master Suite with a large closet, French doors leading to the Patio and a private Bath

■ Two additional Bedrooms sharing a full Bath

■ An optional basement or slab foundation — please specify when ordering.

Main floor — 1,050 sq. ft.
Garage — 261 sq. ft.

■ *Total living area 1,515 sq. ft.* ■ *Price Code B* ■

No. 96522

■ **This plan features:**

— Three bedrooms

— Two full baths

■ The triple arched front Porch adds to the curb appeal of the home

■ The expansive Great Room is accented by a cozy gas fireplace

■ The efficient Kitchen includes an eating bar that separates it from the Great Room

■ The Master Bedroom is highlighted by a walk-in closet and a whirlpool Bath

■ The rear Porch extends dining to the outdoors

■ An optional slab or crawlspace foundation — please specify when ordering.

Main floor — 1,515 sq. ft.
Garage — 528 sq. ft.

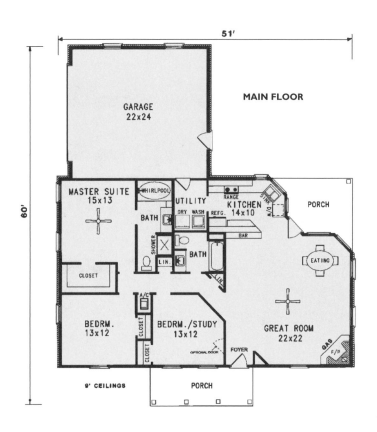

For the Discriminating Buyer

■ Total living area 1,710 sq. ft. ■ Price Code B ■

No. 92625

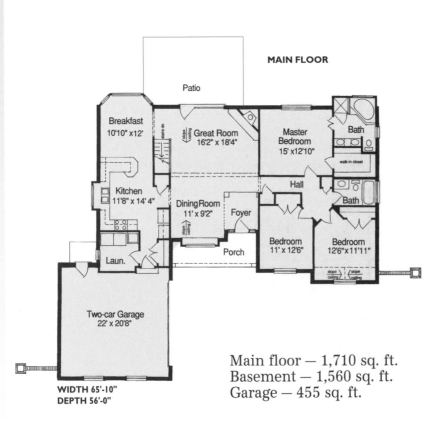

MAIN FLOOR

Patio

Breakfast 10'10" x 12'

Great Room 16'2" x 18'4"

Master Bedroom 15' x 12'10"

Bath

walk-in closet

Kitchen 11'8" x 14' 4"

Dining Room 11' x 9'2"

Foyer

Hall

Bath

Laun.

Porch

Bedroom 11' x 12'6"

Bedroom 12'6" x 11'11"

Two-car Garage 22' x 20'8"

WIDTH 65'-10"
DEPTH 56'-0"

Main floor — 1,710 sq. ft.
Basement — 1,560 sq. ft.
Garage — 455 sq. ft.

■ This plan features:

— Three bedrooms

— Two full baths

■ An attractive, classic brick design with wood trim, multiple gables, and wing walls

■ A sheltered entrance into the Foyer

■ A sloped ceiling adding elegance to the formal Dining Room which flows easily into the Great Room

■ A sloped ceiling and a corner fireplace enhancing the Great Room

■ A Kitchen with a garden window above the double sink

■ A peninsula counter joins the Kitchen and the Breakfast Room in an open layout

■ A Master Suite, equipped with a large walk-in closet and a private Bath with an oval corner tub

■ This home comes with a basement foundation.

Distinctive Brick with Room to Expand

■ *Total living area 2,645 sq. ft.* ■ *Price Code F* ■

No. 93206

■ **This plan features:**

- Four bedrooms

- Two full and one half baths

■ Arched entrance with decorative glass leads into two-story Foyer

■ Formal Dining Room with tray ceiling above decorative window

■ Efficient Kitchen with island cooktop, built-in desk and Pantry

■ Master Bedroom topped by tray ceiling with French door to Patio, huge private Bath with garden tub and two walk-in closets

■ Optional space for Storage and Future Bedroom with full Bath

■ An optional basement, crawlspace or slab foundation — please specify when ordering

First Floor — 2,577 sq. ft.
Future Second Floor — 619 sq. ft.
Bridge — 68 sq. ft.
Basement — 2,561 sq. ft.
Garage — 560 sq. ft.

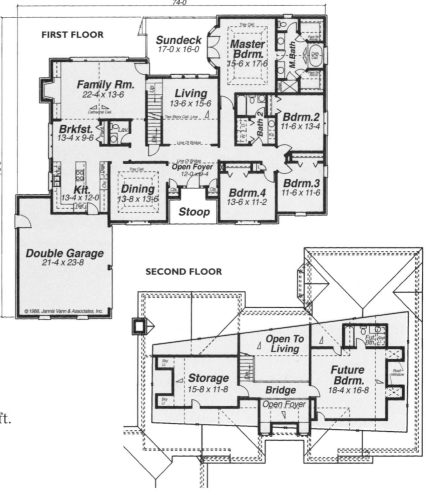

Cozy Traditional with Style

Total living area 1,830 sq. ft. ■ Price Code C

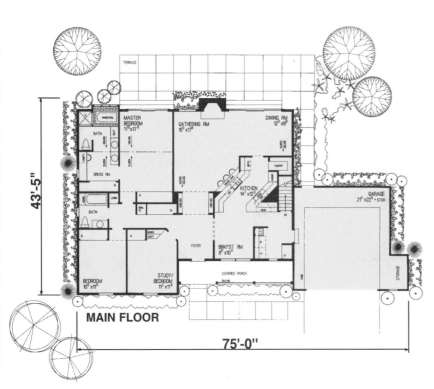

MAIN FLOOR

43'-5"

75'-0"

No. 99208

■ **This plan features:**

— Three bedrooms

— Two full baths

■ A convenient one-level design

■ A galley-style Kitchen that shares a snack bar with the spacious Gathering Room

■ Inviting focal point fireplace in Gathering Room

■ An ample Master Suite with a luxurious Bath which includes a whirlpool tub and separate Dressing Room

■ Two additional Bedrooms, one that could double as a Study, located at the front of the house

■ This home comes with a basement foundation.

Main floor — 1,830 sq. ft.
Basement — 1,830 sq. ft.

■ *Total living area 1,531 sq. ft.* ■ *Price Code B* ■

No. 90358

This plan features:

- Three bedrooms

- Two full baths

- A vaulted ceiling in the Great Room and a fireplace

- An efficient Kitchen with a peninsula counter and double sink

- A Family Room with easy access to the Deck

- A Master Bedroom with private Bath entrance

- Convenient laundry facilities outside the Master Bedroom

- Two additional Bedrooms upstairs with walk-in closets and the use of the full hall Bath

- This home comes with a basement foundation.

First floor — 1,062 sq. ft.
Second floor — 469 sq. ft.

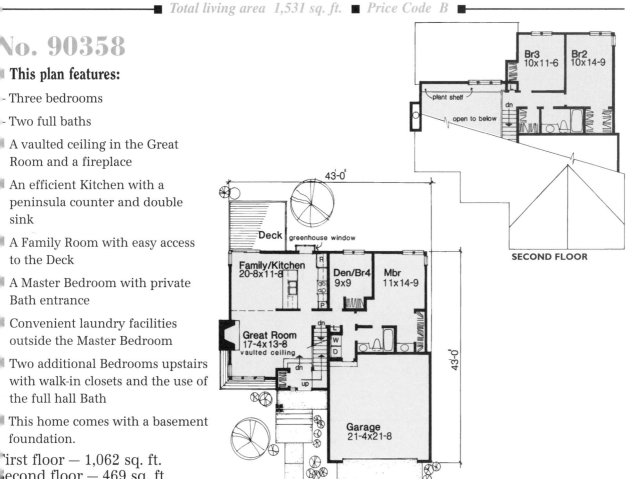

Spectacular Stucco and Stone

■ *Total living area 4,106 sq. ft.* ■ *Price Code L* ■

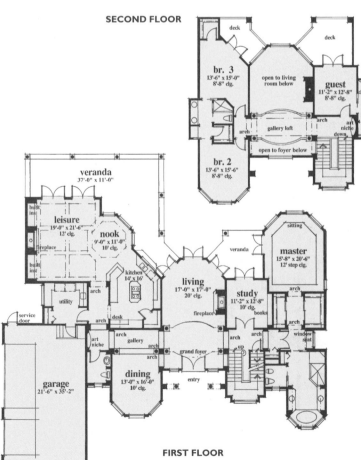

SECOND FLOOR

deck

deck

br. 3
13'-6" x 15'-0"
8'-8" clg.

open to living room below

guest
11'-2" x 12'-8"
8'-8" clg.

arch

gallery loft

arch

art niche down

br. 2
13'-6" x 15'-6"
8'-8" clg.

open to foyer below

veranda
37'-0" x 11'-0"

built ins

leisure
19'-0" x 21'-6"
12' clg.

nook
9'-0" x 11'-0"
10' clg.

fireplace

built ins

kitchen
14' x 16'

sitting

veranda

master
15'-8" x 20'-6"
12' step clg.

living
17'-0" x 17'-0"
20' clg.

study
11'-2" x 12'-8"
10' clg.

books

arch

arch

arch

utility

arch

desk

fireplace

service door

art niche

arch

gallery

arch

arch

arch

arch

window seat

up

grand foyer

dining
13'-0" x 16'-0"
10' clg.

entry

garage
21'-6" x 35'-2"

FIRST FLOOR

No. 94239

■ This plan features:

— Four bedrooms

— One full, two three-quarter and one half baths

■ Arches and columns accent Entry Grand Foyer, Gallery, Living and Dining rooms

■ Open Living Room with fireplace and multiple glass doors

■ Angled Kitchen with walk-in Pantry and peninsula counter

■ An optional slab or combo basement/crawlspace foundation — please specify when ordering.

■ Alternate foundation options available at an additional charge, call 1.800.235.5700 for more information.

First floor — 3,027 sq. ft.
Second floor — 1,079 sq. ft.
Basement — 3,027 sq. ft.
Garage — 802 sq. ft.

Rustic Warmth

■ *Total living area 1,764 sq. ft.* ■ *Price Code C* ■

No. 90440

■ **This plan features:**

— Three bedrooms

— Two full baths

■ A fireplaced Living Room with built-in bookshelves

■ A fully-equipped Kitchen with an island

■ A sunny Dining Room with glass sliders to the Deck

■ A first floor Master Suite with walk-in closet and lavish Master Bath

■ An optional basement or crawlspace foundation — please specify when ordering.

First floor — 1,100 sq. ft.
Second floor — 664 sq. ft.
Basement — 1,100 sq. ft.

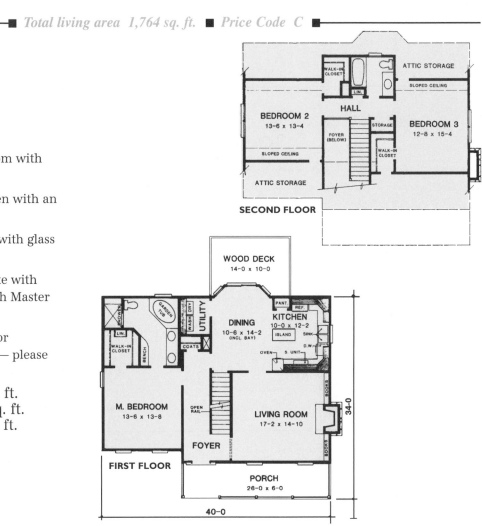

Perfect Home for Narrow Lot

© Donald A. Gardner Architects, Inc.

B. NATHAN

■ *Total living area 1,669 sq. ft.* ■ *Price Code F* ■

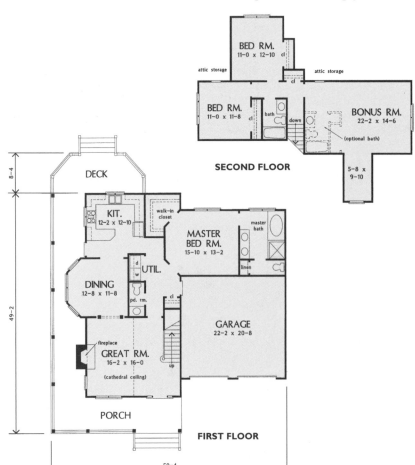

SECOND FLOOR

BED RM.
11-0 x 12-10 cl

attic storage

attic storage

BED RM.
11-0 x 11-8 cl

bath

down

BONUS RM.
22-2 x 14-6

(optional bath)

5-8 x
9-10

FIRST FLOOR

DECK

KIT.
12-2 x 12-10

walk-in closet

master bath

MASTER BED RM.
15-10 x 13-2

linen

UTIL.

d
w

DINING
12-8 x 11-8

pd. rm.

cl

GARAGE
22-2 x 20-8

fireplace

GREAT RM.
16-2 x 16-0

(cathedral ceiling)

up

PORCH

8-4

49-2

50-4

© Donald A. Gardner Architects, Inc.

No. 96487

■ This plan features:

— Three bedrooms

— Two full and one half baths

■ Wraparound Porch and two-car Garage features unusual for narrow lot floor plan

■ Cathedral ceiling above inviting fireplace accent spacious Great Room

■ Efficient Kitchen with peninsula counter accesses side Porch and Deck

■ This home comes with a crawlspace foundation.

■ Alternate foundation options available at an additional charge, call 1.800.235.5700 for more information.

First floor — 1,219 sq. ft.
Second floor — 450 sq. ft.
Bonus Room — 406 sq. ft.
Garage — 473 sq. ft.

■ *Total living area 3,381 sq. ft.* ■ *Price Code I* ■

No. 98514

This plan features:

- Five bedrooms
- Two full, one three-quarter and one half baths
- The Entry/Gallery features a grand spiral staircase
- The Study has built-in bookcases
- Formal Living and Dining Rooms each have palladian windows
- The large Family Room has a fireplace
- The first floor Master Bedroom contains a luxurious Bath with a cathedral ceiling
- An optional slab or crawlspace foundation — please specify when ordering

First floor — 2,208 sq. ft.
Second floor — 1,173 sq. ft.
Bonus — 224 sq. ft.
Garage — 520 sq. ft.

SECOND FLOOR

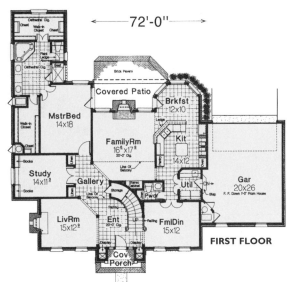

FIRST FLOOR

Small, Yet Lavishly Appointed

■ *Total living area 1,845 sq. ft.* ■ *Price Code C* ■

No. 98425

■ **This plan features:**

— Three bedrooms

— Two full and one half baths

■ The Dining Room, Living Room, Foyer and Master Bath all topped by high ceilings

■ Master Bedroom includes a decorative tray ceiling and a walk in closet

■ Kitchen open to the Breakfast Room and enhanced by a serving bar and a Pantry

■ Living Room with a large fireplace and a French door to the rear yard

■ An optional basement or crawlspace foundation — please specify when ordering.

Main floor — 1,845 sq. ft.
Bonus — 409 sq. ft.
Basement — 1,845 sq. ft.
Garage — 529 sq. ft.

■ *Total living area 1,767 sq. ft.* ■ *Price Code C* ■

No. 99045

This plan features:

- Three bedrooms

- Two full and one half baths

- Full front Porch provides comfortable visiting and a sheltered entrance

- Expansive Living Room with an inviting fireplace opens to bright Dining Room and Kitchen

- U-shaped Kitchen with peninsula serving counter and nearby Pantry

- Secluded Master Bedroom with two closets and a double vanity Bath

- Two second floor Bedrooms share a full Bath

- This home comes with a basement foundation.

First floor — 1,108 sq. ft.
Second floor — 659 sq. ft.
Basement — 875 sq. ft.

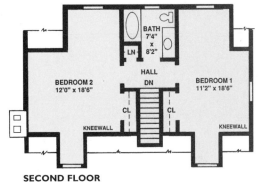

SECOND FLOOR

WIDTH 67'-0"
DEPTH 30'-0"

FIRST FLOOR

Vacation Retreat or Year Round Living

Total living area 1,024 sq. ft. ■ Price Code A ■

MAIN FLOOR

No. 1078

■ **This plan features:**

— Two bedrooms

— One full bath

■ A long hallway dividing Bedrooms and living areas assuring privacy

■ A centrally located Utility Room and Bath

■ An open Living/Dining Room area with exposed beams, sloping ceilings and optional fireplace

■ This home comes with a crawlspace foundation.

Main floor — 1,024 sq. ft.
Carport & Storage — 387 sq. ft.
Deck — 411 sq. ft.

Elegant Elevation

Total living area 2,217 sq. ft. ■ Price Code D ■

FIRST FLOOR

SECOND FLOOR

No. 92622

■ **This plan features:**

— Three bedrooms

— Two full and one half baths

■ Brick trim, sidelights and a transom window give a warm welcome to this hom

■ High ceilings continue from Foyer into Great Room which counts among it's amenities a fireplace and entertainment center

■ The Kitchen serves the formal and inform. Dining Areas with ease

■ The Master Suite is positioned for privacy on the first floor

■ The second floor has loads of possibilities with a Bonus space and a Study

■ Two Bedrooms, each with walk-in closet, share a full Bath

■ This home comes with a basement foundation.

First floor — 1,134 sq. ft.
Second floor — 1,083 sq. ft.
Basement — 931 sq. ft.
Garage — 554 sq. ft

■ *Total living area 1,322 sq. ft.* ■ *Price Code A* ■

No. 93072

This plan features:

Three bedrooms

Two full baths

The cozy Kitchen with a Pantry, and cooking island has an area for a table

Ten-foot ceilings are found in all the main living areas

A well proportioned Living Room has a fireplace

The Bedrooms are grouped for convenience

A two-car Garage is tucked away in the rear to provide a pleasing front elevation

An optional crawlspace or slab foundation — please specify when ordering

Main floor — 1,322 sq. ft.
Garage — 528 sq. ft.

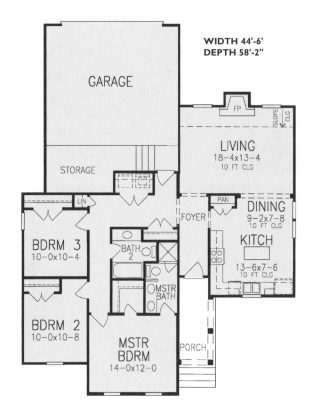

WIDTH 44'-6'
DEPTH 58'-2"

GARAGE

STORAGE

LIN

BDRM 3
10-0x10-4

BDRM 2
10-0x10-8

MSTR BDRM
14-0x12-0

BATH 2

MSTR BATH

FOYER

PORCH

FP

LIVING
18-4x13-4
10 FT CLG

SLOPE CLG

PAN

DINING
9-2x7-8
10 FT CLG

KITCH
13-6x7-6
10 FT CLG

MAIN FLOOR

European Flair

■ *Total living area 1,544 sq. ft.* ■ *Price Code B* ■

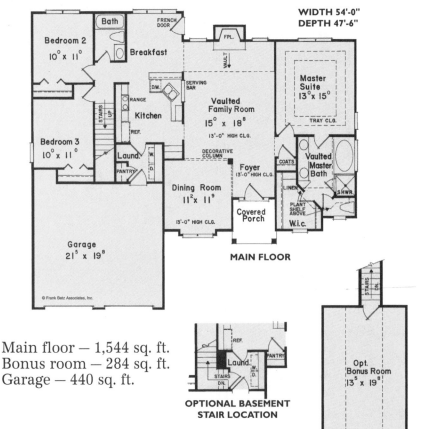

WIDTH 54'-0"
DEPTH 47'-6"

Bath

Bedroom 2
10⁰ x 11⁰

FRENCH DOOR

Breakfast

FPL.

VAULT

Master Suite
13⁰ x 15⁰

SERVING BAR

D.W.

RANGE

Kitchen

REF.

Vaulted Family Room
15⁰ x 18⁸
13'-0" HIGH CLG.

TRAY CLG.

STAIRS UP

Bedroom 3
10⁰ x 11⁰

Laund.

DECORATIVE COLUMN

COATS

Vaulted Master Bath

PANTRY

Foyer
13'-0" HIGH CLG.

LINEN

SHWR.

Dining Room
11² x 11⁹

Covered Porch

PLANT SHELF ABOVE

W.i.c.

13'-0" HIGH CLG.

Garage
21⁵ x 19⁸

MAIN FLOOR

© Frank Betz Associates, Inc.

Main floor — 1,544 sq. ft.
Bonus room — 284 sq. ft.
Garage — 440 sq. ft.

REF.

Laund.

W. D.

PANTRY

STAIRS DN.

OPTIONAL BASEMENT STAIR LOCATION

STAIRS DN.

Opt. Bonus Room
13⁵ x 19⁸

OPTIONAL BONUS ROOM

No. 98460

■ **This plan features:**

— Three bedrooms

— Two full baths

■ Large fireplace serving as an attractive focal point for the vaulted Family Room

■ Decorative column defining the elegant Dining Room

■ Kitchen including a serving bar for the Family Room and a Breakfast Area

■ Master Suite topped by a tray ceiling over the Bedroom and a vaulted ceiling over the five-piece Master Bath

■ Optional Bonus Room for future expansion

■ An optional basement or crawlspace foundation — please specify when ordering

Simplicity at its Finest

No. 99420

This plan features:

Three bedrooms

Two full and one half baths

A covered Porch gives the home a nostalgic feel

The volume Great Room offers a fireplace with transom windows on either side

A built-in planning desk and Pantry in the Breakfast Area

A snack bar for informal meals highlights the Kitchen

The formal Dining Room overlooks the porch, which has easy access to the Kitchen

An isolated Master Suite has a five-piece Bath and a walk-in closet

This home comes with a basement foundation.

First floor — 1,298 sq. ft.

Second floor — 396 sq. ft.

Basement — 1,298 sq. ft.

Garage — 513 sq. ft.

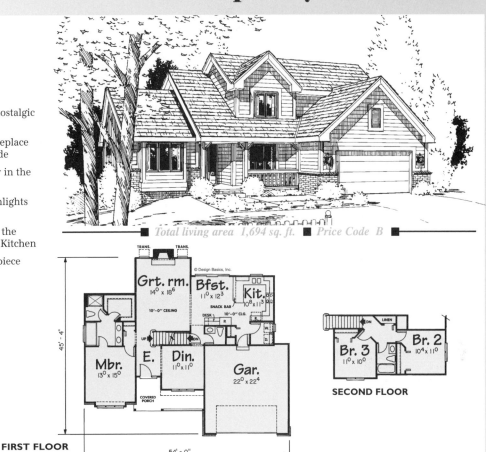

Total living area 1,694 sq. ft. ■ *Price Code B* ■

FIRST FLOOR

SECOND FLOOR

Versatile Chalet

No. 90847

This plan features:

Two bedrooms

Two full baths

A Sun Deck entry into a spacious Living Room/Dining Room with a fieldstone fireplace, a large window and a sliding glass door

A well-appointed Kitchen with extended counter space and easy access to the Dining Room and the Utility Area

A first floor Bedroom adjoins a full hall Bath

A spacious Master Bedroom, with a private Deck, a suite Bath and plenty of storage

This home comes with a basement foundation.

First floor — 864 sq. ft.

Second floor — 496 sq. ft.

Basement — 864 sq. ft.

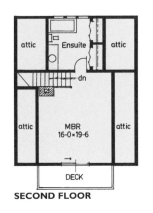

Total living area 1,360 sq. ft. ■ *Price Code A* ■

SECOND FLOOR

FIRST FLOOR

WIDTH 27'-0"
DEPTH 32'-0"

125

Three Bedroom Traditional Country Cape

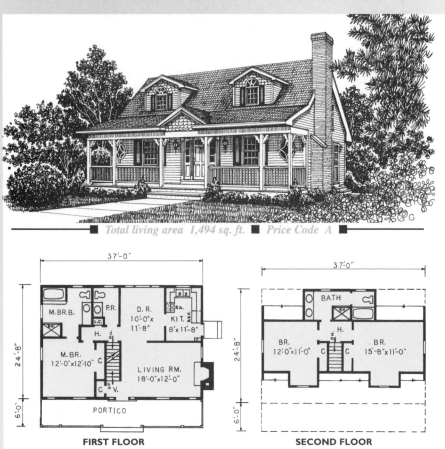

Total living area 1,494 sq. ft. ■ *Price Code A*

FIRST FLOOR

SECOND FLOOR

No. 99022

■ **This plan features:**

— Three bedrooms

— Two full and one half baths

■ Entry area with a coat closet

■ An ample Living Room with a fireplace

■ A Dining Room with a view of the rear yard and located conveniently close to the Kitchen and Living Room

■ A U-shaped Kitchen with a double sink, ample cabinet and counter space and a side door to the outside

■ A first floor Master Suite with a private Master Bath

■ Two additional, second floor Bedrooms that share a full, double vanity Bath with a separate shower

■ This home comes with a basement foundation.

First floor — 913 sq. ft.
Second floor — 581 sq. ft.

Spanish Influence

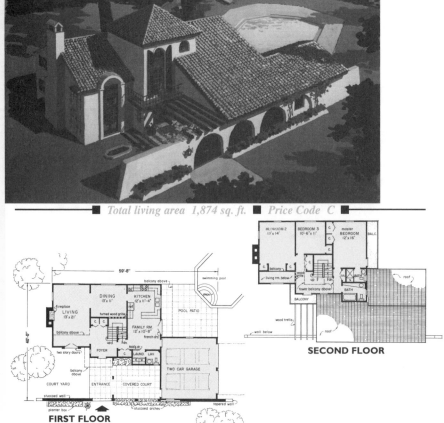

Total living area 1,874 sq. ft. ■ *Price Code C*

FIRST FLOOR

SECOND FLOOR

No. 90000

■ **This plan features:**

— Three bedrooms

— One full, one three-quarter and one half baths

■ A fireplace and two-story doors to the courtyard highlight the Living Room

■ The Dining Room is located between the Living Room and the Kitchen

■ The Family Room is separated from the Kitchen by a peninsula counter

■ French doors to a Patio area enhance the Family Room

■ The Master Suite has a private three-quarter Bath

■ Two additional Bedrooms share the use of a full Bath in the hall

■ This home comes with a basement foundation.

First floor — 969 sq. ft.
Second floor — 905 sq. ft.
Basement — 969 sq. ft.
Garage — 420 sq. ft.

■ *Total living area 1,883 sq. ft.* ■ *Price Code F* ■

No. 96479

This plan features:

Three bedrooms

Two full baths

Columns accenting the Dining Room, adjacent to the Foyer

Great room, open to the Kitchen and Breakfast Room, enlarged by a cathedral ceiling

Master Suite topped by a tray and includes a skylit Bath with garden tub and a double vanity

This home comes with a crawlspace foundation.

Alternate foundation options available at an additional charge, call 1.800.235.5700 for more information.

First floor — 1,803 sq. ft.

Second floor — 80 sq. ft.

Garage & storage — 569 sq. ft.

Bonus Space — 918 sq. ft.

Impressive Fieldstone Facade

■ *Total living area 3,110 sq. ft.* ■ *Price Code H* ■

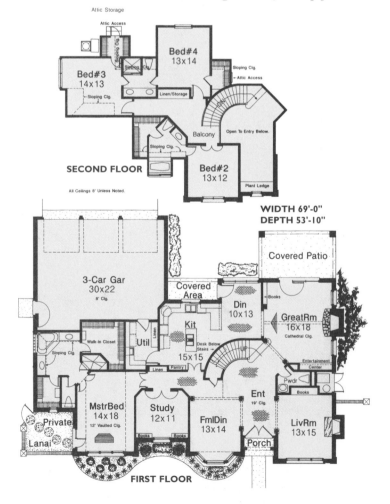

Attic Storage

Attic Access

Bed#4
13x14

Sloping Clg.

Attic Access

Bed#3
14x13

Sloping Clg.

Linen/Storage

Sloping Clg.

Balcony

Open To Entry Below.

Sloping Clg.

SECOND FLOOR

Bed#2
13x12

Plant Ledge

All Ceilings 8' Unless Noted.

WIDTH 69'-0"
DEPTH 53'-10"

Covered Patio

3-Car Gar
30x22
8' Clg.

Covered Area

Din
10x13

Books

GreatRm
16x18
Cathedral Clg.

Kit
15x15

Desk Below Stairs

Util

Walk-In Closet

Sloping Clg.

Linen Pantry

Entertainment Center

Pwdr

Books

Ent
19' Clg.

MstrBed
14x18
12' Vaulted Clg.

Private Lanai

Study
12x11

Books Books

FmlDin
13x14

Porch

LivRm
13x15

Books

FIRST FLOOR

No. 92277

■ This plan features:

— Four bedrooms

— Three full and one half baths

■ Double-door leads into two-story Entry with an exquisite curved staircase

■ Formal Living Room features a marble hearth fireplace, triple window and built-in book shelve

■ Formal Dining Room defined by columns and a lovely bay window

■ Expansive Great Room with entertainment center, fieldstone fireplace and cathedral ceiling

■ Vaulted ceiling crowns Master Bedroom suite offering a plush Bath and two walk-in closets

■ An optional basement or slab foundation — please specify whe ordering.

First floor — 2,190 sq. ft.
Second floor — 920 sq. ft.
Garage — 624 sq. ft.

Contemporary Classic with a Custom Look

No. 99314

This plan features:

- Two bedrooms
- Two full and one half baths
- A well-appointed Kitchen with an angular Nook
- A two-story Great Room accentuated by a massive fireplace and glass sliders to the rear Deck
- A bump-out window seat and private bath with double vanities in the Master Suite
- This home comes with a basement foundation.

First floor — 1,044 sq. ft.
Second floor — 454 sq. ft.
Basement — 1,044 sq. ft.
Garage — 380 sq. ft.

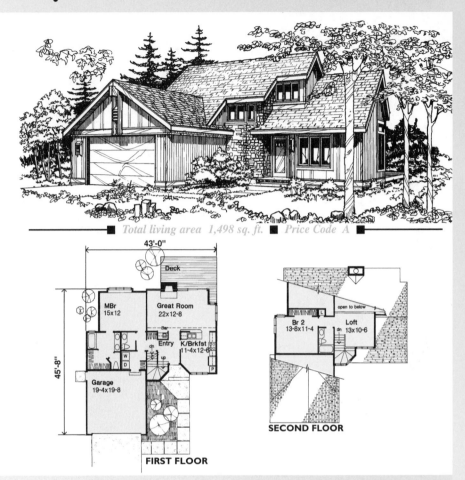

Total living area 1,498 sq. ft. ■ Price Code A

FIRST FLOOR

SECOND FLOOR

Loads of Natural Light

No. 24705

This plan features:

- Three bedrooms
- Two full baths
- Double French doors with arched transom windows access an elevated Deck
- Spacious feeling created by open Great Room, Dining Area and Kitchen
- Two first floor Bedrooms with ample closets, share a full Bath
- Secluded Master Bedroom with covered Deck, plush Bath, loads of storage and a Loft
- Lower floor offers an optional Recreation Room with Patio, fireplace and wetbar
- This home comes with a basement foundation.

First floor — 1,062 sq. ft.
Second floor — 500 sq. ft.
Bonus — 678 sq. ft.
Basement — 384 sq. ft.

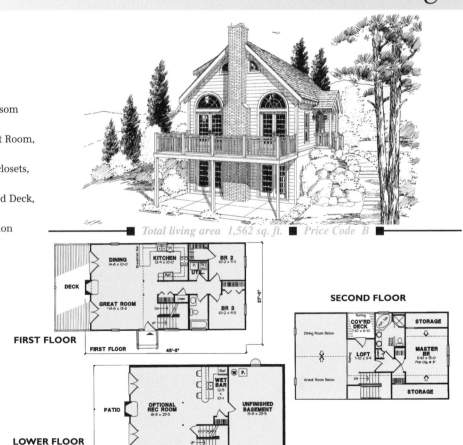

Total living area 1,562 sq. ft. ■ Price Code B

FIRST FLOOR

SECOND FLOOR

LOWER FLOOR

Adapt this Colonial to Your Lifestyle

Total living area 1,587 sq. ft. ■ **Price Code B**

No. 90671

■ **This plan features:**

— Four bedrooms

— Two full baths

■ A Living Room with a beam ceiling and a fireplace

■ An eat-in Kitchen efficiently serving the formal Dining Room

■ A Master Bedroom with his and her closets

■ Two upstairs Bedrooms sharing a split Bath

■ This home comes with a basement foundation.

First floor — 1,056 sq. ft.
Second floor — 531 sq. ft.

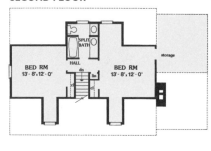

FIRST FLOOR

SECOND FLOOR

The Town House

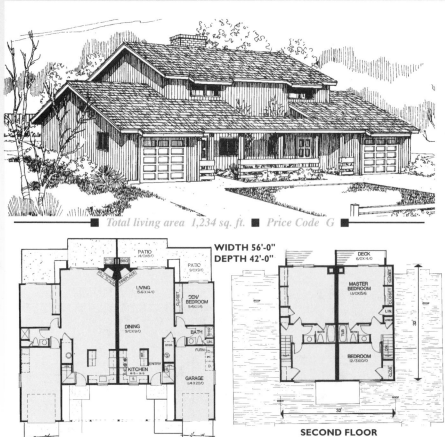

Total living area 1,234 sq. ft. ■ **Price Code G**

No. 91325

■ **This plan features (per unit):**

— Two or three bedrooms

— One full and one three-quarter baths

■ Sheltered entrance leads to spacious Living/Dining Area

■ Living area enhanced by a corner fireplace and sliding glass door to Patio with built-in barbecue

■ Efficient, U-shaped Kitchen easily serves Dining Area

■ Den/Bedroom with a large closet and easy access to Patio and full Bath

■ Spacious Master Bedroom offers three closets, a private Deck and full Bath access

■ Secondary Bedroom with a large closet and easy access to a full Bath

■ This home comes with a slab foundation.

First floor — 722 sq. ft.
Second floor — 512 sq. ft.

WIDTH 56'-0"
DEPTH 42'-0"

FIRST FLOOR

SECOND FLOOR

Exciting Three-Bedroom

© Donald A. Gardner Architects, Inc.

B. NATHAN

■ *Total living area 1,787 sq. ft.* ■ *Price Code F* ■

No. 99805

This plan features:

- Three bedrooms

- Two full baths

■ A Great Room enhanced by a fireplace, cathedral ceiling and built-in bookshelves

■ A Kitchen designed for efficiency with a food preparation island and a Pantry

■ A Master Suite topped by a cathedral ceiling and pampered by a luxurious Bath and a walk-in closet

■ This home comes with a crawlspace foundation.

■ Alternate foundation options available at an additional charge. Please call 1.800.235.5700 for more information.

Main floor — 1,787 sq. ft.
Garage & storage — 521 sq. ft.
Bonus room — 326 sq. ft.

SCREEN PORCH

BRKFST. 8-6 x 9-6

master bath

MASTER BED RM. 12-4 x 15-2

storage

GARAGE 20-4 x 24-4

DINING RM. 12-8 x 12-0

KITCHEN 10-6 x 13-6

pantry

walk-in closet

GREAT RM. 14-6 x 21-2

fireplace

UTIL.

cl

cl

BED RM. 10-6 x 11-4

FOYER

up

PORCH

bath

skylights

BED RM./ STUDY 11-8 x 12-0

walk-in closet

66-8

66-2

MAIN FLOOR

© 1994 Donald A Gardner Architects, Inc.

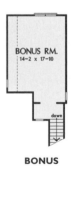

BONUS RM. 14-2 x 17-10

down

BONUS

131

Home on a Hill

■ *Total living area 1,908 sq. ft.* ■ *Price Code C* ■

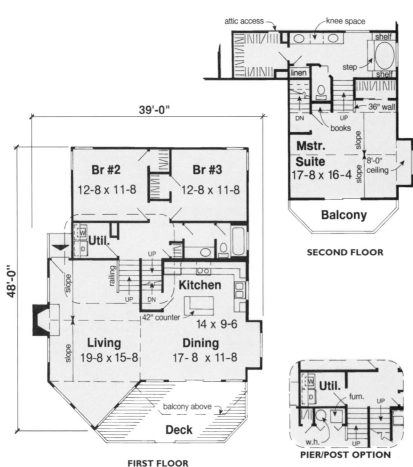

SECOND FLOOR

FIRST FLOOR

PIER/POST OPTION

No. 20501

■ **This plan features:**

— Three bedrooms

— Two full baths

■ Window walls combining with sliders to unite active areas with a huge outdoor deck

■ Interior spaces flowing together for an open feeling, that is accentuated by the sloping ceilings and towering fireplace in the Living Room

■ An island Kitchen with easy access to the Dining Room

■ A Master Suite complete with a garden spa and a balcony

■ This home comes with a slab foundation.

■ An optional pier/post or combo basement/crawlspace foundation. — please specify when ordering.

First floor — 1,316 sq. ft.
Second floor — 592 sq. ft.

Comfortable Vacation Living

No. 98714

This plan features:

— Three bedrooms

— One full, two three-quarter and one half baths

■ A wrap-around Deck offering views and access into the Living Room

■ A sunken Living Room with a vaulted ceiling, and a raised-hearth fireplace adjoining the Dining Area

■ An open Kitchen with a corner sink and windows, an eating bar and a walk-in storage/Pantry

■ Two private Bedroom suites with sliding glass doors leading to a Deck, walk-in closets and plush Baths

■ A Loft Area with a walk-in closet, attic access, a private Bath and a Deck

■ This home comes with a crawlspace foundation.

First floor — 1,704 sq. ft.
Second floor — 313 sq. ft.

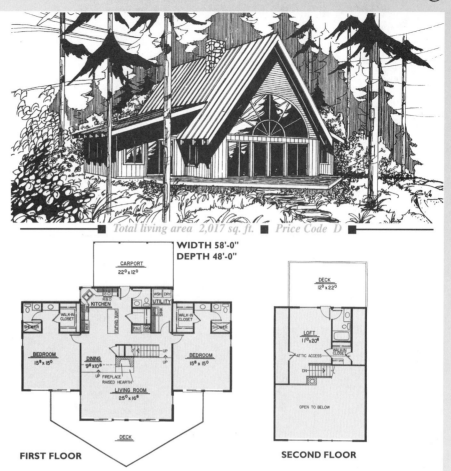

Total living area 2,017 sq. ft. ■ Price Code D

WIDTH 58'-0"
DEPTH 48'-0"

FIRST FLOOR

SECOND FLOOR

Breathtaking Cathedral Ceilings

No. 24402

This plan features:

— Three bedrooms

— Two full baths

■ A spacious Living Room with a cathedral ceiling and elegant fireplace

■ A Dining Room that adjoins both the Living Room and the Kitchen

■ An efficient Kitchen, with double sinks, ample cabinet space and peninsula counter that doubles as an eating bar

■ A convenient hallway laundry center

■ A Master Suite with a cathedral ceiling and a private Master Bath

■ An optional slab or crawlspace foundation — please specify when ordering.

Main Area — 1,346 sq. ft.
Garage — 449 sq. ft.

Total living area 1,346 sq. ft. ■ Price Code A

MAIN FLOOR

Distinctive Detailing

Total living area 1,972 sq. ft. ■ Price Code F

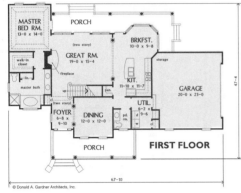

FIRST FLOOR

© Donald A. Gardner Architects, Inc.

SECOND FLOOR

No. 99829

■ **This plan features:**

– Three bedrooms

– Two full and one half baths

■ Interior columns distinguishing the inviting two-story Foyer from the Dining Room

■ Spacious Great Room set off by two-story windows and opening to the Kitchen and Breakfast Bay

■ Nine-foot ceilings adding volume and drama to the first floor

■ Secluded Master Suite topped by a space amplifying tray ceiling and enhanced by a plush Bath

■ Two generous additional Bedrooms with ample closet and storage space

■ Skylit Bonus Room enjoying second floor access

■ This home comes with a crawlspace foundation.

■ Alternate foundation options available at an additional charge. Please call 1.800.235.5700 for more information.

First floor — 1,436 sq. ft.
Second floor — 536 sq. ft.
Garage & storage — 520 sq. ft.
Bonus room — 296 sq. ft.

Design Features Six Sides

Total living area 1,040 sq. ft. ■ Price Code A

MAIN FLOOR

No. 1074

■ **This plan features:**

– Three bedrooms

– One full and one three-quarter baths

■ Active Living Area is centrally located between two quiet Bedroom and Bath areas

■ A Living Room that can be closed off from Bedroom wings giving privacy to both areas

■ A Bath located behind a third Bedroom

■ A Bedroom complete with washer/dryer facilities.

■ This home comes with a crawlspace foundation.

Main floor — 1,040 sq. ft.
Storage — 44 sq. ft.
Deck — 258 sq. ft.
Carport — 230 sq. ft.

Varied Roof Heights Create Interesting Lines

■ Total living area 1,613 sq. ft. ■ Price Code B ■

No. 90601

■ **This plan features:**

– Three bedrooms

– Two full and one half baths

■ A spacious Family Room with a heat-circulating fireplace, which is visible from the Foyer

■ A large Kitchen with a cooktop island, opening into the Dinette bay

■ A Master Suite with his-n-her closets and a private Master Bath

■ Two additional Bedrooms which share a full hall Bath

■ Formal Dining and Living Rooms, flowing into each other for easy entertaining

■ An optional basement or slab foundation — please specify when ordering.

Main floor — 1,613 sq. ft.
Basement — 1,060 sq. ft.
Garage — 461 sq. ft.

MAIN FLOOR

Home With Many Views

■ *Total living area 1,710 sq. ft.* ■ *Price Code B* ■

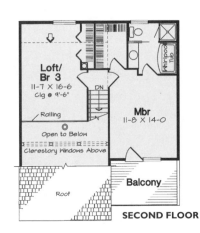

Util Rm
10-11 X 5-9

Wet Bar

Garage
11-8 x 19-0

Rec Rm
11-1 X 20-2

Storage

Optional Hot Tub

Step

UP

LOWER FLOOR

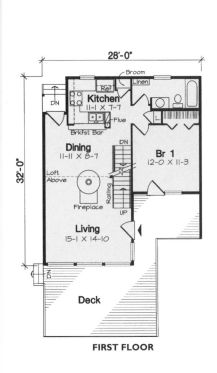

28'-0"

Broom

Ref.

Linen

Kitchen
11-1 X 7-7

DN

Flue

Brkfst Bar

Dining
11-11 X 8-7

DN

Br 1
12-0 X 11-3

Loft Above

Fireplace

UP

Living
15-1 X 14-10

32'-0"

Deck

FIRST FLOOR

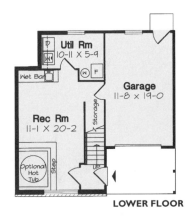

Loft/ Br 3
11-7 X 16-6
Clg @ 9'-6"

Railing

Open to Below

Clerestory Windows Above

DN

Whirlpool Tub

Mbr
11-8 X 14-0

Roof

Balcony

SECOND FLOOR

No. 24319

■ **This plan features:**

— Three bedrooms

— Two full baths

■ Large Decks and windows taking full advantage of the view

■ A fireplace that divides the Living Room from the Dining Room

■ A Kitchen flowing into the Dining Room

■ A Master Bedroom with full Master Bath

■ A Recreation Room sporting a whirlpool tub and a bar

■ This home comes with a basement foundation.

First floor — 728 sq. ft.
Second floor — 573 sq. ft.
Lower floor — 409 sq. ft.
Garage — 244 sq. ft.

A Plus in Any Neighborhood

No. 98802

This plan features:

– Three bedrooms

– Two full and one half baths

■ An open railed staircase creates openness throughout the Foyer

■ A spacious hillside design that captures the view of the rear of the lot

■ An efficient Kitchen serves the formal and informal rooms equally with ease

■ The Living Room includes a cozy corner fireplace

■ The layout between the Family Room and the nook create an open, airy atmosphere

■ The luxurious Master Suite is accented by French doors, and includes a five-piece Bath

■ The Den is highlighted by a bay window

■ This home comes with a basement foundation.

Main floor — 2,035 sq. ft.
Basement — 2,021 sq. ft.
Garage — 528 sq. ft.

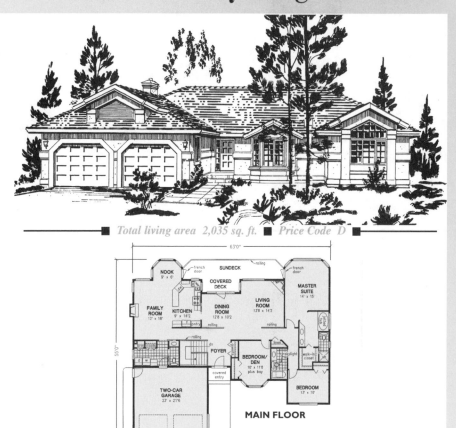

■ Total living area 2,035 sq. ft. ■ Price Code D ■

MAIN FLOOR

Master Suite with Private Sun Deck

No. 91411

This plan features:

– Four bedrooms

– Two and one half baths

■ A sunken Living Room, formal Dining Room, and island Kitchen enjoying an expansive view of the Patio and backyard

■ A fireplaced Living Room keeping the house toasty after the sun goes down

■ Skylights brightening the balcony and Master Bath

■ An optional basement, slab or crawl space foundation — please specify when ordering

Main level — 1,249 sq. ft.
Upper level — 890 sq. ft.
Garage — 462 sq. ft.

■ Total living area 2,139 sq. ft. ■ Price Code D ■

FIRST FLOOR

SECOND FLOOR

Detailed Brick and Fieldstone Facade

Total living area 2,205 sq. ft. ■ Price Code D

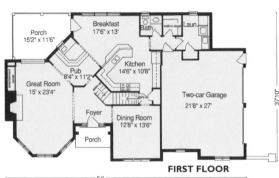

FIRST FLOOR

64'

- Porch 15'2" x 11'6"
- Breakfast 17'6" x 13'
- Bath
- walk-in closet
- Laun.
- Pub 8'4" x 11'2"
- Kitchen 14'6" x 10'8"
- Great Room 15' x 23'4"
- Two-car Garage 21'8" x 27'
- Foyer
- Dining Room 12'8" x 13'6"
- Porch

SECOND FLOOR

37'10"

- Bedroom 11' x 13'2"
- Master Bedroom 12'6" x 16'
- Bath
- walk-in closet
- Hall
- Bath
- Bedroom 12'8" x 11'1"

No. 92675

■ **This plan features**

— Three bedrooms

— Two full and one half baths

■ Open Foyer enhanced by a graceful, banister staircase

■ Great Room highlighted by a twelve-foot ceiling topping an alcove of windows, fireplace, built-in entertainment center and Porch access

■ Spacious Kitchen and Breakfast Area with extended counter/snackbar and nearby Pub, walk-in closet, Laundry and Garage

■ Comfortable Master Bedroom with a large walk-in closet and double vanity Bath

■ Two additional Bedrooms share a double vanity Bath

■ This home comes with a basement foundation.

First floor — 1,192 sq. ft.
Second floor — 1,013 sq. ft.
Basement — 1,157 sq. ft.

Rich Classic Lines

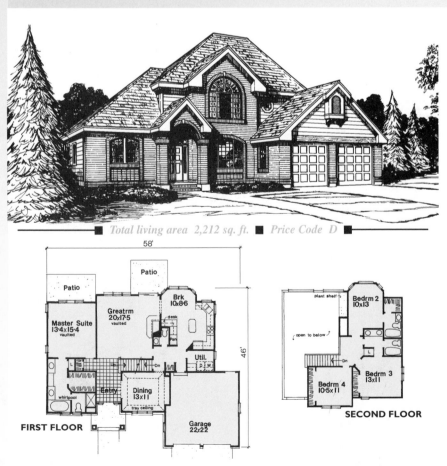

Total living area 2,212 sq. ft. ■ Price Code D

FIRST FLOOR

58'

46'

- Patio
- Patio
- Master Suite 13'4 x 15'4 vaulted
- Greatrm 20x17'5 vaulted
- Brk 10x8'6
- desk
- Util.
- whirlpool
- Entry
- Dining 13x11 tray ceiling
- Garage 22x22

SECOND FLOOR

- plant shelf
- Bedrm 2 10x13
- open to below
- Bedrm 3 13x11
- Bedrm 4 10·5x11

No. 91901

■ **This plan features:**

— Four bedrooms

— Three full and one half baths

■ A two-story Foyer flooded by light through an arched transom

■ A vaulted ceiling in the Great Room that continues into the Master Suite

■ A corner fireplace in the Great Room with French doors to the Breakfast/Kitchen Area

■ A center island in the Kitchen with an angled sink and a built-in desk and Pantry

■ A tray ceiling and recessed hutch area in the formal Dining Room

■ A Master Suite with a walk-in closet, a whirlpool tub and two vanities

■ This home comes with a basement foundation.

First floor — 1,496 sq. ft.
Second floor — 716 sq. ft.
Basement — 1,420 sq. ft.
Garage — 460 sq. ft.

Inexpensive Ranch Design

■ *Total living area 1,500 sq. ft.* ■ *Price Code A* ■

No. 20062

■ **This plan features:**

— Three bedrooms

— Two full baths

■ A large picture window brightening the Breakfast Area

■ A well-planned Kitchen

■ A Living Room which is accented by an open beam across the sloping ceiling and wood burning fireplace

■ A Master Bedroom with an extremely large Bath Area

■ An optional basement, slab or crawlspace foundation — please specify when ordering.

Main floor — 1,500 sq. ft.
Basement — 1,500 sq. ft.
Garage — 482 sq. ft.

MAIN FLOOR

Large Front Window Provides Streaming Light

■ *Total living area   1,707 sq. ft.* ■ *Price Code B* ■

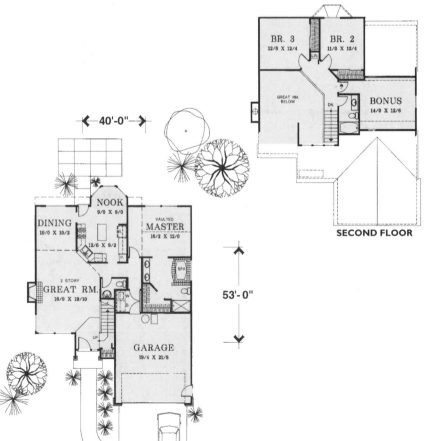

← 40'-0" →

NOOK
9/0 X 9/0

DINING
10/0 X 10/2

VAULTED
MASTER
16/2 X 12/0

12/6 X 9/2

2 STORY
GREAT RM.
16/0 X 19/10

SPA

53'-0"

UP

GARAGE
19/4 X 21/8

FIRST FLOOR

BR. 3
12/8 X 12/4

BR. 2
11/0 X 12/4

GREAT RM.
BELOW

DN.

BONUS
14/0 X 12/6

SECOND FLOOR

No. 91514

■ **This plan features:**

— Three bedrooms

— Two full and one half baths

■ A two-story Great Room with a floor-to-ceiling, corner front window and cozy hearth fireplace

■ An efficient Kitchen with a work island, Pantry and a corner, double sink

■ A quiet Master Suite with a vaulted ceiling and a plush Bath with a double vanity, spa tub and walk-in closet

■ On the second floor, two additional Bedrooms share a full hall Bath and a Bonus area for multiple uses

■ This home comes with a crawlspace foundation.

First floor — 1,230 sq. ft.
Second floor — 477 sq. ft.
Bonus area — 195 sq. ft.

Gabled Roofline and Arched Windows

No. 91063

This plan features:

- Three bedrooms
- Two full baths
- Vaulted ceilings and an open interior creating a spacious feeling
- A private Master Bedroom with a generous closet and Master Bath
- Two additional Bedrooms sharing the second full Bath
- A Kitchen with ample storage, countertops and a built-in Pantry
- This home comes with a crawlspace foundation.

Main floor — 1,207 sq. ft.
Garage — 440 sq. ft.

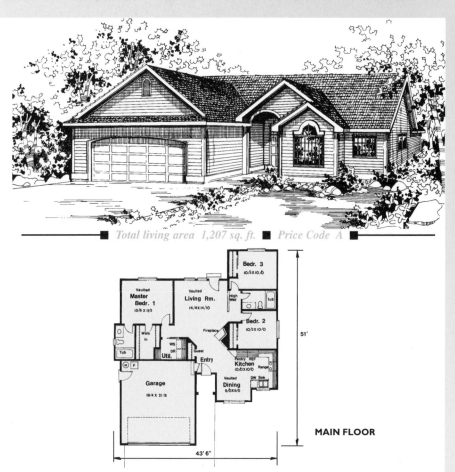

Total living area 1,207 sq. ft. ■ *Price Code A*

MAIN FLOOR

Spanish Style Affordable Home

No. 91340

This plan features:

- Two bedrooms
- Two full baths
- A beautiful arched entry leads guests to the Porch and Great Room within
- A large Master Suite with vaulted ceilings and a handicap accessible private Bath
- Vaulted ceilings in the Great Room
- An open Kitchen area with an eating bar
- A large wrap-around Porch punctuated by columns, spanning the length of the home
- Easy access from the Carport to the central hallway
- An optional slab or crawlspace foundation — please specify when ordering.

Main floor — 1,111 sq. ft.

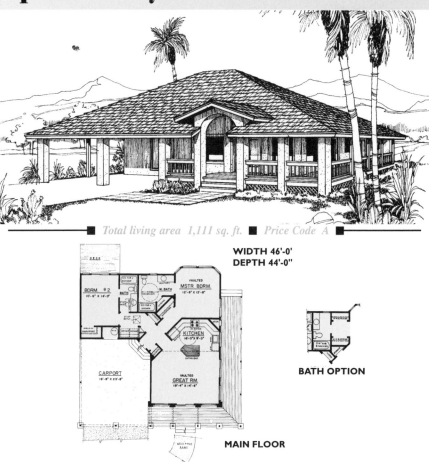

Total living area 1,111 sq. ft. ■ *Price Code A*

WIDTH 46'-0'
DEPTH 44'-0"

BATH OPTION

MAIN FLOOR

141

Brick Abounds

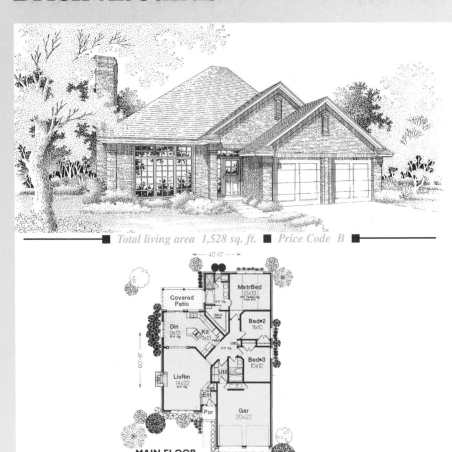

Total living area 1,528 sq. ft. ■ Price Code B ■

MAIN FLOOR

No. 98522

■ **This plan features:**

— Three bedrooms

— Two full baths

■ The covered front Porch opens into the entry that has a 10-foot ceiling and a coat closet

■ The large Living Room is distinguished by a fireplace and a front window wall

■ The Dining Room features a 10-foot ceiling and access to the rear covered Patio

■ The Kitchen is angled and has a Pantry, and a cooktop island

■ The Master Bedroom is located in the rear for privacy and boasts a triangular walk-in closet, plus a private Bath

■ Two more Bedrooms each have large closets and share a hallway Bath

■ This home has a two-car Garage that is accessed through the Utility Room

■ This home comes with a slab foundation.

Main floor — 1,528 sq. ft.
Garage — 440 sq. ft.

Notable Windows

Total living area 2,198 sq. ft. ■ Price Code D ■

SECOND FLOOR

FIRST FLOOR

No. 94950

■ **This plan features:**

— Four bedrooms

— Two full and one three-quarter and one half baths

■ Gables accenting arches enhance this brick and wood home

■ Open Entry between formal Living and Dining rooms provide ease in entertaining

■ Comfortable Family Room offers a fireplace a wetbar, and a wall of windows

■ Kitchen includes an island counter and adjoins the Breakfast bay with the Laundry/Garage nearby

■ Luxurious Master Bedroom with a skylit Bath

■ Three secondary Bedrooms, two with window seats, share full Bath

■ This home comes with a slab foundation.

■ Alternate foundation options available at an additional charge. Please call 1.800.235.5700 for more information.

First floor — 1,179 sq. ft.
Second floor — 1,019 sq. ft.
Basement — 1,179 sq. ft.
Garage — 466 sq. ft.

An Open Concept Home

■ *Total living area 1,282 sq. ft.* ■ *Price Code A* ■

No. 93021

■ **This plan features:**

— Three bedrooms

— Two full baths

■ An angled Entry creating the illusion of space

■ Two square columns that flank the bar and separate the Kitchen from the Living Room

■ A Dining Room that may service both formal and informal occasions

■ A Master Bedroom with a large walk-in closet

■ A large Master Bath with double vanity, linen closet and whirlpool tub/shower combination

■ Two additional Bedrooms that share a full Bath

■ An optional slab or crawlspace foundation — please specify when ordering.

Main floor — 1,282 sq. ft.
Garage — 501 sq. ft.

WIDTH 48-10

OPTIONAL BAY WINDOW

FP

DINING
9-8 X 9-6
10 FT CLG

LIVING ROOM
16-0 X 17-6
10 FT CLG

BEDRM 3
10-0 X 10-0

SLOPE

MASTER BATH

LIN

DEPTH 52-6

MASTER BEDRM
11-0 X 14-0
10 FT CLG

SLOPE

10 FT CLG
KITCHEN
13-4 X 9-6

FOYER

ARCH

ARCH

BATH 2

LIN

BEDRM 2
10-0 X 12-0

PORCH

MAIN FLOOR

STORAGE

GARAGE

© Larry E. Belk

Pleasing to the Eye

■ *Total living area 1,202 sq. ft.* ■ *Price Code A* ■

No. 93073

■ **This plan features:**

— Three bedrooms

— Two full baths

■ A large covered front Porch opening to a Foyer with nine-foot ceilings

■ Kitchen with a built-in desk, sunny window over the sink and Dining Area with a bay window

■ Living Room with a corner fireplace and ten-foot ceilings

■ Master Suite topped by a sloped ceiling

■ Two-car Garage with optional door locations located at the rear of the home

■ An optional slab or crawlspace foundation — please specify when ordering.

Main floor — 1,202 sq. ft.
Garage — 482 sq. ft.

WIDTH 51'-10'
DEPTH 43'-10"

OPTIONAL GARAGE DOOR LOCATION

MSTR BDRM
11-0x13-8
10 FT CLG

LIVING
13-0x17-8
10 FT CLG

GARAGE

MSTR BATH

BATH 2

STOR

BDRM 3
10-10x11-6

FOYER
9 FT CLG

STORAGE

LIN

BDRM 2
10-4x10-2

© Larry E. Belk

COVERED PORCH

DESK

DINING
11-0x9-2
9 FT CLG

KITCH
11-6x 8-0
9 FT CLG

MAIN FLOOR

Thoroughly Modern Split-Level

No. 99123

This plan features:

- Three bedrooms
- One full, one three-quarter and one half baths
- The covered Entry leads to the Foyer and on into the Living Room
- The formal Living Room is topped by a vaulted ceiling and adjoins the Nook
- The Kitchen includes a Pantry and is designed in an efficient U-shape
- The Family Room is complemented by a fireplace
- The Master Bedroom includes a three-quarter Bath and a walk-in closet
- Two additional Bedrooms share a full Bath
- This home comes with a basement foundation.

Upper floor — 1,289 sq. ft.
Lower floor — 443 sq. ft.
Basement — 552 sq. ft.

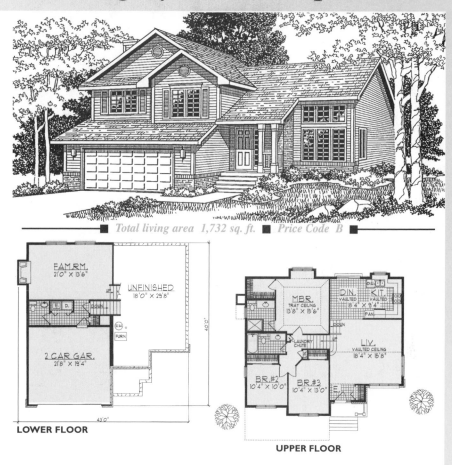

Total living area 1,732 sq. ft. ■ Price Code B

LOWER FLOOR

UPPER FLOOR

First Floor Master Suite

No. 98357

This plan features:

- Three bedrooms
- Two full and one half baths
- Front porch and dormer add to the Country appeal of this home
- Elegant Dining Room is topped by a decorative ceiling and has direct Kitchen access
- Kitchen/Breakfast Room includes a cooktop island, a double corner sink, a walk-in Pantry, a built-in desk and a vaulted ceiling
- Great Room accented by a vaulted ceiling and a fireplace
- A double door entrance, a box bay window, a vaulted ceiling and a plush five-piece Bath are all features of the Master Suite
- Two additional Bedrooms share use of the full Bath in the hall
- This home comes with a basement foundation.

First floor — 1,490 sq. ft.
Second floor — 436 sq. ft.
Basement — 1,490 sq. ft.
Garage — 400 sq. ft.

Total living area 1,926 sq. ft. ■ Price Code C

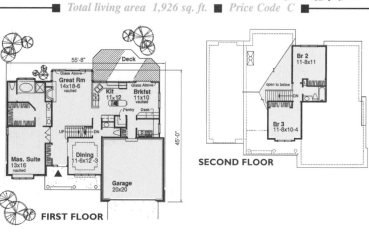

FIRST FLOOR

SECOND FLOOR

Columned Entry

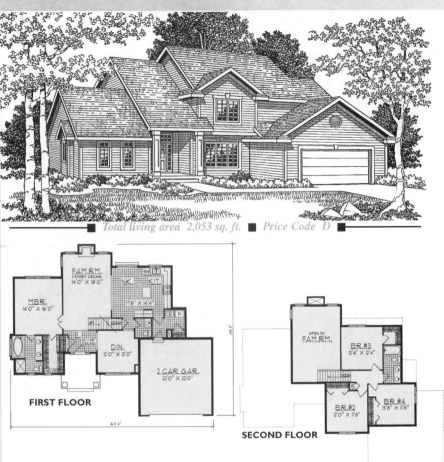

■ Total living area 2,053 sq. ft. ■ Price Code D ■

FIRST FLOOR

SECOND FLOOR

No. 99131

■ **This plan features:**

— Four bedrooms

— Two full and one half baths

■ The covered set back entry of this two-story home welcomes visitors

■ The formal Dining Room to the right of the Foyer is perfect for special dinners

■ A fireplace and rear facing windows highlight the Family Room

■ A large Nook and Kitchen are open to each other and then flow into the Family Room

■ A Laundry/Mud room separates the Kitchen from the two-car Garage

■ The Master Suite is enhanced by a large walk-in closet and a private Bath

■ Three additional Bedrooms share a full Bath in the hall

■ This home comes with a basement foundation.

First floor — 1,386 sq. ft.
Second floor — 667 sq. ft.
Basement — 1,386 sq. ft.

Compact Ranch Loaded with Living Space

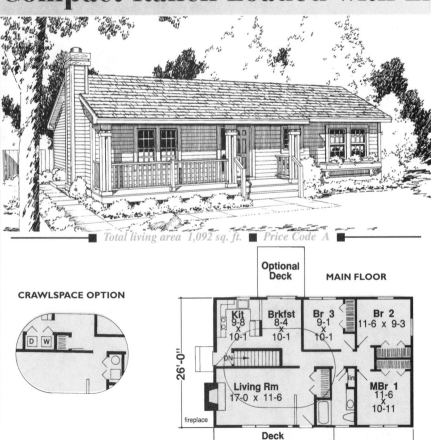

■ Total living area 1,092 sq. ft. ■ Price Code A ■

CRAWLSPACE OPTION

MAIN FLOOR

No. 34328

■ **This plan features:**

— Three bedrooms

— One full bath

■ A central entrance, opening to the Living Room with ample windows

■ A Kitchen, featuring a Breakfast Area with sliding doors to the backyard and an optional Deck

■ An optional basement, slab or crawlspace foundation — please specify when ordering.

Main floor — 1,092 sq. ft.
Basement — 1,092 sq. ft.

Traditional That Has It All

■ *Total living area 2,759 sq. ft.* ■ *Price Code G* ■

No. 90443

■ **This plan features:**

- Three bedrooms

- Three full and two half baths

■ A Master Suite with two closets and Bath with separate shower, corner tub and dual vanity

■ A large Dining Room with a bay window, adjacent to the Kitchen

■ A formal Living Room for entertaining and a cozy Family Room with fireplace

■ Two upstairs Bedrooms with walk-in closets and private Baths

■ A Bonus Room to allow the house to grow with your needs

■ An optional basement, slab or crawlspace foundation — please specify when ordering

First floor — 1,927 sq. ft.
Second floor — 832 sq. ft.
Bonus room — 624 sq. ft.
Basement — 1,674 sq. ft.

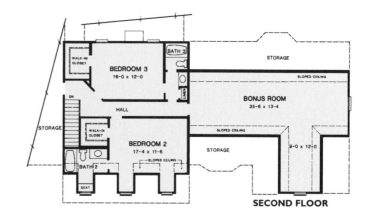

SECOND FLOOR

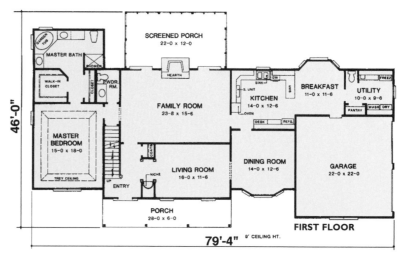

FIRST FLOOR

Skylight Brightens Master Bedroom

■ *Total living area 1,686 sq. ft.* ■ *Price Code B* ■

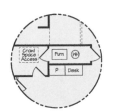

SLAB/CRAWLSPACE OPTION

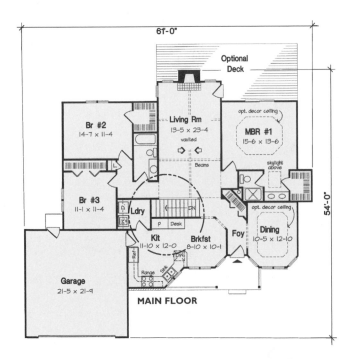

MAIN FLOOR

No. 34029

■ **This plan features:**

— Three bedrooms

— Two full baths

■ A covered Porch entry

■ A foyer separating the Dining Room from the Breakfast Area and Kitchen

■ A Living Room enhanced by a vaulted beam ceiling and a fireplace

■ A Master Bedroom with a decorative ceiling and a skylight in the private Bath

■ An optional Deck accessible through sliding doors off the Master Bedroom

■ An optional basement, slab or crawlspace foundation — please specify when ordering.

Main floor — 1,686 sq. ft.
Basement — 1,676 sq. ft.
Garage — 484 sq. ft.

Plan Yields Lots of Living Space

No. 10519

■ **This plan features:**

– Three bedrooms

– Two full and one half baths0

■ Sloped ceilings and an open central stairway

■ An efficient, U-shaped Kitchen with easy access to the Dining Room and a Laundry facility

■ Ample closet space throughout the home

■ This home comes with a basement foundation.

First floor — 872 sq. ft.
Second floor — 483 sq. ft.

■ *Total living area 1,355 sq. ft.* ■ *Price Code A* ■

FIRST FLOOR

SECOND FLOOR

Eye-Catching Elevation

No. 94305

■ **This plan features:**

– Two bedrooms

– Two three-quarter baths

■ An entrance to a Spa Deck with hot tub and a few steps down to an open Living Area with a cozy fireplace, a vaulted ceiling and atrium door to the side Deck

■ An efficient Kitchen with a peninsula counter/eating bar opens to Living Area

■ A first floor Bedroom next to the full Bath and Utility Area

■ A second floor Master Bedroom with an over-sized and private Bath

■ This home comes with a crawlspace foundation.

First floor — 680 sq. ft.
Second floor — 345 sq. ft.

■ *Total living area 1,025 sq. ft.* ■ *Price Code A* ■

FIRST FLOOR

SECOND FLOOR

Built-In Beauty

Total living area 1,687 sq. ft. • Price Code B

No. 91507

■ **This plan features:**

— Three bedrooms

— Two full baths

■ A sky-lit Foyer

■ A bump-out window enhancing the wide-open arrangement in the Living/Dining Room

■ An efficient island Kitchen with a built-in Pantry, and a corner double sink

■ An informal Family Room with a lovely fireplace

■ A Master Suite with elegant double doors, and a luxurious private Master Bath

■ Two additional Bedrooms flanking the Laundry Area

■ An optional basement or crawl space foundation — please specify when ordering

Main floor — 1,687 sq. ft.
Garage — 419 sq. ft.

WIDTH 50'-0"
DEPTH 52'-0"

FAMILY 13/0 X 17/0

MASTER 12/0 X 15/0

SPA

PANTRY

10/0 X 13/0

LINEN

13/4 X 10/0

SKYLITE

BR. 2 12/0 X 10/0

LIVING 13/4 X 14/0

BR. 3 10/10 12/0

GARAGE 19/2 X 21/8

MAIN FLOOR

Columns Enhance Entry

Total living area 2,107 sq. ft. • Price Code D

No. 91537

■ **This plan features:**

— Four bedrooms

— Two full and one half baths

■ The formal areas flow into each other while a fireplace accents the Living Room

■ A spacious, island Kitchen efficiently serves both the Dining Room and the Nook

■ The Family Room conveniently flows from the Kitchen/Nook and includes a second fireplace

■ The second floor Master Suite has a private Bath and a walk-in closet

■ Three additional Bedrooms have ample closet space and easy access to the full Bath in the hall

■ This home comes with a crawlspace foundation.

Main floor — 1,032 sq. ft.
Upper floor — 1,075 sq. ft.

◄ 49' ►

DINING 10/4 X 11/10

NOOK 7/8 X 10/0

▲ 40' ▼

PAN. Q. DESK

FAMILY 13/6 X 15/2

LIVING 13/0 X 16/2

UP

GARAGE 19/4 X 21/4

PORCH

MAIN FLOOR

SPA

DEN/BR. 2 10/3 X 9/10

BR. 3 11/6 X 13/4

LIN.

LINEN

MASTER 13/0 X 16/8

FOYER BELOW

BR. 4 11/0 X 12/6

UPPER FLOOR

■ *Total living area 1,567 sq. ft.* ■ *Price Code B* ■

No. 99641

■ **This plan features:**

— Three bedrooms

— Two full baths

■ The Living Room is enhanced by nine-foot ceilings and a bookcase flanked fireplace

■ Two mullioned French doors from the Dining Room to the rear Terrace

■ Laundry Area serving as a Mudroom between the Garage and Kitchen

■ A Master Suite with a compartmented Bath has a separate shower, whirlpool tub, double vanity and linen closet

■ An optional basement or slab foundation — please specify when ordering.

Main floor — 1,567 sq. ft.
Future bonus area — 462 sq. ft.
Basement — 1,567 sq. ft.
Garage — 504 sq. ft.

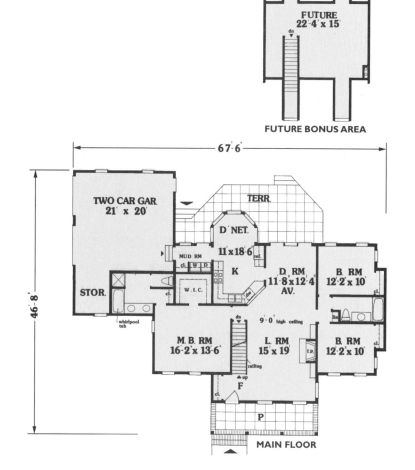

FUTURE BONUS AREA

FUTURE
22'-4" x 15'

MAIN FLOOR

151

Keystone Arches and Decorative Windows

■ *Total living area 1,666 sq. ft.* ■ *Price Code B* ■

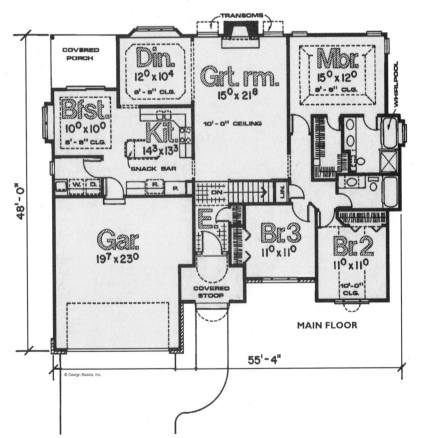

MAIN FLOOR

© Design Basics, Inc.

No. 94923

■ **This plan features:**

— Three bedrooms

— Two full baths

■ Brick and stucco enhance the dramatic front elevation and volume entrance

■ Inviting Entry leads into expansive Great Room with hearth fireplace framed by transom window

■ Corner Master Suite enjoys a tray ceiling, roomy walk-in closet and a plush Bath with a double vanity and whirlpool window tub

■ This home comes with a basement foundation.

Main floor — 1,666 sq. ft.
Basement — 1,666 sq. ft.
Garage — 496 sq. ft.

Spacious Elegance

No. 98455

This plan features:

- Four bedrooms

- Three full baths

■ This appealing home has gables, a hip roof, and keystone window accents

■ The two-story Foyer with palladian window illuminates a lovely staircase and the Dining Room Entry way

■ The Family Room has a vaulted ceiling and an inviting fireplace

■ Vaulted ceiling and a radius window highlight the Breakfast Area and the efficient Kitchen

■ The Master Bedroom Suite boasts a tray ceiling, luxurious Bath and a walk-in closet

■ An optional basement or crawlspace foundation — please specify when ordering

First floor — 1,761 sq. ft.
Second floor — 588 sq. ft.
Bonus room — 267 sq. ft.
Basement — 1,761 sq. ft.
Garage — 435 sq. ft.

■ *Total living area 2,349 sq. ft.* ■ *Price Code E* ■

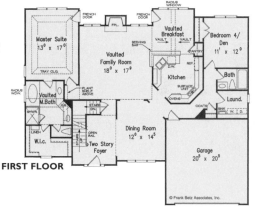

FIRST FLOOR

© Frank Betz Associates, Inc.

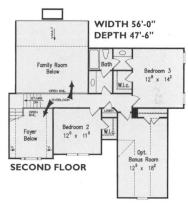

WIDTH 56'-0"
DEPTH 47'-6"

SECOND FLOOR

Spacious Family Areas

No. 93220

This plan features:

- Three bedrooms

- Two full and one half baths

■ Two-story Foyer with landing staircase leads to formal Living and Dining Rooms

■ Open layout for Kitchen/Breakfast Area and Family Room offers a spacious feeling and easy interaction

■ Efficient Kitchen with cooktop peninsula, built-in Pantry and a glassed Breakfast Area

■ Comfortable Family Room with a focal point fireplace and a wall of windows with access to Sun Deck

■ Master Bedroom enhanced by decorative ceiling and French doors into private Bath and walk-in closet

■ Two additional Bedrooms, full Bath, Laundry closet and Bonus Room complete second floor

■ An optional basement, slab or crawlspace foundation — please specify when ordering

First floor — 902 sq. ft.
Second floor — 819 sq. ft.
Finished staircase — 28 sq. ft.
Bonus room — 210 sq. ft.
Basement — 874 sq. ft.
Garage — 400 sq. ft.

■ *Total living area 1,749 sq. ft.* ■ *Price Code B* ■

SECOND FLOOR

FIRST FLOOR

Affordable Living

■ *Total living area 984 sq. ft.* ■ *Price Code A* ■

OPTIONAL BASEMENT STAIR LOCATION

Kitchen 8-0 x 8-3
BATH
Ref.
Flue
DN

MAIN FLOOR

54'-0"

Mstr. Br. 13-7 x 11-8
Kitchen 8-0 x 8-3
Dining 8-10 x 8-3
Covered Patio
Ref.
Furn
Linen
Crawl Access
Br 2 9-8 x 11-8
Br 3 11-0 x 10-2
Living Rm 15-8 x 11-7
Garage 13-9 x 19-5

28'-0"

No. 24303

■ **This plan features:**

— Three bedrooms

— One full and one three quarter baths

■ A simple, yet gracefully designed exterior

■ A sheltered entrance into a roomy Living Room graced with a large front window

■ A formal Dining Room flowing from the Living Room, allowing for ease in entertaining

■ A well-appointed U-shaped Kitchen with double sinks and adequate storage

■ A Master Bedroom equipped with a full Bath

■ Two additional Bedrooms that share a full hall Bath complete with a convenient Laundry center

■ A covered Patio, tucked behind the Garage, perfect for a cook-out or picnic

■ An optional basement or crawlspace foundation — please specify when ordering.

Main floor — 984 sq. ft.
Basement — 960 sq. ft.
Garage — 280 sq. ft.

First Floor Master Suite is Special

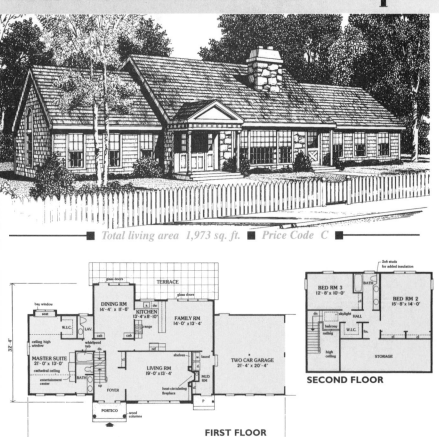

■ *Total living area 1,973 sq. ft.* ■ *Price Code C* ■

FIRST FLOOR

75'-0"
32'-4"

bay window seat
W.I.C.
LAV.
ceiling high window
whirlpool tub
MASTER SUITE 21'-0" x 13'-0"
cathedral ceiling
BATH
entertainment center
FOYER
PORTICO
wood columns
DINING RM 14'-4" x 11'-6"
glass doors
TERRACE
glass doors
KITCHEN 13'-4" x 8'-10"
range
cab
cab
dw
FAMILY RM 14'-0" x 13'-4"
shelves
laund
LIVING RM 19'-0" x 13'-4"
heat-circulating fireplace
MUD RM
up
TWO CAR GARAGE 21'-4" x 20'-4"

SECOND FLOOR

2x6 studs for added insulation
BED RM 3 12'-8" x 10'-0"
BATH
BED RM 2 15'-8" x 14'-0"
dn
skylight HALL
balcony railing
W.I.C.
lin.
high ceiling
STORAGE

No. 90624

■ **This plan features:**

— Three bedrooms

— Two full and one half baths

■ A two-story Foyer lit from above by a skylight

■ Access to the terrace or Garage through the Family Room

■ A heat-circulating fireplace

■ A Master Suite with vaulted ceilings and spectacular windows

■ This home comes with a basement foundation.

First floor — 1,360 sq. ft.
Second floor — 613 sq. ft.
Basement — 1,340 sq. ft.
Garage — 462 sq. ft.

Wide Open and Convenient

■ Total living area 1,737 sq. ft. ■ Price Code B ■

No. 20100

■ **This plan features:**

— Three bedrooms

— Two full baths

■ Vaulted ceilings in the Dining Room and Master Bedroom

■ A sloped ceiling in the fireplaced Living Room

■ A skylight illuminating the Master Bath

■ A large Master Bedroom with a walk-in closet

■ An optional basement, slab or crawlspace foundation — please specify when ordering.

Main floor — 1,737 sq. ft.
Basement — 1,727 sq. ft.
Garage — 484 sq. ft.

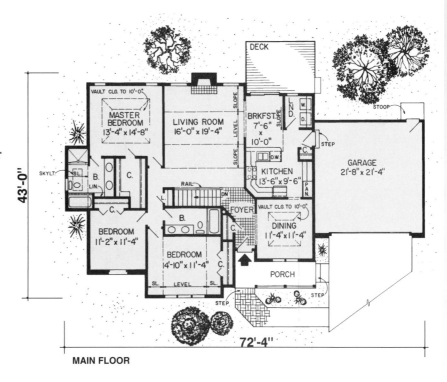

National Treasure

■ *Total living area 1,978 sq. ft.* ■ *Price Code C* ■

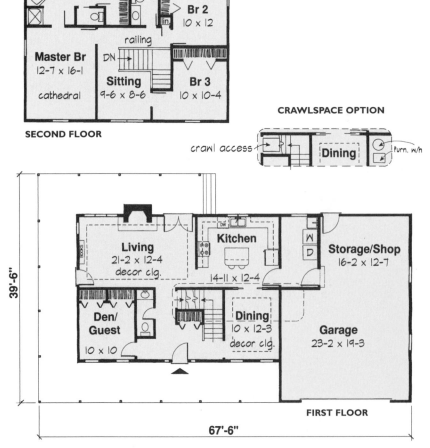

Br 2
10 x 12

railing

Master Br
12-7 x 16-1

DN

Sitting
9-6 x 8-6

Br 3
10 x 10-4

cathedral

SECOND FLOOR

CRAWLSPACE OPTION

crawl access

Dining

Furn. w/h

Living
21-2 x 12-4
decor clg.

Kitchen
14-11 x 12-4

W
D

Storage/Shop
16-2 x 12-7

Den/Guest
10 x 10

Dining
10 x 12-3
decor clg.

Garage
23-2 x 19-3

39'-6"

67'-6"

FIRST FLOOR

No. 24400

■ **This plan features:**

— Three bedrooms

— Two full and one half baths

■ A wrap-around covered Porch

■ Decorative vaulted ceilings in the fireplaced Living Room

■ A large Kitchen with central island/Breakfast Bar

■ A sun-lit Sitting Area

■ An optional basement, slab or crawlspace foundation — please specify when ordering.

First floor — 1,034 sq. ft.
Second floor — 944 sq. ft.
Basement — 944 sq. ft.
Garage & storage — 675 sq. ft.

Recreation Room Houses Fireplace

No. 9964

This plan features:

- Four bedrooms

- Two full baths

- A wood-burning fireplace warming the Living/Dining Room, which is accessible to the large wooden Sun Deck

- Two first floor Bedrooms with access to a full hall Bath

- Two ample-sized second floor Bedrooms

- A Recreation Room with a cozy fireplace and convenient half Bath

- This home comes with a basement foundation.

Main floor — 906 sq. ft.
Upper floor — 456 sq. ft.
Lower floor — 594 sq. ft.
Basement — 279 sq. ft.

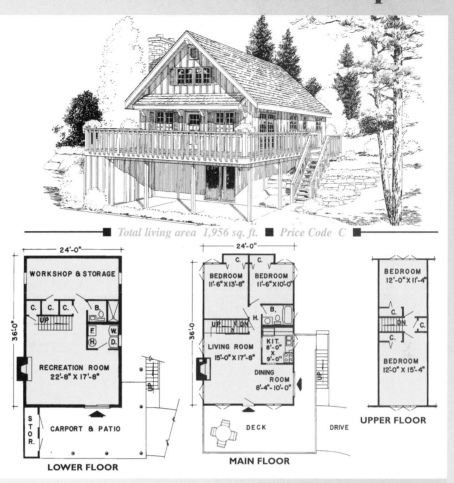

■ *Total living area 1,956 sq. ft.* ■ *Price Code C* ■

LOWER FLOOR

MAIN FLOOR

UPPER FLOOR

Expandable Home

No. 34077

This plan features:

- Four bedrooms

- Three full baths

- Front Entry into open Living Room highlighted by double window

- Bright Dining Area with sliding glass door to optional Patio

- Compact, efficient Kitchen with peninsula serving/snackbar, Laundry closet and outdoor access

- Two first floor Bedrooms with ample closet share a full Bath

- Second floor Master Bedroom and additional Bedroom feature dormer windows, private Baths and walk-in closets

- An optional basement, slab or crawlspace foundation — please specify when ordering.

First floor — 957 sq. ft.
Second floor — 800 sq. ft.

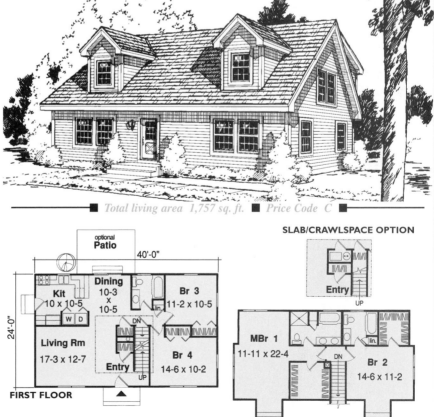

■ *Total living area 1,757 sq. ft.* ■ *Price Code C* ■

SLAB/CRAWLSPACE OPTION

FIRST FLOOR

SECOND FLOOR

Early American Exterior

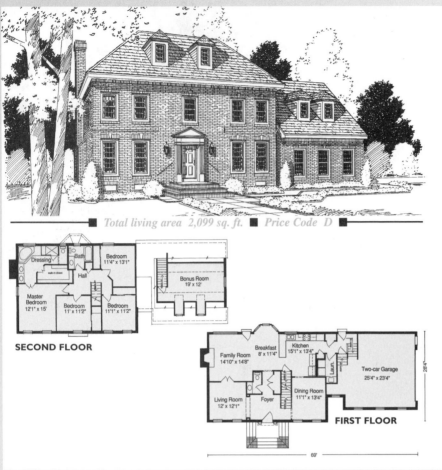

Total living area 2,099 sq. ft. ■ **Price Code D**

SECOND FLOOR

Dressing
Bath
Bedroom 11'4" x 13'1"
walk-in closet
Hall
Master Bedroom 12'1" x 15'
Bedroom 11' x 11'2"
Bedroom 11'1" x 11'2"

Bonus Room 19' x 12'

Breakfast 8' x 11'4"
Kitchen 15'1" x 13'4"
Family Room 14'10" x 14'8"
Laun.
Two-car Garage 25'4" x 23'4"
Living Room 12' x 12'1"
Foyer
Dining Room 11'1" x 13'4"

FIRST FLOOR

69'

No. 92672

■ **This plan features:**

— Four bedrooms

— Two full and one half baths

■ Open Foyer leads into the formal Living and Dining Rooms

■ Multiple windows accentuate the open Family Room and Breakfast Nook

■ The L-shaped Kitchen is open and arranged for maximum convenience

■ The large Master Suite with a private Bath and a walk-in closet

■ Three additional Bedrooms share a full Bath on the second floor

■ A Bonus Room is located over the garage for future consideration

■ This home comes with a basement foundation.

First floor — 1,095 sq. ft.
Second floor — 1,004 sq. ft
Bonus — 323 sq. ft.
Basement — 1,082 sq. ft.

Living Room Features Vaulted Ceiling

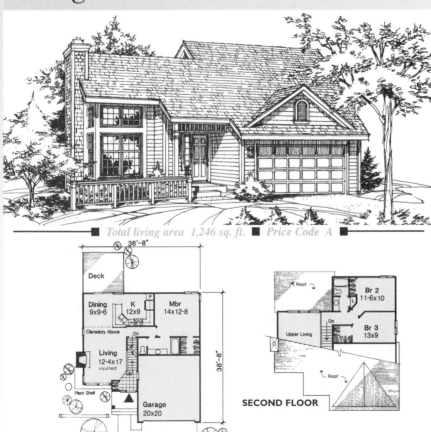

Total living area 1,246 sq. ft. ■ **Price Code A**

36'-8"

Deck

Dining 9x9-6
K 12x9
P
Mbr 14x12-8
Clerestory Above
Living 12-4x17 vaulted
Dn
Plant Shelf
Garage 20x20

38'-6"

FIRST FLOOR

Roof
Br 2 11-6x10
Upper Living
On
Br 3 13x9
Roof

SECOND FLOOR

No. 90353

■ **This plan features:**

— Three bedrooms

— Two full baths

■ A vaulted ceiling in the Living Room and the Dining Room, with a clerestory above

■ A Master Bedroom with a walk-in closet and private full Bath

■ An efficient Kitchen, with a corner double sink and peninsula counter

■ A Dining Room with sliding doors to the Deck

■ A Living Room with a fireplace that adds warmth to open areas

■ Two additional Bedrooms that share a full hall Bath

■ This home comes with a basement foundation.

First floor — 846 sq. ft.
Second floor — 400 sq. ft.

■ *Total living area 1,393 sq. ft.* ■ *Price Code A* ■

No. 90680

■ This plan features:

— Three bedrooms

— Two full baths

■ A covered Porch leading into an open Foyer and Living/Dining Room with skylights and front to back exposure

■ An efficient Kitchen with a bay window Dinette Area, a walk-in Pantry and adjacent to the Mudroom, Garage Area

■ A private Master Bedroom with a luxurious Master Bath leading to a private Deck

■ Two additional Bedrooms with access to a full hall Bath

■ An optional basement or slab foundation — please specify when ordering.

Main floor — 1,393 sq. ft.
Basement — 1,393 sq. ft.

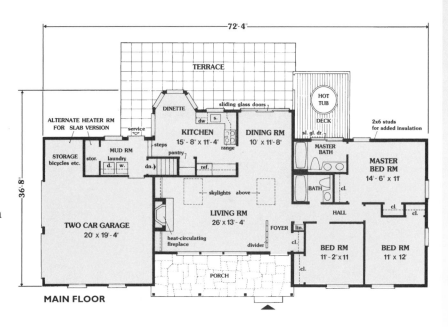

Country Style For Today

■ *Total living area 2,406 sq. ft.* ■ *Price Code E* ■

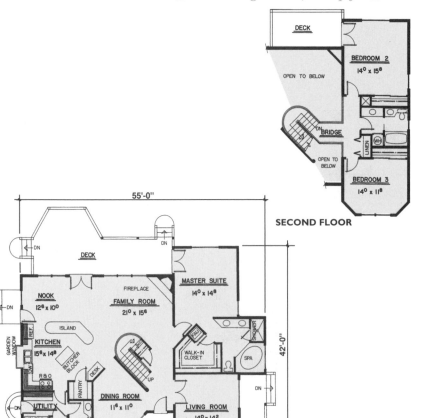

DECK

BEDROOM 2
14⁰ x 15⁸

OPEN TO BELOW

BRIDGE

OPEN TO BELOW

BEDROOM 3
14⁰ x 11⁸

SECOND FLOOR

55'-0"

DECK

NOOK
12⁶ x 10⁰

ISLAND

KITCHEN
15⁶ x 14⁸

GARDEN WINDOW

BUTCHER BLOCK

DESK

PANTRY

FIREPLACE
FAMILY ROOM
21⁰ x 15⁶

MASTER SUITE
14⁰ x 14⁸

WALK-IN CLOSET

SHOWER

SPA

UP

DINING ROOM
11⁶ x 11⁰

UTILITY
WSH DRY

LIVING ROOM
14⁰ x 14²

42'-0"

PORCH

DN

FIRST FLOOR

No. 91700

■ **This plan features:**

— Three bedrooms

— Two full and one half baths

■ A wide wrap-around Porch for a farmhouse style

■ A spacious Living Room with double doors and a large front window

■ A garden window over the double sink in the huge, Country Kitchen with two islands, one a butcher block and the other an eating bar

■ A Master Suite with a Spa tub, and a huge walk-in closet as well as a shower and double vanity

■ An optional basement or crawlspace foundation — please specify when ordering.

First floor — 1,785 sq. ft.
Second floor — 621 sq. ft.

Especially Surprising

No. 99106

This plan features:

- Three bedrooms
- Two full baths
- Graceful columns support the covered Entry
- The tiled Foyer leads directly into the Great Room that has a rear wall fireplace, and a cathedral ceiling
- The Kitchen has an arched pass through to the Great Room and is open to the Dining Room with a cathedral ceiling
- The screened Porch is accessed from the Dining Room
- The Master Suite has a plant ledge, a fireplace, a tray ceiling, a walk-in closet and a fully appointed Bath
- Two other Bedrooms have access to a full Bath in the hall
- A two-car Garage
- This home comes with a basement foundation.

Main floor — 1,495 sq. ft.
Basement — 1,495 sq. ft.

■ *Total living area 1,495 sq. ft.* ■ *Price Code A* ■

MAIN FLOOR

A Nest for Empty-Nesters

No. 90934

This plan features:

- Two bedrooms
- One full bath
- An economical design
- A covered Sun Deck adding outdoor living space
- A Mudroom/Laundry Area inside the side door, trapping dirt before it can enter the house
- An open layout between the Living Room with fireplace, Dining Room and Kitchen
- This home comes with a slab foundation.

Main floor — 884 sq. ft.
Width — 34'-0"
Depth — 28'-0"

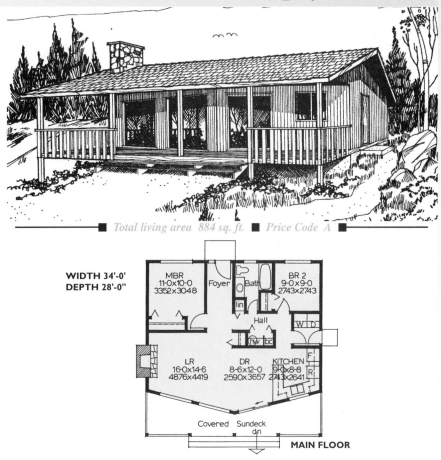

■ *Total living area 884 sq. ft.* ■ *Price Code A* ■

WIDTH 34'-0"
DEPTH 28'-0"

MAIN FLOOR

Exterior Shows Attention to Detail

■ Total living area 2,165 sq. ft. ■ Price Code D ■

MAIN FLOOR

No. 94811

■ **This plan features:**

— Three bedrooms

— Two full and one half baths

■ Privately located Master Suite is complimented by a luxurious Bath with two walk-in closets

■ Two additional Bedrooms have ample closet space and share a full Bath

■ The Activity Room has a sloped ceiling, large fireplace and is accented with columns

■ Access to Sun Deck from the Dining Room

■ The island Kitchen and Breakfast Area have access to Garage for ease when bringing in groceries

■ This home comes with a basement foundation.

Main floor — 2,165 sq. ft.
Basement — 2,165 sq. ft.
Garage — 484 sq. ft.

A Modern Look At Colonial Styling

■ Total living area 2,024 sq. ft. ■ Price Code D ■

No. 93287

■ **This plan features:**

— Three bedrooms

— Two full and one half baths

■ Brick detailing and keystones highlight elevation

■ Two-story Foyer opens to formal Living and Dining rooms

■ Expansive Family Room with a hearth fireplace between built-in shelves and Deck access

■ U-shaped Kitchen with serving counter, Breakfast alcove, and nearby Garage Entry

■ Elegant Master Bedroom with a decorative ceiling, large walk-in closet and a double vanity Bath

■ Two additional Bedrooms share a full Bath, Laundry and Bonus Area

■ This home comes with a basement foundation.

First floor — 987 sq. ft.
Second floor — 965 sq. ft.
Finished staircase — 72 sq. ft.
Basement — 899 sq. ft.

SECOND FLOOR

FIRST FLOOR

■ *Total living area 1,388 sq. ft.* ■ • *Price Code A* ■

No. 93279

■ **This plan features:**

- Three bedrooms

- Two full baths

■ A central, double fireplace adding warmth and atmosphere to the Family Room, Kitchen and the Breakfast Area

■ An efficient Kitchen highlighted by a peninsula counter that doubles as a snack bar

■ A Master Suite that includes a walk-in closet, a double vanity, separate shower and tub in the Bath

■ Two additional Bedrooms sharing a full hall Bath

■ A wooden Deck that can be accessed from the Breakfast Area

■ An optional crawlspace or slab foundation — please specify when ordering

Main floor — 1,388 sq. ft.
Garage — 400 sq. ft.

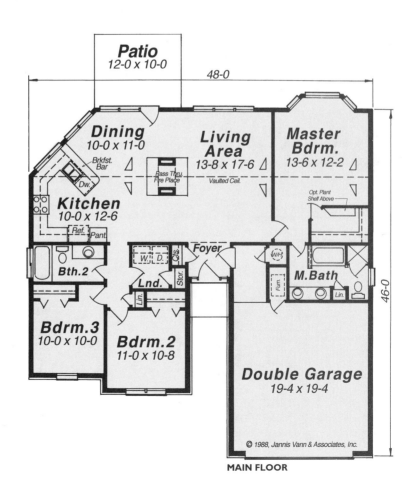

MAIN FLOOR

© 1988, Jannis Vann & Associates, Inc.

Distinctive Detail and Design

■ *Total living area 1,897 sq. ft.* ■ *Price Code C* ■

walk-in closet

Master Bedroom
12' x 14'11"

Bedroom
10'6" x 11'2"

Great Room Below

Bath

Bath

computer desk

Balcony

Bedroom
11' x 12'

stairs dn.

window seat

SECOND FLOOR

French doors w/ arched window above

Laun.

hanging space

Bath

Breakfast
10'8" x 11'

Great Room
14'10" x 17'1"

10'6" x 13'6"
Kitchen

pantry

high ceiling

38'

Two-car Garage
20' x 21'

furniture alcove

Dining Room
11' x 13'7"

Foyer

wood rail

stairs up

stairs dn.

FIRST FLOOR

48'

No. 92644

■ **This plan features:**

— Three bedrooms

— Two full and one half baths

■ Impressive pilaster Entry into open Foyer with landing staircase

■ Great Room accented by hearth fireplace and French doors

■ Formal Dining Room enhanced by furniture alcove

■ Efficient, L-shaped Kitchen with work island, walk-in Pantry and bright Breakfast Area

■ Master Bedroom offers a walk-in closet, and plush Bath with two vanities and whirlpool tub

■ Two additional Bedrooms share a full Bath and computer desk

■ This home comes with a basemen foundation.

First floor — 1,036 sq. ft.
Second floor — 861 sq. ft.
Garage — 420 sq. ft.

Nostalgia Returns

No. 99321

This plan features:

- Three bedrooms

- Two full baths

- Arched transom window with quarter-round detail and a vaulted ceiling in the Great Room

- A cozy corner fireplace which brings warmth to the Great Room

- A vaulted ceiling in the Kitchen/Breakfast Area

- A Master Suite with a walk-in closet and a private Master Bath

- Two additional Bedrooms which share a full hall Bath

- This home comes with a basement foundation.

Main floor — 1,368 sq. ft.

Garage — 412 sq. ft.

■ *Total living area 1,368 sq. ft.* ■ *Price Code A* ■

MAIN FLOOR

With Room to Expand

No. 98431

This plan features:

- Three bedrooms

- Two full and one half baths

- An impressive two-story Foyer

- The Kitchen is equipped with ample cabinet and counter space

- Spacious Family Room flows from the Breakfast Bay and is highlighted by a fireplace and a French door to the rear yard

- The Master Suite is topped by a tray ceiling and is enhanced by a vaulted, five-piece Master Bath

- Two additional Bedrooms share the full Bath in the hall

- An optional basement, crawlspace or slab foundation — please specify when ordering

First floor — 882 sq. ft.

Second floor — 793 sq. ft.

Bonus room — 416 sq. ft.

Basement — 882 sq. ft.

Garage — 510 sq. ft.

■ *Total living area 1,675 sq. ft.* ■ *Price Code B* ■

FIRST FLOOR

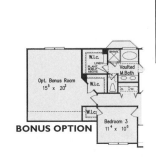

BONUS OPTION

SECOND FLOOR

Outstanding Four-Bedroom

■ Total living area 1,945 sq. ft. ■ Price Code C ■

WIDTH 56'-6"
DEPTH 52'-6"

MAIN FLOOR

© Frank Betz Associates, Inc.

No. 98435

■ **This plan features:**

— Four bedrooms

— Two full baths

■ Radius window highlighting the exterior and the formal Dining Room

■ High ceiling topping the Foyer for a grand first impression

■ Vaulted ceiling enhances the Great Room accented by a fireplace framed by window to either side

■ Arched opening to the Kitchen from the Great Room

■ Breakfast Room topped by a vaulted ceilin and enhanced by an elegant French door t the rear yard

■ Tray ceiling and a five-piece compartmental Bath gives a luxurious presence to the Master Suite

■ Three additional Bedrooms share a full, double vanity Bath in the hall

■ An optional basement or crawlspace foundation — please specify when ordering

Main floor — 1,945 sq. ft.

Quoin Accents Distinguish this Plan

■ Total living area 1,142 sq. ft. ■ Price Code A ■

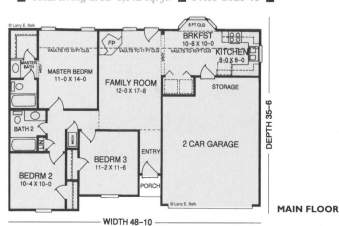

MAIN FLOOR

WIDTH 48-10

No. 93017

■ **This plan features:**

— Three bedrooms

— Two full baths

■ A traditional brick elevation with quoin accents

■ A large Family Room with a corner fireplac and direct access to the outside

■ An arched opening leading to the Breakfas Area

■ A bay window illuminating the Breakfast Area with natural light

■ An efficiently designed U-shaped kitchen with ample cabinet and counter space

■ A Master Suite with a private Master Bath

■ Two additional Bedrooms that share a full hall Bath

■ An optional slab or crawlspace foundation please specify when ordering.

Main floor — 1,142 sq. ft.
Garage — 428 sq. ft.

166

Old-Fashioned With Contemporary Interior

■ *Total living area 2,052 sq. ft.* ■ *Price Code D* ■

No. 98407

This plan features:

Four bedrooms

Three full baths

A two-story Foyer is flanked by the Living Room and the Dining Room

The Family Room features a fireplace and a French door

The bayed Breakfast Nook and Pantry are adjacent to the Kitchen

The Master Suite with a trayed ceiling has an attached Bath with a vaulted ceiling

Upstairs are two additional Bedrooms, a full Bath, a Laundry closet, and a Bonus Room

An optional basement, slab or crawlspace foundation — please specify when ordering

First floor — 1,135 sq. ft.

Second floor — 917 sq. ft.

Bonus — 216 sq. ft.

Basement — 1,135 sq. ft.

Garage — 452 sq. ft.

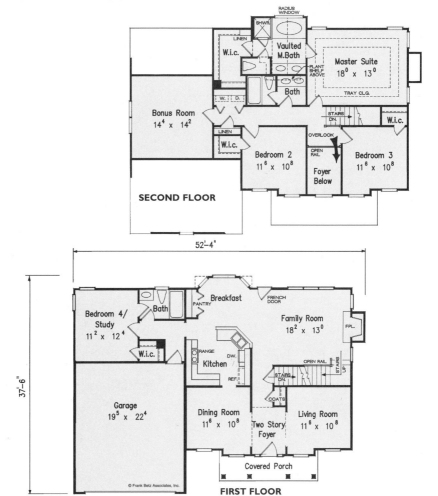

Cozy Country Ranch

■ *Total living area 1,576 sq. ft.* ■ *Price Code B* ■

No. 24708

■ **This plan features:**

— Three bedrooms

— Two full baths

■ Front Porch shelters outdoor visiting and entrance into Living Room

■ Expansive Living Room highlighted by a boxed window and hearth fireplace between built-ins

■ Columns frame entrance to Dining Room which has access to backyard

■ Efficient, U-shaped Kitchen with direct access to the Screened Porch and the Dining Room

■ Master Bedroom wing enhanced by a large walk-in closet and a double vanity Bath with a whirlpool tub

■ Two additional Bedrooms with large closets share a double vanity Bath with Laundry center

■ An optional basement, slab or crawlspace foundation — please specify when ordering.

MAIN FLOOR

Main floor — 1,576 sq. ft.
Garage — 576 sq. ft.
Basement — 1,454 sq. ft.

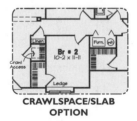

CRAWLSPACE/SLAB OPTION

No. 99871

■ This plan features:

– Three bedrooms

– Two full baths

■ Charm and personality radiate throughout this Country style home

■ Interior columns dramatically open the Foyer and Kitchen to the spacious Great Room

■ Drama is heightened by the Great Room cathedral ceiling and fireplace

■ Master Suite with a tray ceiling combines privacy with access to the rear Deck with Spa, while the skylit Bath has all the amenities expected in a quality home

■ Tray ceilings with round-top picture windows bring a special elegance to the Dining Room and the front swing room

■ This home comes with a crawlspace foundation.

■ Alternate foundation options available at an additional charge. Please call 1.800.235.5700 for more information.

Main floor — 1,655 sq. ft.
Garage — 434 sq. ft.

© Donald A. Gardner Architects, Inc.

■ Total living area 1,655 sq. ft. ■ Price Code F ■

MAIN FLOOR

© 1994 Donald A Gardner Architects, Inc.

Studio Enhances Dutch Colonial

No. 10016

■ This plan features:

– Three bedrooms

– One full and one three-quarter and one half baths

■ A convenient Foyer area leads to a large Terrace Living Room with a fireplace and sliding doors

■ The U-shaped Kitchen offers efficiency and easy access to the Family Room and a half bath with Laundry Center

■ The informal, airy Family Room opens onto the front Porch and a second Terrace and leads to an upstairs multi-purpose Studio

■ Three Bedrooms with two full Baths, one private, complete the upstairs level

■ This home comes with a basement foundation.

First floor — 1,256 sq. ft.
Second floor — 815 sq. ft.
Game room — 384 sq. ft.
Garage — 576 sq. ft.
Basement — 936 sq. ft.

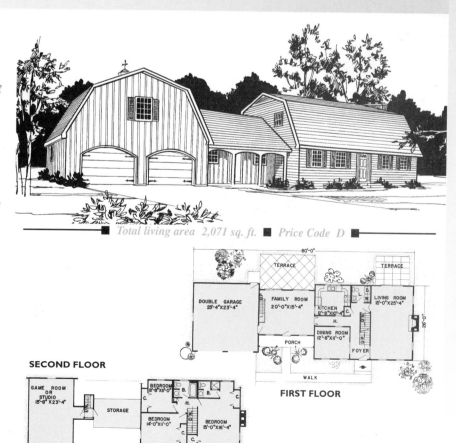

■ Total living area 2,071 sq. ft. ■ Price Code D ■

SECOND FLOOR

FIRST FLOOR

Sense of Spaciousness

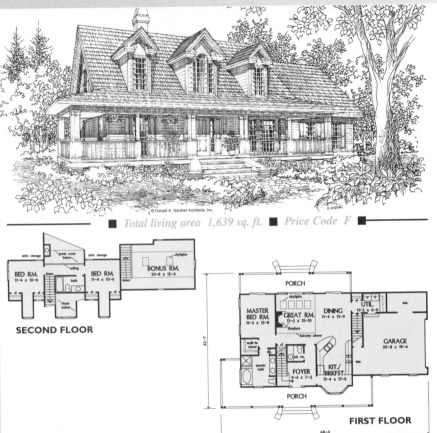

Total living area 1,639 sq. ft. ■ Price Code F ■

SECOND FLOOR

attic storage
great room below
ceiling
attic storage

skylights

BED RM.
11-4 x 10-0

BED RM.
11-4 x 10-0

BONUS RM.
20-8 x 15-4

bath

down

foyer below

FIRST FLOOR

© Donald A. Gardner Architects, Inc.

PORCH

skylights

MASTER BED RM.
11-4 x 13-8

GREAT RM.
13-2 x 15-10

DINING
11-4 x 13-9

UTIL
11-2 x 6-0

GARAGE
20-8 x 19-4

fireplace

balcony above

walk-in closet

pd. rm.

master bath

FOYER
9-4 x 7-5

KIT./BRKFST.
11-4 x 17-6

PORCH

68-0

42-7

No. 96456

■ **This plan features:**

— Three bedrooms

— Two full and one half baths

■ Creative use of natural lighting gives a feeling of spaciousness to this Country style home

■ Traffic flows easily from the bright Foyer into the Great Room which has a vaulted ceiling and skylights

■ The open floor plan is efficient for Kitchen/Breakfast area and the Dining Room

■ Master Bedroom suite features a walk-in closet and a private Bath with whirlpool tub

■ This home comes with a crawlspace foundation.

■ Alternate foundation options available at an additional charge, call 1.800.235.5700 for more information.

First floor — 1,180 sq. ft.
Second floor — 459 sq. ft.
Bonus room — 385 sq. ft.
Garage & storage — 533 sq. ft.

Two Choices for Courtyard Home

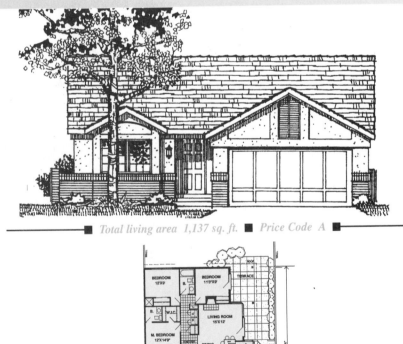

Total living area 1,137 sq. ft. ■ Price Code A ■

MAIN FLOOR

BEDROOM
12'X9'

BEDROOM
11'3"X9'

TERRACE

W.I.C.

LIVING ROOM
15'X12'

M. BEDROOM
12'X14'9'

DINING
9'X9'

SERVICE COURT

KITCHEN
12'X9'

GARAGE
19'X19'

38'

34'6"

No. 94302

■ **This plan features:**

— Three bedrooms

— One full and one three-quarter baths

■ A tiled Entry leading to an open Dining/Living Room Area with hearth fireplace and a wall of windows with an atrium door to Terrace

■ An efficient Kitchen with a corner window and eating bar adjoins Dining Area, Garage and Terrace

■ A Master Bedroom with walk-in closet and private Bath featuring either recessed, decorative window or atrium door to Terrace

■ One or two additional Bedrooms with ample closets near full Bath

■ This home comes with a crawlspace foundation.

Main floor — 1,137 sq. ft.
Garage — 390 sq. ft.

Whimsical Two-Story Farmhouse

© Donald A. Gardner Architects, Inc.

B. NATHAN

■ *Total living area 2,182 sq. ft.* ■ *Price Code G* ■

No. 96442

This plan features:

- Four bedrooms

- Three full and one half baths

- Double gable with palladian, clerestory window and wrap-around Porch provide Country appeal

- First floor enjoys nine-foot ceilings throughout

- Palladian windows flood two-story Foyer and Great Room with natural light

- Both Master Bedroom and Great Room access covered, rear Porch

- This home comes with a crawlspace foundation.

- Alternate foundation options available at an additional charge, call 1.800.235.5700 for more information.

First floor — 1,346 sq. ft.
Second floor — 836 sq. ft.

171

Stately Manor

Total living area 2,380 sq. ft. ■ *Price Code E* ■

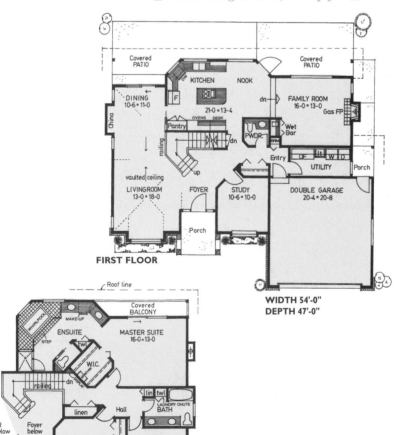

FIRST FLOOR

WIDTH 54'-0"
DEPTH 47'-0"

SECOND FLOOR

No. 90966

■ **This plan features:**

— Three bedrooms

— Two full and one half baths

■ A very spacious Foyer with an open staircase and lots of angles

■ A beautiful Kitchen equipped with a cooktop island and a full bay window wall that includes a roomy Breakfast Nook

■ A Living Room with a vaulted ceiling that flows into the formal Dining Room for ease in entertaining

■ A grand Master Suite equipped with a walk-in closet and five-piece private Bath

■ This home comes with a basement foundation.

First floor — 1,383 sq. ft.
Second floor — 997 sq. ft.
Basement — 1,374 sq. ft.
Garage — 420 sq. ft.

Expansive, Not Expensive

No. 90623

This plan features:

Three bedrooms

Two full baths

A Master Suite with his and her closets and a private Master Bath

Two additional Bedrooms that share a full hall closet

A pleasant Dining Room that overlooks a rear garden

A well-equipped Kitchen with a built-in planning corner and eat-in space

This home comes with a basement foundation.

Main floor — 1,474 sq. ft.

Basement — 1,370 sq. ft.

Garage — 563 sq. ft.

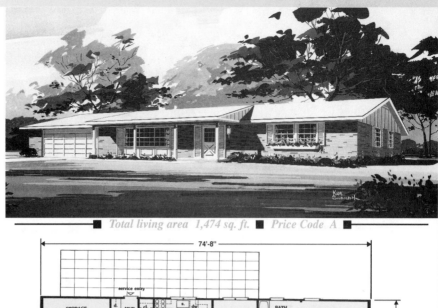

■ *Total living area 1,474 sq. ft.* ■ *Price Code A* ■

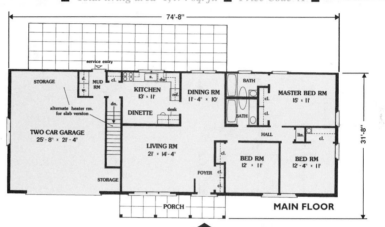

MAIN FLOOR

Outdoor-Lovers' Delight

No. 10748

This plan features:

Three bedrooms

Two full baths

A roomy Kitchen and Dining Room

A massive Living Room with a fireplace and access to the wrap-around Porch via double French doors

An elegant Master Suite and two additional spacious Bedrooms closely located to the Laundry Area

An optional slab or crawlspace foundation — please specify when ordering.

Main Floor — 1,540 sq. ft.

Porches — 530 sq. ft.

■ *Total living area 1,540 sq. ft.* ■ *Price Code B* ■

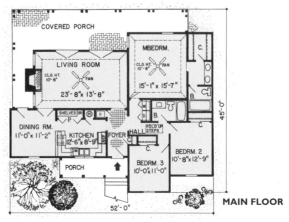

MAIN FLOOR

173

Nostalgic of a More Relaxed Time

■ Total living area 1,513 sq. ft. ■ Price Code B ■

WIDTH 49'-8"
DEPTH 30'-6"

SECOND FLOOR

Bedroom 10'8" x 10'4"
Bedroom 10'9" x 10'8"
walk-in closet
Bonus Room 17'9" x 11'
Hall
Bath
Bath
Master, Bedroom 12' x 16'
walk-in closet
plant shelf
slope ceiling
slope ceiling

FIRST FLOOR

Laun.
Kitchen 10'4" x 13'4"
Dining Room 12' x 12'8"
Two-car Garage 19' x 20'
Great Room 20' x 14'6"
Porch

No. 92684

■ **This plan features:**

– Three bedrooms

– One full one three quarter and one half baths

■ Large rooms and a clean, easy floor plan offer value and efficiency to the new family

■ First floor Laundry, two-car Garage, counter space with seating availability, a Pantry and a fireplace are just a few of the amenities

■ Spacious second floor boasts a generous sized Master Bedroom with a private Bath and walk-in closet

■ Two additional Bedrooms that share a full hall Bath

■ Large Bonus Room can be finished later

■ This home comes with a basement foundation.

First floor — 790 sq. ft.
Second floor — 723 sq. ft.
Bonus room — 285 sq. ft.

Soaring Ceilings Add Space and Drama

No. 90288

■ Total living area 1,387 sq. ft. ■ Price Code A ■

■ **This plan features:**

– Two bedrooms (with optional third bedroom)

– Two full baths

■ A sunny Master Suite with a sloping ceiling, private terrace entry, and luxurious garden Bath with an adjoining Dressing Room

■ A Gathering Room with a fireplace, study and formal Dining Room, flowing together for a more spacious feeling

■ A convenient pass-through that adds to the efficiency of the galley Kitchen and adjoining Breakfast Room

■ This home comes with a basement foundation.

Main floor — 1,387 sq. ft.
Garage 440 — sq. ft.

49'-8"
50'-0"

TERRACE
TERRACE
FORMAL DINING
GATHERING RM 23' x 19'8"
STUDY 9' x 11'
MASTER BEDROOM 13' x 11'8"
BRKFST RM 8' x 10'4"
OPEN OVER CLOSET
KITCHEN 12' x 9'8"
DRESSING RM
LAUNDRY
FOYER
BATH
BATH
COVERED PORCH
BEDROOM 10' x 10'
ENTRANCE COURT
GARAGE 19'4" x 21'8"

MAIN FLOOR

■ *Total living area 1,778 sq. ft.* ■ *Price Code F* ■

No. 99873

This plan features:

Three bedrooms

Two full and one half baths

An exterior Porch giving the home a traditional flavor

Great Room highlighted by a fireplace and a balcony above as well as a pass-through into the Kitchen

Kitchen eating area with skylights and bow windows overlooking the Deck with Spa

This home comes with a crawlspace foundation.

Alternate foundation options available at an additional charge. Please call 1.800.235.5700 for more information.

First floor — 1,325 sq. ft.
Second floor — 453 sq. ft.

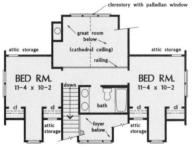

SECOND FLOOR

FIRST FLOOR

175

Comfort and Style

■ *Total living area 1,423 sq. ft.* ■ *Price Code A* ■

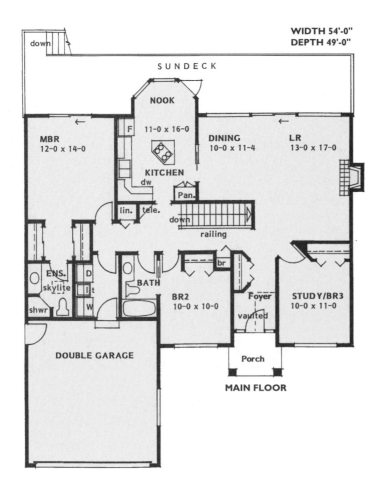

WIDTH 54'-0"
DEPTH 49'-0"

SUNDECK

NOOK
11-0 x 16-0

MBR
12-0 x 14-0

DINING
10-0 x 11-4

LR
13-0 x 17-0

KITCHEN
dw

Pan.

lin.   tele.

down
railing

ENS.
skylite

br

BATH

BR2
10-0 x 10-0

Foyer
vaulted

STUDY/BR3
10-0 x 11-0

shwr

DOUBLE GARAGE

Porch

MAIN FLOOR

No. 90990

■ **This plan features:**

— Two bedrooms with possible third bedroom/den

— One full and one three quarter baths

■ An unfinished daylight basement providing possible space for family recreation

■ A Master Suite complete with private Bath and skylight

■ A large Kitchen including an Eating Nook

■ A Sundeck that is easily accessible from the Master Suite, Nook and the Living/Dining Area

■ This home comes with a basement foundation.

Main floor — 1,423 sq. ft.
Basement — 1,423 sq. ft.
Garage — 399 sq. ft.

Spread Out Ranch

No. 91720

This plan features:

Three bedrooms

Two full baths

The covered front Porch protects from the elements

The Living Room has a vaulted ceiling, bright windows, and a corner fireplace

The Dining Room features a bay with windows

The Kitchen has an island with a range, and adjoins the unique angled Nook

The Master Suite has a closet that spans the entire rear wall, plus a private Bath

Two additional Bedrooms share a full Bath with a dual vanity

This home comes with a crawlspace foundation.

Main floor — 1,870 sq. ft.

Garage — 588 sq. ft.

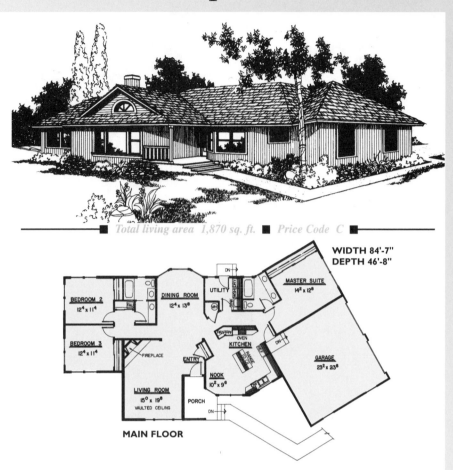

■ *Total living area 1,870 sq. ft.* ■ *Price Code C* ■

WIDTH 84'-7"
DEPTH 46'-8"

MAIN FLOOR

Deserving of a Beautiful Setting

No. 90208

This home features:

Three bedrooms

Two full baths

Rustic and modern elements combine to create a home worthy of a beautiful setting

A covered front Porch leads into an Entry Hall with a staircase to the left

The Gathering Room features a sloped ceiling and a towering wall of windows

Located off the Dining Room is a Deck, perfect for outdoor entertaining

The convenient U-shaped Kitchen offers a Pantry and a snackbar

The Master Bedroom on the first floor offers privacy with a Bath and Dressing Room

Upstairs find two secondary Bedrooms, a full Bath, and a lounge that overlooks the Gathering Room

This home comes with a basement foundation.

First floor — 1,113 sq. ft.

Second floor — 543 sq. ft.

Basement — 1,113 sq. ft.

■ *Total living area 1,656 sq. ft.* ■ *Price Code B* ■

FIRST FLOOR

SECOND FLOOR

Country Charmer

■ Total living area 1,438 sq. ft. ■ Price Code A ■

MAIN FLOOR

No. 96509

■**This plan features:**

— Three bedrooms

— Two full baths

■ Quaint front Porch is perfect for sitting and relaxing

■ Great Room opening into Dining Area and Kitchen

■ Corner Deck in rear of home accessed from Kitchen and Master Suite

■ Master Suite with a private Bath, walk-in closet and built-in shelves

■ Two large secondary Bedrooms in the front of the home share a hall Bath

■ Two-car Garage located in the rear of the home

■ An optional slab or crawlspace foundation — please specify when ordering.

Main floor — 1,438 sq. ft.
Garage — 486 sq. ft.

Victorian Styling Accents the Exterior

© Donald A. Gardner Architects, Inc.

■ Total living area 1,865 sq. ft. ■ Price Code F ■

MAIN FLOOR

No. 99857

■**This plan features:**

— Three bedrooms

— Two full baths

■ The covered wrap-around Porch connects to the rear Deck

■ The Foyer opens into the octagonal Great Room that is warmed by a fireplace

■ The Dining Room has a tray ceiling and convenient access to the Kitchen

■ The galley Kitchen opens into the Breakfast Bay

■ The Master Bedroom has a bay area in the rear, a walk-in closet and a fully appointed Bath

■ Two more Bedrooms complete this plan as does another full Bath

■ Alternate foundation options available at an additional charge. Please call 1.800.235.5700 for more information.

■ This home comes with a crawlspace foundation.

Main floor — 1,865 sq. ft.
Garage — 505 sq. ft.

Arched Windows Accent Sophisticated Design

Total living area 2,551 sq. ft. ■ Price Code F

No. 92509

This plan features:

- Four bedrooms

- Two full and one half baths

- Graceful columns and full-length windows highlight front Porch

- Spacious Great Room with decorative ceiling over hearth fireplace between built-in cabinets

- Kitchen with peninsula counter and Breakfast Alcove

- Secluded Master Bedroom offers access to back Porch, and has a decorative ceiling and plush Bath

- Three additional Bedrooms with loads of closets space share double vanity Bath

- An optional crawlspace or slab foundation — please specify when ordering

Main floor — 2,551 sq. ft.
Garage — 532 sq. ft.

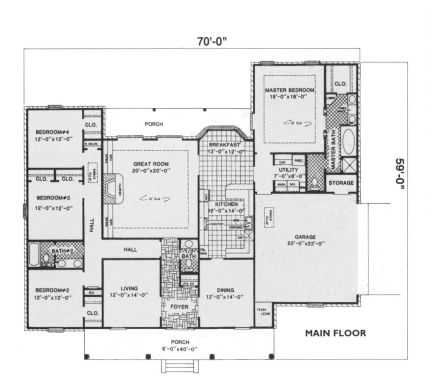

Fieldstone Facade and Arched Windows

■ *Total living area 1,858 sq. ft.* ■ *Price Code C* ■

No. 94911

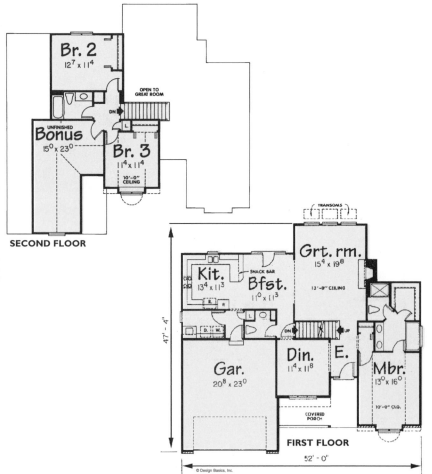

■ This plan features:

— Three bedrooms

— Two full and one half baths

■ Inviting Covered Porch shelters entrance

■ Expansive Great Room enhanced by warm fireplace and three transom windows

■ A first floor Master Bedroom with an arched window below a sloped ceiling and a double vanity Bath

■ This home comes with a basement foundation.

■ Alternate foundation options available at an additional charge, call 1.800.235.5700 for more information.

First floor — 1,405 sq. ft.
Second floor — 453 sq. ft.
Bonus room — 300 sq. ft.
Basement — 1,405 sq. ft.
Garage — 490 sq. ft.

Distinguished Look

No. 98429

This plan features:

Three bedrooms

Two full and one half baths

The Family Room, Breakfast Room and the Kitchen are presented in an open layout

A fireplace in the Family Room provides a warm atmosphere

The plush Master Suite pampers the owner and features a trapezoid glass above the tub

Two additional Bedrooms share the use of the double vanity Bath in the hall

Please specify a basement, crawlspace or slab foundation when ordering

First floor — 1,028 sq. ft.

Second floor — 878 sq. ft.

Bonus room — 315 sq. ft.

Basement — 1,028 sq. ft.

Garage — 497 sq. ft.

■ *Total living area 1,906 sq. ft.* ■ *Price Code C* ■

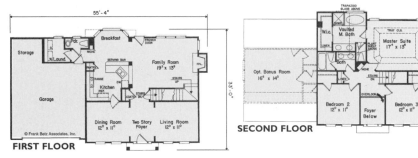

Traditional Transom Windows Add Appeal

No. 90396

This plan features:

Three bedrooms

Two full and one half baths

A vaulted ceiling in both the Living and adjoining Dining Rooms, accentuated by a fireplace

A well-appointed, sky-lit Kitchen which easily serves the Dining Room

A first floor Master Suite with a dramatic vaulted ceiling and private patio access

A private Master Bath with double vanity and walk-in closet

This home comes with a basement foundation.

First floor — 1,099 sq. ft.

Second floor — 452 sq. ft.

Basement — 1,099 sq. ft.

Garage — 412 sq. ft.

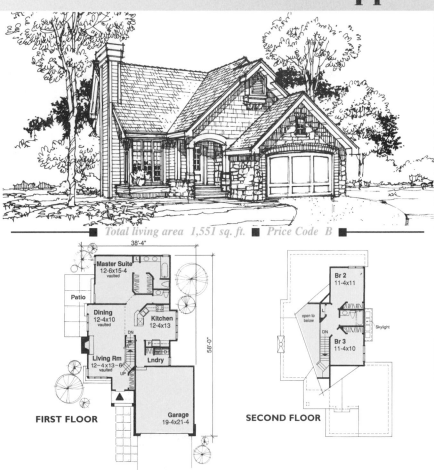

■ *Total living area 1,551 sq. ft.* ■ *Price Code B* ■

Comfortable Contemporary

Total living area 1,591 sq. ft. ■ Price Code B ■

46'-2"

TERR.

D.R. 10'-10"x 11' | KIT. 10'x 11' | D'NET 7' x 11' | MUD RM | STOR. 7 x 11'

ref. | dw

L.R. 14'-10"x 15'
high ceiling

2 CAR GAR. 20' x 20'

P.

F.

32'-4"

FIRST FLOOR

B.R. 10'-10"x 11' | cl. | cl. | lin. | B.R. 11' x 10' | whirlpool tub

W.I.C.

H

upper part of living rm.

M.B.R. 15' x 13'

dn.

cl.

roof

SECOND FLOOR

No. 99652

■ **This plan features:**

— Three bedrooms

— Two full and one half baths

■ Covered Porch entrance into convenient Foyer with closet and Powder Room

■ High ceiling accenting arched window in Living Room which opens to Dining Room with sliding glass door to Patio

■ Efficient U-shaped Kitchen with serving counter, Dinette Area and indispensable Mudroom

■ Private, corner Master Bedroom with two closets and plush Bath with whirlpool tub

■ Two additional Bedrooms with ample closets share a full Bath

■ An optional basement or slab foundation — please specify when ordering.

First floor — 810 sq. ft.
Second floor — 781 sq. ft.
Basement — 746 sq. ft.
Garage/Storage — 513 sq. ft.

Impressive Brick and Wood Facade

Total living area 1,651 sq. ft. ■ Price Code B ■

WHIRLPOOL | LIN.

Mbr. 14' x 13' | Grt. rm. 17' x 17' | Bfst. 11' x 11'

Den 10' x 10' OPTIONAL BEDROOM | WET BAR

Kit. 13' x 11'

Din. 12' x 11'

Br.2 11' x 10'

Gar. 30' x 20'

COVERED PORCH

COVERED PORCH

56'-0"

MAIN FLOOR

62'-0"

© Design Basics, Inc.

Br.3 10' x 10'

BEDROOM OPTION

No. 94921

■ **This plan features:**

— Two or three bedrooms

— Two full baths

■ Covered front and rear Porches expand living space outside

■ Handy serving area located between formal Dining Room and expansive Great Room

■ Transom windows frame hearth fireplace in Great Room and highlight Breakfast Room

■ Hub Kitchen with built-in Pantry, snack bar and adjoining Laundry/Garage Entry

■ French doors lead into Den with wetbar, which can easily convert to third Bedroom

■ Exclusive Master Suite includes decorative ceiling, walk-in closet, dual vanity and a corner whirlpool tub

■ This home comes with a basement foundation.

Main floor — 1,651 sq. ft.
Basement — 1,651 sq. ft.
Garage — 480 sq. ft.

© Donald A. Gardner Architects, Inc.

G. NATHAN

Total living area 2,211 sq. ft. ■ *Price Code G* ■

No. 96449

This home features:

- Three bedrooms

- Two full baths

■ Exciting roof lines and brick detailing fit in the finest neighborhood

■ Great Room also offers cathedral ceiling above arched windows and fireplace nestled between built-ins

■ Private Master Suite features walk-in closet and plush Bath with twin vanities, shower and corner window tub

■ This home comes with a crawlspace foundation.

■ Alternate foundation options available at an additional charge, call 1.800.235.5700 for more information.

Main floor — 2,211 sq. ft.
Bonus room — 408 sq. ft.
Garage & storage — 700 sq. ft.

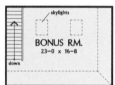

BONUS

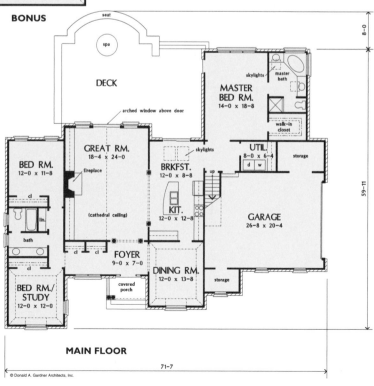

MAIN FLOOR

© Donald A. Gardner Architects, Inc.

Perfect Plan for Busy Family

■ Total living area 1,756 sq. ft. ■ Price Code C ■

No. 93191

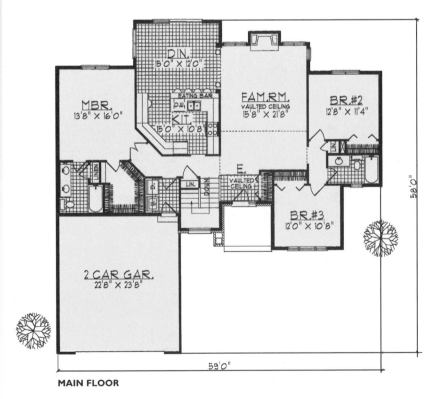

MAIN FLOOR

■ **This plan features:**

— Three bedrooms

— Two full baths

■ Covered Entry opens to vaulted Foyer and Family Room

■ Family Room with a vaulted ceiling and central fireplace

■ Angular Kitchen with an eating bar, built-in desk and nearby Laundry and Garage Entry

■ Secluded Master Bedroom with a large walk-in closet and double vanity Bath

■ Two additional Bedrooms with easy access to a full Bath

■ Plenty of room for growing family to expand on lower level

■ This home comes with a basement foundation.

Main floor — 1,756 sq. ft.
Basement — 1,756 sq. ft.

For the Young at Heart

No. 99324

This plan features:

- Three bedrooms

- Two full baths

- Arched transom windows, divided-light windows, bay windows and a covered Porch Entry

- A Great Room with a vaulted ceiling, a fireplace and a transom window

- A Kitchen with a vaulted ceiling and a Breakfast Area with sliding doors to the Deck

- A Master Suite with ample closet space and a private full Master Bath

- This home comes with a basement foundation.

Main floor — 1,307 sq. ft.
Basement — 1,307 sq. ft.
Garage — 374 sq. ft.

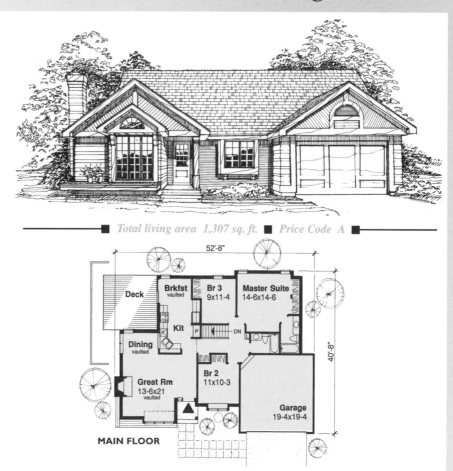

■ *Total living area 1,307 sq. ft.* ■ *Price Code A* ■

MAIN FLOOR

For a Small Lot

No. 92052

This plan features:

- Three bedrooms

- Two full and one half baths

- At 36' wide this home still has a double Garage, a Great Room and a large Dining Area

- The Great Room is topped by a cathedral ceiling and flows into the Dining Area

- The Dining Area has direct access to the rear Patio

- Three ample-sized Bedrooms and two full Baths are on the second floor

- The Master Bedroom is highlighted by a cathedral ceiling and a wardrobe closet

- Secondary Bedrooms share the full Bath in the hall

- This home comes with a basement foundation.

First floor — 615 sq. ft.
Second floor — 574 sq. ft.
Basement — 615 sq. ft.

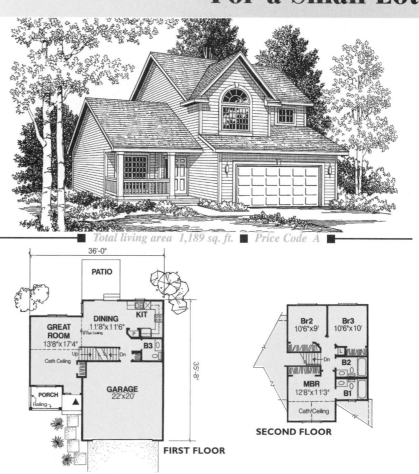

■ *Total living area 1,189 sq. ft.* ■ *Price Code A* ■

FIRST FLOOR

SECOND FLOOR

No Wasted Space

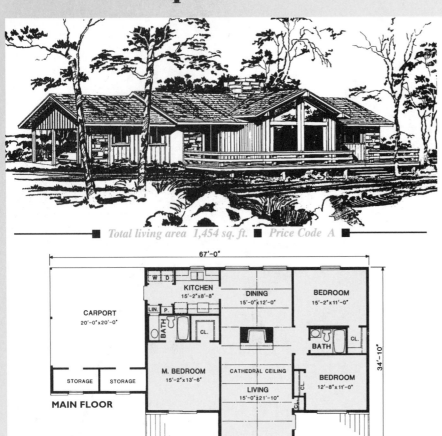

Total living area 1,454 sq. ft. ■ Price Code A

MAIN FLOOR

CARPORT
20'-0"x20'-0"

STORAGE   STORAGE

67'-0"

W D

KITCHEN
15'-2"x8'-8"

LIN. P.

BATH

CL.

DINING
15'-0"x12'-0"

BEDROOM
15'-2"x11'-0"

BATH

CL.

M. BEDROOM
15'-2"x13'-6"

CATHEDRAL CEILING

LIVING
15'-0"x21'-10"

BEDROOM
12'-8"x11'-0"

CL.

34'-10"

DECK

No. 90412

■ **This plan features:**

– Three bedrooms

– Two full baths

■ A centrally located Great Room with a cathedral ceiling, exposed wood beams, and large areas of fixed glass

■ The Living and Dining Areas separated by a massive stone fireplace

■ A secluded Master Suite with a walk-in closet and private Master Bath

■ An efficient Kitchen with a convenient Laundry Area

■ An optional basement, slab or crawlspace foundation — please specify when ordering.

Main floor — 1,454 sq. ft.

Attractive Combination of Brick and Siding

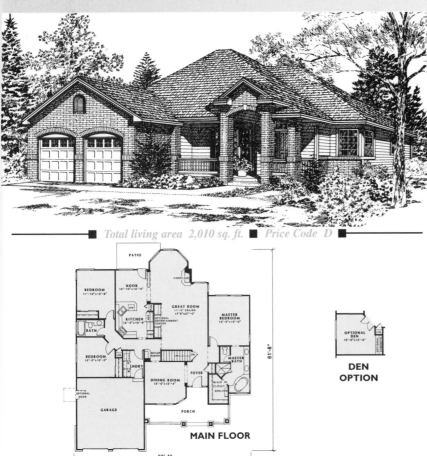

Total living area 2,010 sq. ft. ■ Price Code D

PATIO

BEDROOM
11'-10"x12'-6"

NOOK
10'-10"x10'-0"

FIREPLACE

GREAT ROOM
11'-0" CEILING
17'-6"x21'-0"

MASTER
BEDROOM
13'-0"x16'-0"

KITCHEN
12'-0"x10'-6"

OPTIONAL
ENTERTAINMENT
CENTER

BATH

BEDROOM
12'-0"x12'-0"

BUTLER'S
PANTRY

LNDRY

DINING ROOM
13'-0"x12'-4"

FOYER

MASTER
BATH

WALK IN
CLOSET
SHELVES

GARAGE

PORCH

61'-8"

56'-4"

MAIN FLOOR

OPTIONAL
DEN
12'-0"x12'-0"

DEN OPTION

No. 24259

■ **This plan features:**

– Three bedrooms

– Two full baths

■ Great Room with a sunny bayed area, fireplace and built-in entertainment center

■ A private Master Bedroom with luxurious Master Bath and walk-in closet

■ Dining Room has a Butler's Pantry

■ Two additional Bedrooms have use of hall full Bath

■ An optional basement, slab or crawlspace foundation — please specify when ordering.

Main floor — 2,010 sq. ft.
Basement — 2,010 sq. ft.

© Donald A. Gardner Architects, Inc.

■ *Total living area 2,692 sq. ft.* **■** *Price Code H* **■**

No. 99853

This plan features:

- Four bedrooms

- Three full and one half baths

- Impressive double gable roof with front and rear palladian windows and wrap-around Porch

- Vaulted ceilings in two-story Foyer and Great Room accommodates Loft/Study Area

- Spacious, first floor Master Bedroom offers walk-in closet and luxurious Bath

- Alternate foundation options available at an additional charge. Please call 1.800.235.5700 for more information.

- This home comes with a crawlspace foundation.

First floor — 1,734 sq. ft.
Second floor — 958 sq. ft.

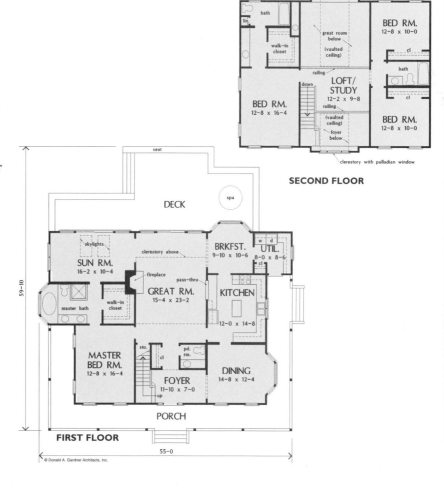

SECOND FLOOR

FIRST FLOOR

© Donald A. Gardner Architects, Inc.

Stately Stone and Stucco

■ *Total living area 3,027 sq. ft.* ■ *Price Code H* ■

FIRST FLOOR

62'- 4"

54'- 6"

Vaulted M. Bath
W.i.c.
PLANT SHELF ABOVE
Two Story Great Room 19⁰ x 18⁰
Keeping Room 13⁵ x 15⁹
Breakfast
Master Suite 14⁵ x 17⁵
Pdr
Kitchen
Study / Opt. Sitting Room 12⁵ x 12⁰
Two Story Foyer
Dining Room 13⁵ x 16⁰
Laundry
Storage
Garage 20⁰ x 20⁰

© Frank Betz Associates, Inc.

SECOND FLOOR

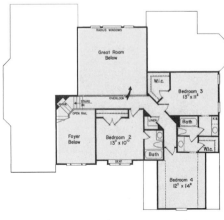

RADIUS WINDOWS
Great Room Below
W.i.c.
Bedroom 3 13⁰ x 11²
OVERLOOK
Foyer Below
OPEN RAIL
Bedroom 2 13⁵ x 10⁰
Bath
Linen
Bath
W.i.c.
Bedroom 4 12⁵ x 14⁰

No. 98402

■ **This plan features:**

— Four bedrooms

— Three full and one half baths

■ Two-story Foyer with angled staircase welcomes all

■ Large Great Room has a fireplace, wetbar and French doors

■ Kitchen with a cooktop island, Pantry and Breakfast Alcove

■ Open Keeping Room accented by a wall of windows

■ Master Suite wing offers a tray ceiling, a plush Bath and roomy walk-in closet

■ An optional basement, slab or crawlspace foudation — please specify when ordering

First floor — 2,130 sq. ft.
Second floor — 897 sq. ft.
Garage — 494 sq. ft.
Basement — 2,130 sq. ft.

Large Living in a Small Space

No. 24304

This plan features:

Three bedrooms

One full and one three-quarter baths

A sheltered entrance leads into an open Living Room with a corner fireplace and a wall of windows

A well-equipped Kitchen features a peninsula counter with a Nook, a laundry and clothes closet, and a built-in Pantry

A Master Bedroom with a private Bath

Two additional Bedrooms that share full hall Bath

An optional basement or crawlspace foundation — please specify when ordering.

Main floor — 993 sq. ft.

Garage — 390 sq. ft.

Basement — 987 sq. ft.

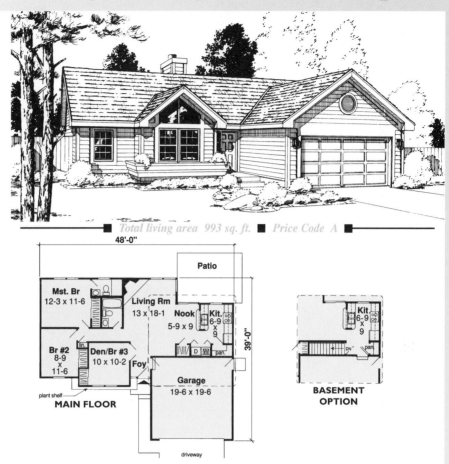

Total living area 993 sq. ft. ■ Price Code A

Fireplace Center of Circular Living Area

No. 10274

This plan features:

Three bedrooms

One full and one three quarter baths

A dramatically positioned fireplace as a focal point for the main Living Area

The Kitchen, Dining and Living Rooms form a circle that allows work areas to flow into Living Areas

Sliding glass doors accessible to wood a Deck

A convenient Laundry Room located off the Kitchen

A double Garage providing excellent storage

This home comes with a slab foundation.

Main floor — 783 sq. ft.

Garage — 576 sq. ft.

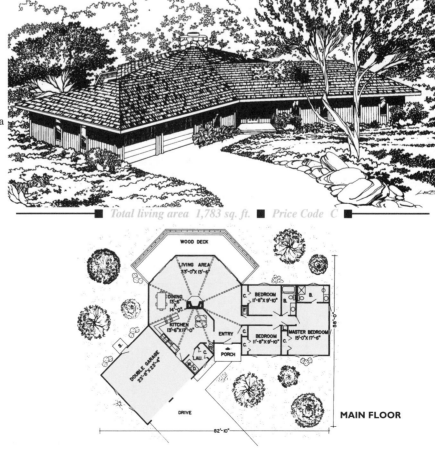

Total living area 1,783 sq. ft. ■ Price Code C

189

Traditional Beauty

■ *Total living area 1,576 sq. ft.* ■ *Price Code F* ■

No. 99802

■ **This plan features:**

— Three bedrooms

— Two full baths

■ Traditional beauty with large arched windows, round columns, covered Porch, brick veneer and an open floor plan

■ Clerestory dormers above covered Porch lighting the Foyer

■ Cathedral ceiling enhancing the Great Room along with a cozy fireplace

■ Island Kitchen with Breakfast Area accessing the large Deck with an optional Spa

■ Columns defining spaces

■ Tray ceiling over the Master Bedroom, Dining Room and Bedroom/Study

■ Dual vanity, separate shower and whirlpool tub in the Master Bath

■ This home comes with a crawlspace foundation.

■ Alternate foundation options available at an additional charge. Please call 1.800.235.5700 for more information.

Main floor — 1,576 sq. ft.
Garage — 465 sq. ft.

MAIN FLOOR

Compact Home is Surprisingly Spacious

No. 90905

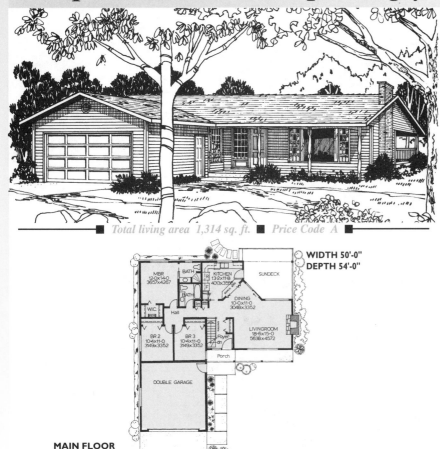

■ *Total living area 1,314 sq. ft.* ■ *Price Code A* ■

■ **This plan features:**

— Three bedrooms

— One full and one three-quarter baths

■ A spacious Living Room warmed by a fireplace

■ A Dining Room flowing off the Living Room, with sliding glass doors to the Deck

■ An efficient, well-equipped Kitchen with a snack bar, double sink, and ample cabinet and counter space

■ A Master Suite with a walk-in closet and private full Bath

■ Two additional, roomy Bedrooms with ample closet space and protection from street noise from the two-car Garage

■ This home comes with a basement foundation.

Main floor — 1,314 sq. ft.
Basement — 1,488 sq. ft.
Garage — 484 sq. ft.

WIDTH 50'-0"
DEPTH 54'-0"

MAIN FLOOR

Total living area 3,480 sq. ft. ■ **Price Code I** ■

No. 98508

■ This plan features:

- Four bedrooms

- Three full and one half baths

■ Formal Living and Dining Rooms gracefully defined with columns and decorative windows

■ Wood plank flooring and a massive fireplace accent the Great Room

■ Hub Kitchen with brick pavers and extended serving counter

■ Private Master Bedroom offers a Private Lanai and plush Dressing Area

■ Three second floor Bedrooms with walk-in closets and private access to a full Bath

■ This home comes with a slab foundation.

First floor — 2,441 sq. ft.
Second floor — 1,039 sq. ft.
Bonus — 271 sq. ft.
Garage — 660 sq. ft.

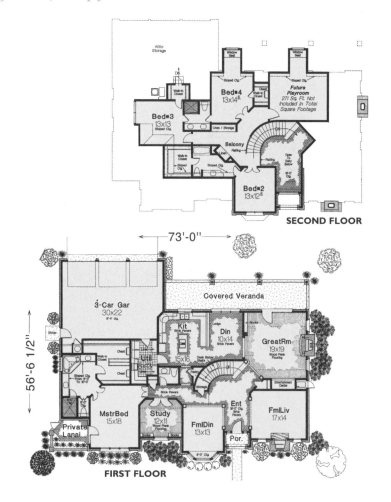

Southern Hospitality

■ *Total living area 1,830 sq. ft.* ■ *Price Code C* ■

No. 92220

■ **This plan features:**

— Three bedrooms

— Two full baths

■ Covered Veranda catches breezes

■ Tiled Entry leads into Great Room with fieldstone fireplace, a cathedral ceiling and atrium door to another Covered Veranda

■ A bright Kitchen/Dining Room includes a stovetop island/snackbar, built-in Pantry and desk

■ Vaulted ceiling crowns Master Bedroom that offers a plush Bath and huge walk-in closet

■ Two additional Bedrooms with ample closets share a double vanity Bath

■ An optional basement, slab or crawlspace foundation — please specify when ordering.

Main floor — 1,830 sq. ft.
Garage — 759 sq. ft.

WIDTH 75'-0'
DEPTH 52'-3"

COVERED VERANDA

MSTR. BDRM.
14 X 16
VAULTED CLG.
9" TO 11"

SLOPED CLGS.
9" TO 11"

WALK-IN-CLOS.

KITCHEN/DINING
21 X 15
9" CLGS.

PANTRY

HALL
9" CLGS.

LAUND.

3 CAR GARAGE
23 X 33

ENT.
10" CLGS.

LIN.

BDRM. #3
11 X 12
9" CLGS.

GREAT ROOM
22 X 16
CATHEDRAL CLGS.

BDRM #2
12 X 13
10" CLGS.

SERVICE PORCH

COVERED VERANDA

MAIN FLOOR

European Sophistication

No. 99831

■ This plan features:

— Three bedrooms

— Two full baths

■ Keystone arches, gables, and stucco give the exterior European sophistication

■ Large Great Room with fireplace, and U-shaped Kitchen and a large Utility Room nearby

■ Octagonal tray ceiling dresses up the Dining Room

■ Special ceiling treatments include a cathedral ceiling in the Great Room and tray ceilings in the Master and front Bedrooms

■ Indulgent Master Bath with a separate toilet area, a garden tub, shower and dual vanity

■ Bonus Room over the Garage adds flexibility

■ Alternate foundation options available at an additional charge. Please call 1.800.235.5700 for more information.

■ This home comes with a crawlspace foundation.

Main floor — 1,699 sq. ft.
Bonus room — 386 sq. ft.
Garage — 637 sq. ft.

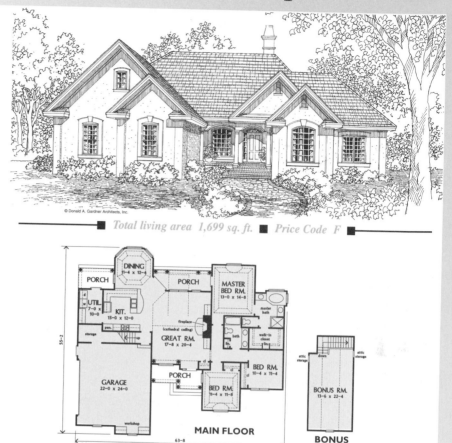

Total living area 1,699 sq. ft. ■ *Price Code F*

MAIN FLOOR

BONUS

© Donald A. Gardner Architects, Inc.

Foyer Isolates Bedroom Wing

No. 20087

■ This plan features:

— Three bedrooms

— Two full baths

■ A Living Room complete with a window wall, flanking a massive fireplace

■ A Dining Room with recessed ceilings and a pass-through for convenience

■ A Master Suite tucked behind the two-car Garage for maximum noise protection

■ A spacious Kitchen with built-ins and access to the two-car Garage

■ This home comes with a basement foundation.

Main floor —1,568 sq. ft.
Basement — 1,568 sq. ft.
Garage — 484 sq. ft.

Total living area 1,568 sq. ft. ■ *Price Code B*

MAIN FLOOR

With All the Amenities

No. 98430

This plan features:

- Three bedrooms
- Two full and one half baths
- A sixteen-foot high ceiling over the Foyer
- Arched openings highlight the hallway accessing the Great Room which is further enhanced by a fireplace
- A French door to the rear yard and decorative columns at its arched entrance
- Another vaulted ceiling topping the Dining Room, convenient to both the Living Room and the Kitchen
- An expansive Kitchen features a center work island, a built-in Pantry and a Breakfast Area defined by a tray ceiling
- A Master Suite also has a tray ceiling treatment and includes a lavish private Bath and a huge walk-in closet
- Secondary Bedrooms have private access to a full Bath
- An optional basement, slab or crawlspace foundation — please specify when ordering

Main floor – 1,884 sq. ft.
Basement – 1,908 sq. ft.
Garage – 495 sq. ft.

Total living area 1,884 sq. ft. • Price Code C

MAIN FLOOR

© Frank Betz Associates, Inc.

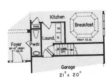

BASEMENT OPTION

Appealing Master Suite

No. 92239

This plan features:

- Three bedrooms
- Two full baths
- Sheltered Entry into spacious Living Room with a corner fireplace and Patio access
- Efficient Kitchen with a serving counter for Dining Area and nearby Utility/Garage Entry
- Private Master Bedroom offers a vaulted ceiling and pampering Bath with two vanities and walk-in closets and a garden window tub
- Two additional Bedrooms with ample closets, share a full Bath
- An optional slab or crawlspace foundation — please specify when ordering.

Main floor — 1,198 sq. ft.

Total living area 1,198 sq. ft. • Price Code A

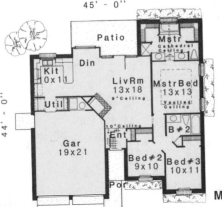

MAIN FLOOR

A Very Distinctive Ranch

No. 99115

■ **This plan features:**

— Three bedrooms

— Two full and one half baths

■ This hip roofed ranch has an exterior mixing brick and siding

■ The recessed entrance has sidelights which work to create a formal Entry

■ The formal Dining Room has a butler's Pantry for added convenience

■ The Great Room features a vaulted ceiling and a fireplace for added atmosphere

■ The large open Kitchen has ample cupboard space and a spacious Breakfast Area

■ The Master Suite includes a walk-in closet, private Bath and an elegant bay window

■ A Laundry Room is on the main floor between the three-car Garage and the Kitchen

■ This home comes with a basement foundation.

Main floor — 1,947 sq. ft.
Basement — 1,947 sq. ft.

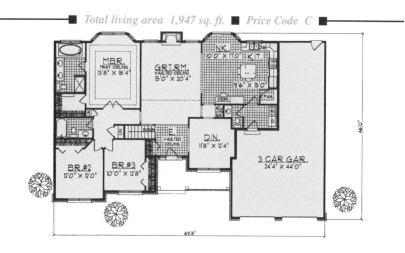

■ Total living area 1,947 sq. ft. ■ Price Code C ■

Deck Surrounds House on Three Sides

No. 91304

■ **This plan features:**

— Three bedrooms

— One full, one three-quarter and one half baths

■ A sunken, circular Living Room with windows on four sides and a vaulted clerestory for a wide-open feeling

■ Back-to-back fireplaces in the Living Room and the adjoining Great Room

■ A convenient, efficient Kitchen with a sunny Eating Nook

■ A Master Suite with a walk-in closet and a private Master Bath

■ Two additional Bedrooms that share a full hall Bath

■ An optional basement or crawlspace foundation — please specify when ordering.

First floor — 1,439 sq. ft.
Second floor — 873 sq. ft.

■ Total living area 2,312 sq. ft. ■ Price Code E ■

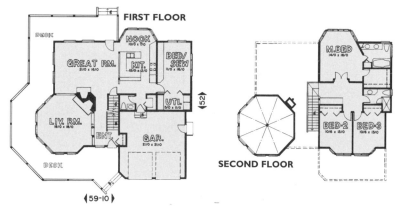

FIRST FLOOR

SECOND FLOOR

Sunny Two-story Foyer

© 1994 Donald A. Gardner Architects, Inc.

Total living area 1,823 sq. ft. ■ **Price Code F**

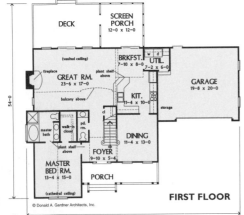

DECK

SCREEN PORCH
12-0 x 12-0

(vaulted ceiling)

fireplace

GREAT RM.
23-6 x 17-0

plant shelf above

balcony above

BRKFST.
7-10 x 8-0

UTIL.
7-2 x 6-0

w d

KIT.
11-4 x 10-0

GARAGE
19-8 x 20-0

storage

cl

master bath

walk-in closet

pd. rm.

plant shelf above

DINING
11-4 x 13-0

MASTER BED RM.
13-4 x 15-0

FOYER
9-10 x 5-4

PORCH

(cathedral ceiling)

FIRST FLOOR

© Donald A. Gardner Architects, Inc.

54-0

great room below

skylight

attic storage

railing

BED RM.
12-2 x 12-0

cl

bath

down

BED RM.
11-4 x 12-0

cl cl

foyer below

SECOND FLOOR

No. 96476

■ **This plan features:**

— Three bedrooms

— Two full and one half baths

■ The two-story Foyer off the formal Dining Room sets an elegant mood in this one-and-a-half story, dormered home

■ The Great Room and Breakfast Area are both topped by a vaulted ceiling

■ The screened Porch has a relaxing atmosphere

■ The Master Suite on the first floor includes a cathedral ceiling and an elegant Bath with whirlpool tub and separate shower

■ There is plenty of attic and Garage Storage space available

■ This home comes with a crawlspace foundation.

■ Alternate foundation options available at an additional charge, call 1.800.235.5700 for more information.

First floor — 1,335 sq. ft.
Second floor — 488 sq. ft.
Garage & Storage — 465 sq. ft.

Distinctive French Door Entrance

Total living area 2,394 sq. ft. ■ **Price Code E**

SUNDECK
16'0"x10'0"

LAV.

BREAKFAST
11'6"x8'6"

M. BATH

FAMILY RM.
19'8"x13'6"

KITCHEN
11'6"x9'0"

M. BDRM.
15'8"x17'6"

DINING RM.
11'6"x13'6"

LIVING RM.
11'6"x15'6"

FOYER
9'8"x12'0"

47'-0"

50'-0"

FIRST FLOOR

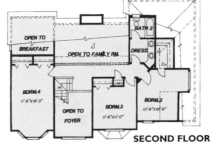

OPEN TO BREAKFAST

OPEN TO FAMILY RM.

BATH 2

DRESS.

BDRM.4
11'6"x19'0"

BDRM.3
11'6"x11'0"

OPEN TO FOYER

BDRM.2
10'8"x8'6"

LINEN

SECOND FLOOR

No. 93210

■ **This plan features:**

— Four bedrooms

— Two full and one half baths

■ French doors open into a two-story foyer topped by a beautiful arched window

■ Both the formal Living and Dining Rooms enjoy plenty of natural light through their bay windows

■ Well-appointed Kitchen includes a peninsula counter and easy access to both Dining Areas

■ Expansive Family Room has a fireplace and opens onto the rear Sun Deck

■ Large Master Suite has a private Bath with double vanity and a walk-in closet

■ Three second floor Bedrooms share a full hall Bath with double vanity

■ This home comes with a basement foundation.

First floor — 1,560 sq. ft.
Second floor — 834 sq. ft.
Basement — 772 sq. ft.
Garage — 760 sq. ft.

Simply Cozy

No. 98912

This plan features:

- Three bedrooms

- Two full baths

- Quaint front Porch sheltering Entry into the Living Area showcased by a massive fireplace and built-ins below a vaulted ceiling

- Formal Dining Room accented by a bay of glass with Sun Deck access

- Efficient, galley Kitchen with Breakfast Area, Laundry facilities and outdoor access

- Secluded Master Bedroom offers a roomy walk-in closet and plush Bath with two vanities and a garden window tub

- Two additional Bedrooms with ample closets, share a full Bath with a skylight

- This home comes with a basement foundation.

Main floor — 1,325 sq. ft.

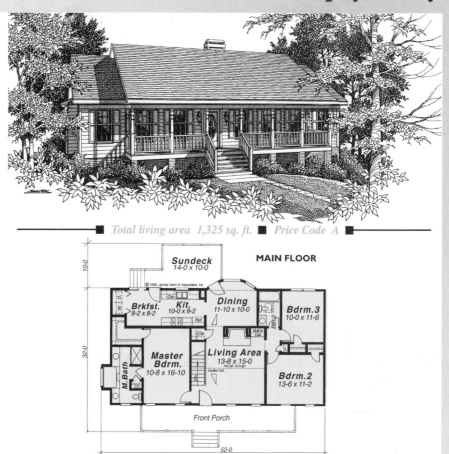

Total living area 1,325 sq. ft. ■ Price Code A

Elegant Design Offers Special Living

No. 10521

This plan features:

- Four bedrooms

- Two full and one half baths

- A balcony overlooking the two-story Foyer

- A Master Suite including a five-piece Bath, an oversized walk-in closet, and a separate linen closet

- A Kitchen including a Breakfast Nook, Pantry and desk

- A formal Living Room with access to a rear Deck

- This home comes with a basement foundation.

First floor — 1,191 sq. ft.
Second floor — 699 sq. ft.
Basement — 1,191 sq. ft.
Garage — 454 sq. ft.

Total living area 1,890 sq. ft. ■ Price Code C

201

Details, Details, Details

Total living area 2,155 sq. ft. ■ *Price Code D* ■

FIRST FLOOR

© Frank Betz Associates, Inc.

SECOND FLOOR

No. 98447

■ **This plan features:**

— Three bedrooms

— Two full and one half baths

■ This elevation is highlighted by stucco, stone and detailing around the arched windows

■ The two-story Foyer allows access to the Dining Room and the Great Room

■ A vaulted ceiling and a fireplace can be found in the Great Room

■ The Breakfast Room has a vaulted ceiling and flows into the Kitchen and the Keeping Room

■ Two secondary Bedrooms, each with a walk-in closet, share a full hall Bath

■ The Master Suite has a tray ceiling a huge walk-in closet and a compartmental Bath

■ An optional basement or crawlspace foundation — please specify when ordering

First floor — 1,628 sq. ft.
Second floor — 527 sq. ft.
Bonus room — 207 sq. ft.
Basement — 1,628 sq. ft.
Garage — 440 sq. ft.

Brick Adds Class

Total living area 1,472 sq. ft. ■ *Price Code A* ■

MAIN FLOOR

No. 93165

■ **This plan features:**

— Three bedrooms

— Two full baths

■ Keystone entrance leads into easy care, tile Entry with plant ledge and convenient closet

■ Expansive Great Room with cathedral ceiling over triple window and a corner gas fireplace

■ Hub Kitchen accented by arches and columns serving Great Room and Dining area, near Laundry Area and Garage

■ Adjoining Dining Area with large windows, access to rear yard and Screen Porch

■ Private Master Bedroom suite with a walk-i closet and plush Bath with corner whirlpoo tub

■ Two additional Bedrooms share a full Bath

■ This plan is not to be built within a 20 mile radius of Iowa City, IA.

■ This home comes with a basement foundation.

Main floor — 1,472 sq. ft.
Basement — 1,472 sq. ft.
Garage — 424 sq. ft.

■ *Total living area 3,352 sq. ft.* ■ *Price Code I* ■

No. 98513

■ **This plan features:**

– Three bedrooms

– Three full and one half baths

■ Brick and stone blend masterfully for an impressive French Country exterior

■ Separate Master Suite with expansive Bath and closet

■ Study containing a built-in desk and bookcase

■ Angled island Kitchen highlighted by walk-in Pantry and open to the Breakfast Bay

■ Fantastic Family Room including a brick fireplace and a built-in entertainment center

■ Three additional Bedrooms with private access to a full Bath

■ This home comes with a slab foundation.

Main floor — 3,352 sq. ft.
Garage — 672 sq. ft.

WIDTH 91'-0'
DEPTH 71'-9"

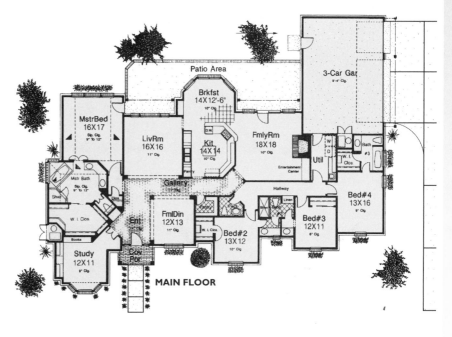

MAIN FLOOR

Elegant Brick Two-Story

■ *Total living area 2,398 sq. ft.* ■ *Price Code E* ■

No. 90450

■ This plan features:

— Four bedrooms

— Two or three full and one half baths

■ A two-story Great Room with a fireplace and access to a Deck

■ Master Suite with two walk-in closets and a private Master Bath

■ A large island Kitchen serving the formal Dining Room and the sunny Breakfast Nook with ease

■ Three additional Bedrooms, two with walk-in closets, sharing a full hall Bath

■ An optional Bonus Room with a private entrance from below

■ An optional basement or crawlspace foundation — please specify when ordering.

First floor — 1,637 sq. ft.
Second floor — 761 sq. ft.
Bonus — 453 sq. ft.

FIRST FLOOR

SECOND FLOOR

No. 90502

This plan features:

- Three bedrooms

- Two full baths

■ Sheltered Entry opens to airy Living/Dining Room with an inviting fireplace

■ Central Family Room with another fireplace opens to glass Nook with access to covered Patio

■ Open Kitchen easily serves nearby Dining Area, Nook and Patio beyond

■ French doors open to Master Suite with Patio access and a private Bath

■ Two additional Bedrooms with ample closets, share a full Bath and Laundry

■ An optional slab or crawlspace foundation — please specify when ordering.

Main floor — 1,642 sq. ft.

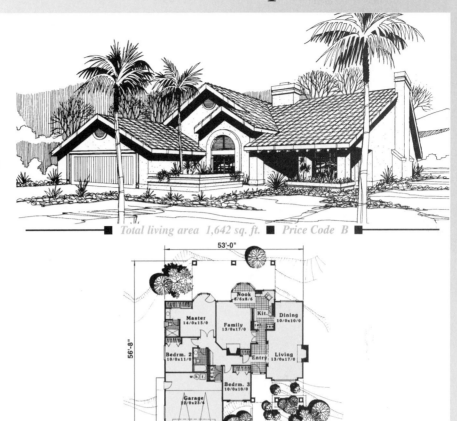

■ Total living area 1,642 sq. ft. ■ Price Code B ■

MAIN FLOOR

No. 20068

This plan features:

- Three bedrooms

- Two full and one half baths

■ A fireplaced Living Room with sloped ceiling

■ A second floor balcony

■ A huge Master Bedroom featuring a lavish Bath

■ Walk-in closets for all Bedrooms

■ An optional basement, slab or crawlspace foundation — please specify when ordering.

First floor — 1,277 sq. ft.
Second floor — 616 sq. ft.
Porch — 32 sq. ft.
Basement — 1,265 sq. ft.
Garage — 477 sq. ft.

■ Total living area 1,893 sq. ft. ■ Price Code C ■

FIRST FLOOR

SECOND FLOOR

205

Flexible Plan Creates Many Options

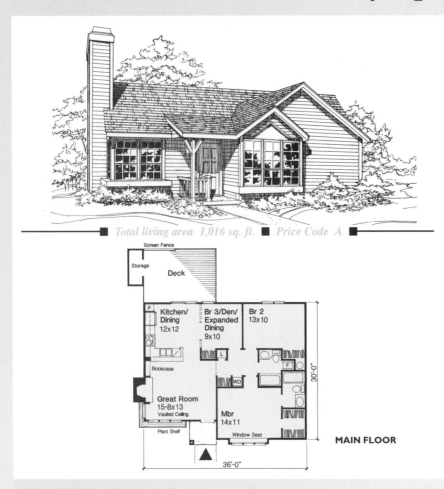

■ **Total living area 1,016 sq. ft.** ■ **Price Code A** ■

MAIN FLOOR

No. 90324

■ **This plan features:**

— Two bedrooms with optional third bedroom/den

— Two full baths

■ A Great Room featuring vaulted ceiling, fireplace, and built-in bookcase

■ An eat-in Kitchen opening onto a partially enclosed Deck through sliding doors

■ An L-shaped design of the Kitchen providing for easy meal preparation

■ A Master Bedroom with private Bath, large walk-in closet and a window seat

■ This home comes with a slab foundation.

Main floor — 1,016 sq. ft.

Half-Round Window Graces Attractive Exterior

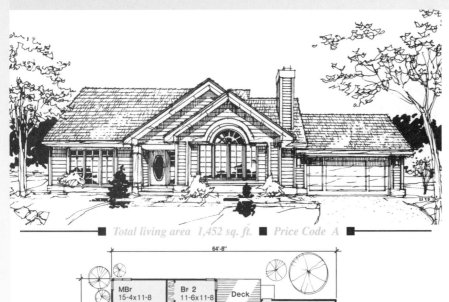

■ **Total living area 1,452 sq. ft.** ■ **Price Code A** ■

MAIN FLOOR

No. 90395

■ **This plan features:**

— Three bedrooms

— Two full baths

■ Soaring ceilings in the Kitchen, Living Room, Dining and Breakfast Rooms

■ An efficient, well-equipped Kitchen with a pass-through to the Dining Room

■ Built-in bookcases flanking the fireplace in the Living Room

■ A Master Suite with a private Master Bath and walk-in closet

■ This home comes with a basement foundation.

Main floor— 1,452 sq. ft.
Basement — 1,452 sq. ft.
Garage — 448 sq. ft.

Moderate Ranch Has Features of a Larger Plan

■ *Total living area 1,811 sq. ft.* ■ *Price Code C* ■

No. 90441

■ **This plan features:**

- Three bedrooms

- Two full baths

■ A large Great Room with a vaulted ceiling and a stone fireplace with bookshelves on either side

■ A spacious Kitchen with ample cabinet space conveniently located next to the large Dining Room

■ A Master Suite having a large Bath with a garden tub, double vanity and a walk-in closet

■ Two other large Bedrooms, each with a walk-in closet and access to the full Bath

■ An optional basement, slab or crawlspace combination — please specify when ordering.

Main floor — 1,811 sq. ft.

MAIN FLOOR

Cozy Traditional

■ *Total living area 1,862 sq. ft.* ■ *Price Code C* ■

No. 93000

■ This plan features:

— Three bedrooms

— Two full baths

■ An angled eating bar separating the Kitchen, Breakfast Room and Great Room, while leaving these areas open for easy entertaining

■ An efficient, well-appointed Kitchen that is convenient to both the formal Dining Room and the sunny Breakfast Room

■ A spacious Master Suite with oval tub, step-in shower, double vanity and walk-in closet

■ Two additional Bedrooms with ample closet space that share a full hall Bath

■ This home comes with a slab foundation.

Main floor — 1,862 sq. ft.
Garage — 520 sq. ft.

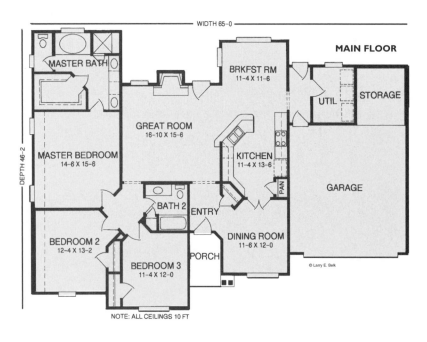

WIDTH 65–0

MAIN FLOOR

MASTER BATH

DEPTH 46–2

MASTER BEDROOM
14–6 X 15–6

GREAT ROOM
16–10 X 15–6

BRKFST RM
11–4 X 11–6

UTIL

STORAGE

KITCHEN
11–4 X 13–6

PAN

GARAGE

BATH 2

ENTRY

BEDROOM 2
12–4 X 13–2

DINING ROOM
11–6 X 12–0

© Larry E. Belk

BEDROOM 3
11–4 X 12–0

PORCH

NOTE: ALL CEILINGS 10 FT

Simply Elegant Design

No. 99268

This plan features:

- Three bedrooms

- Two full and one half baths

- Double door Entry into Foyer and Living Room beyond

- Formal Living Room with Patio access, shares see-through fireplace with Family Room

- Open and efficient Kitchen with Pantry, peninsula snackbar and nearby Laundry/Service Entry

- Private Master Bedroom pampered with two walk-in closets and a Dressing Area with a double vanity and whirlpool tub

- Two additional Bedrooms with arched windows share a full Bath

- This home comes with a basement foundation.

First floor — 1,182 sq. ft.
Second floor — 927 sq. ft.

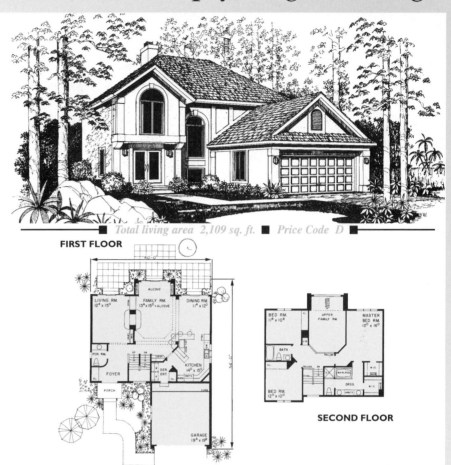

Total living area 2,109 sq. ft. ■ *Price Code D*

FIRST FLOOR

SECOND FLOOR

Brick Home with Four Bedrooms

No. 22004

This plan features:

- Four bedrooms

- Two full and one three-quarter baths

- Four roomy Bedrooms, including the Master Bedroom

- A centrally located Family Room including a fireplace, wetbar, and access to the Patio

- A large Dining Room at the front of the home for entertaining

- An interesting Kitchen and Nook with an adjoining Utility Room

- This home comes with a slab foundation.

Main floor — 2,070 sq. ft.
Garage — 474 sq. ft.

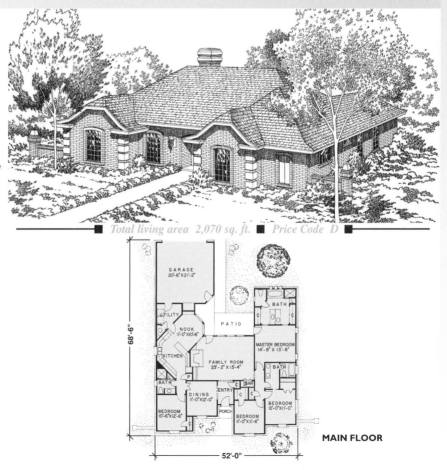

Total living area 2,070 sq. ft. ■ *Price Code D*

MAIN FLOOR

209

Highlighted by Exceptional Windows

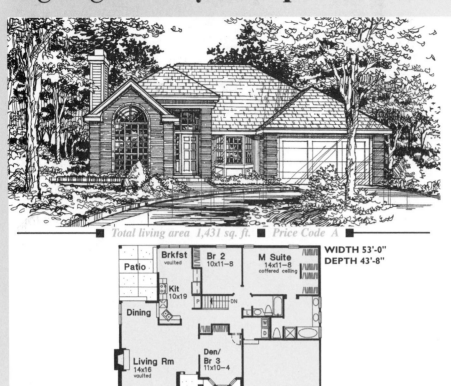

Total living area 1,431 sq. ft. ■ Price Code A

WIDTH 53'-0"
DEPTH 43'-8"

Patio | Brkfst vaulted | Br 2 10x11-8 | M Suite 14x11-8 coffered ceiling

Kit 10x19

Dining

Living Rm 14x16 vaulted | Den/ Br 3 11x10-4 | Garage 19-4x19-8

MAIN FLOOR

No. 98354

■ **This plan features:**

— Two bedrooms

— Two full baths

■ Large arched window in Living Room highlighting both interior and exterior

■ Bay window enhancing the Den

■ Formal Dining Room and the Living Room adjoin for spacious feeling

■ Efficiently arranged Kitchen includes a Breakfast Area topped by a vaulted ceiling

■ Patio accessed from the Dining Room or the Breakfast Area

■ Master Suite topped by a coffered ceiling, and includes two walk-in closets and a private, five-piece Bath

■ Additional Bedroom has easy access to the full Bath in the hall

■ This home comes with a basement foundation.

Main floor — 1,431 sq. ft.
Basement — 1,431 sq. ft.
Garage — 410 sq. ft.

Appealing Front Porch

Total living area 1,842 sq. ft. ■ Price Code C

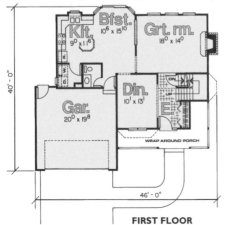

Kit. 9⁰ x 11⁶ | Bfst. 10⁶ x 15¹⁰ | Grt. rm. 18⁰ x 14⁰

Gar. 20⁰ x 19⁸ | Din. 10¹ x 13¹

WRAP AROUND PORCH

40' - 0"

46' - 0"

FIRST FLOOR

© Design Basics, Inc.

Mbr. 12⁰ x 16⁰ 9'-4" CEILING | Br. 4 10⁰ x 11⁶ | Br. 3 10⁰ x 11⁶

WHIRLPOOL | Br. 2 10⁰ x 11⁸ | OPEN TO BELOW | PLANT SHELF

LIN.

SECOND FLOOR

No. 94935

■ **This plan features:**

— Four bedrooms

— Two full and one half baths

■ Appealing wrap-around Porch graces this home

■ Light and airy two-story entrance with a side-light, plant shelf and a closet

■ Wall of windows and fireplace featured in the Great Room

■ Open Kitchen with easy access to the Breakfast Area, Dining Room and the Garage

■ Lovely Master Suite with tiered ceiling, two walk-in closets and a deluxe Bath

■ This home comes with a basement foundation.

First floor — 919 sq. ft.
Second floor — 923 sq. ft.
Basement — 919 sq. ft.
Garage — 414 sq. ft.

A Comfortable Informal Design

■ *Total living area 1,300 sq. ft.* ■ *Price Code A* ■

No. 94801

This plan features:

- Three bedrooms

- Two full baths

- Warm, Country front Porch with wood details

- Spacious Activity Room enhanced by a pre-fab fireplace

- Open and efficient Kitchen/Dining area highlighted by bay window, adjacent to Laundry and Garage Entry

- Corner Master Bedroom offers a pampering Bath with a garden tub and double vanity topped by a vaulted ceiling

- Two additional Bedrooms with ample closets, share a full Bath

- An optional crawlspace or slab foundation available — please specify when ordering

Main floor — 1,300 sq. ft.
Garage — 576 sq. ft.

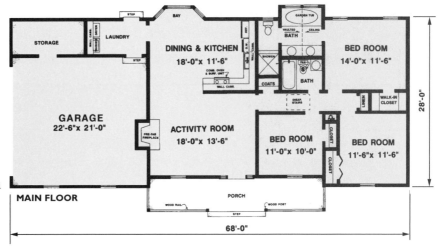

Small, But Not Lacking

■ *Total living area 1,546 sq. ft.* ■ *Price Code B* ■

No. 94116

■ This plan features:

— Three bedrooms

— One full and one three-quarter baths

■ Great Room adjoining the Dining Room for ease in entertaining

■ Kitchen highlighted by a peninsula counter/snack bar extending work space and offering convenience in serving informal meals or snacks

■ Split Bedroom plan allowing privacy for the Master Bedroom with a private Bath and a walk-in closet

■ Garage Entry convenient to the Kitchen

■ This home comes with a basement foundation.

Main floor — 1,546 sq. ft.

Basement — 1,530 sq. ft.
Garage — 440 sq. ft.

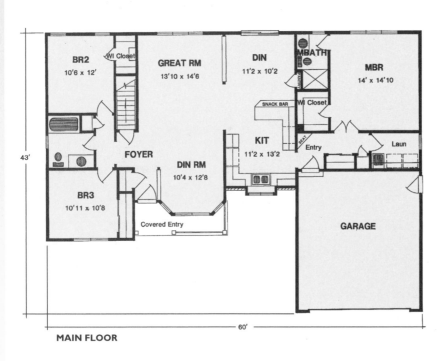

BR2
10'6 x 12'

WI Closet

GREAT RM
13'10 x 14'6

DIN
11'2 x 10'2

MBATH

MBR
14' x 14'10

SNACK BAR

WI Closet

KIT
11'2 x 13'2

FOYER

DIN RM
10'4 x 12'8

Entry

Laun

BR3
10'11 x 10'8

Covered Entry

GARAGE

43'

60'

MAIN FLOOR

Spectacular Sophistication

No. 94944

This plan features:

Four bedrooms

Two full and one half baths

Open Foyer with circular window and a plant shelf leads into the Dining Room

Great Room with an inviting fireplace and windows front and back

Open Kitchen has a work island and accesses the Breakfast Area

Master Bedroom suite features a nine-foot boxed ceiling, a walk-in closet and whirlpool Bath

Three additional Bedrooms share a full Bath with a double vanity

This home comes with a slab foundation.

Alternate foundation options available at an additional charge, call 1.800.235.5700 for more information.

First floor — 941 sq. ft.

Second floor — 992 sq. ft.

Basement — 941 sq. ft.

Garage — 480 sq. ft.

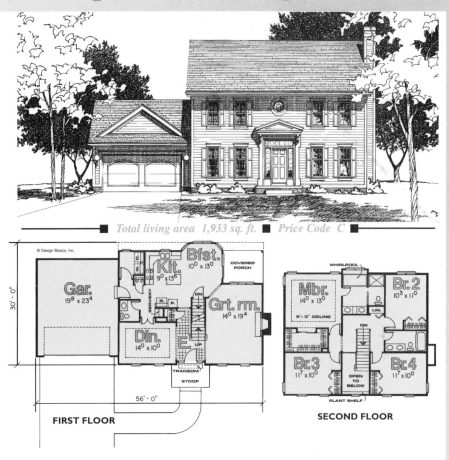

Total living area 1,933 sq. ft. ■ *Price Code C* ■

FIRST FLOOR

SECOND FLOOR

Yesterday's Style for Today's Lifestyle

No. 93704

This plan features:

Three bedrooms

Two full and one half baths

Front Porch shelters entrance into Foyer, Great Room and Study

Great Room with inviting fireplace opens to formal Dining Room

Spacious Kitchen with work island, built-in Pantry and serving/snackbar for Breakfast Area and Porch

Master Bedroom adjoins Study, pampering Bath and Utility Area

Two second floor Bedrooms with double closets, share a double vanity Bath and study alcove

An optional slab or crawlspace foundation — please specify when ordering.

First floor — 1,748 sq. ft.

Second floor — 558 sq. ft.

Garage — 528 sq. ft.

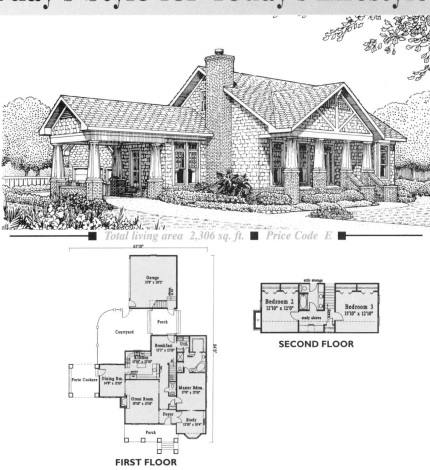

Total living area 2,306 sq. ft. ■ *Price Code E* ■

SECOND FLOOR

FIRST FLOOR

Two-Story Charmer

■ *Total living area 2,124 sq. ft.* ■ *Price Code D* ■

FIRST FLOOR

SECOND FLOOR

No. 99112

■ **This plan features:**

— Three bedrooms

— Two full and one half baths

■ Covered front Porch and vaulted Entry provide a warm welcome

■ Living Room has a vaulted ceiling and a corner fireplace

■ The Dining Room has sliding doors to the backyard

■ The U-shaped Kitchen features a Pantry, serving bar and a double sink

■ The first floor Master Suite spans the width of the home and includes a private Bath

■ Upstairs find two Bedrooms, one with a massive closet, and a full Bath

■ This home comes with a basement foundation.

First floor — 1,498 sq. ft.
Second floor — 626 sq. ft.
Basement — 1,485 sq. ft.

Snug Retreat With A View

■ *Total living area 880 sq. ft.* ■ *Price Code A* ■

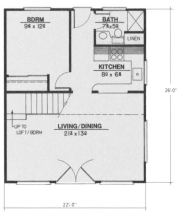

MAIN FLOOR

LOFT

No. 91031

■ **This plan features:**

— One bedroom plus loft

— One three-quarter bath

■ A large front Deck providing views and an expansive entrance

■ A two-story Living/Dining Area with double glass doors leading out to the Deck

■ An efficient, U-shaped Kitchen with a pass through counter to the Dining Area

■ A first floor Bedroom, with ample closet space, located near a full shower Bath

■ A Loft/Bedroom on the second floor offering multiple uses

■ An optional basement, slab or crawlspace foundation — please specify when ordering

Main floor — 572 sq. ft.
Loft — 308 sq. ft.

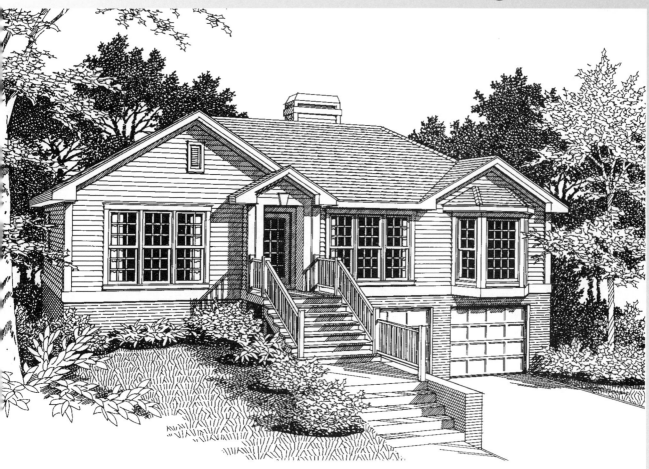

■ *Total living area 1,292 sq. ft.* ■ *Price Code A* ■

No. 93222

This plan features:

Three bedrooms

Two full baths

A bayed formal Dining Room with direct access to the Sun Deck and the Living Room for entertainment ease

An efficient, galley Kitchen, convenient to both formal and informal eating areas

An informal Breakfast Room with direct access to the Sun Deck

A large Master Suite equipped with a walk-in closet and a full private Bath

This home comes with a basement foundation.

Main floor — 1,276 sq. ft.
Finished staircase — 16 sq. ft.
Basement — 392 sq. ft.
Garage — 728 sq. ft.

SUNDECK
14'-0"X10'-0"

BREAKFAST
9'-6"X8'-2"

KITCHEN
10'-0"X8'-2"

DINING RM.
12'-0"X9'-6"

BEDRM.3
10'-0"X11'-6"

M.BEDRM.
16'-0"X11'-6"

LIVING AREA
13'-8"X15'-0"

BEDRM.2
13'-6"X13'-0"

ENTRY

MAIN FLOOR

26'-0"

48'-0"

Columned Keystone Arched Entry

■ *Total living area 2,256 sq. ft.* ■ *Price Code E* ■

No. 96503

■ **This plan features:**

— Three bedrooms

— Two full baths

■ Keystone arches and arched transoms above the windows

■ Formal Dining Room and Study flank the Foyer

■ Fireplace in Great Room

■ Efficient Kitchen with a peninsul counter and bayed Nook

■ A step ceiling in the Master Suite and interesting Master Bath with a triangular area for the oval tub

■ The secondary Bedrooms share a full Bath in the hall

■ An optional slab or crawlspace foundation — please specify whe ordering.

Main floor — 2,256 sq. ft.
Garage — 514 sq. ft.

Dramatic Windows and Gables

No. 99851

This plan features:

Three bedrooms

Two full and one half baths

The barrel vaulted Entrance is flanked by columns

Interior columns add elegance while visually dividing the Foyer from the Dining Room and the Great Room from the Kitchen

The Great Room is enlarged by its cathedral ceiling and a bank of windows

An angled center island and breakfast counter in the Kitchen

The first floor Master Suite has his-n-her closets plus a garden tub with skylight above

This home comes with a crawlspace foundation.

Alternate foundation options available at an additional charge. Please call 1.800.235.5700 for more information.

First floor — 1,416 sq. ft.

Second floor — 445 sq. ft.

Bonus — 284 sq. ft.

Garage — 485 sq. ft.

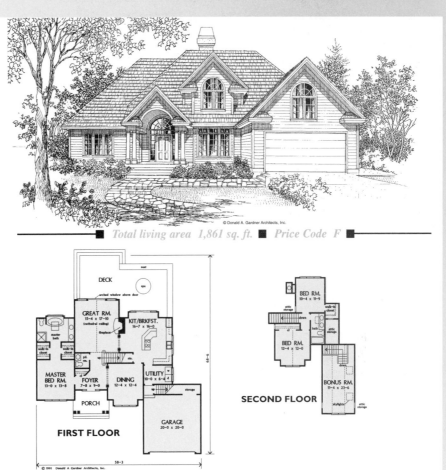

© Donald A. Gardner Architects, Inc.

Total living area 1,861 sq. ft. ■ *Price Code F* ■

Good Things Come in Small Packages

No. 20303

This plan features:

Three bedrooms

Two full baths

An air-lock vestibule Entry that keeps the chill outside

A cozy Sitting Nook in the Living Room

A well-equipped Kitchen with a Breakfast Nook

A sky-lit hall Bath shared by two of the Bedrooms

A Master Suite with his-n-her closets and a private, skylit full Bath

This home comes with a basement foundation.

First floor — 885 sq. ft.

Second floor — 368 sq. ft.

Basement — 715 sq. ft.

Total living area 1,253 sq. ft. ■ *Price Code A* ■

FIRST FLOOR

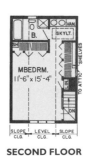

SECOND FLOOR

Flexible Spaces

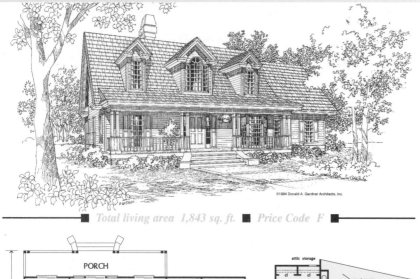

©1994 Donald A Gardner Architects, Inc.

Total living area 1,843 sq. ft. ■ Price Code F

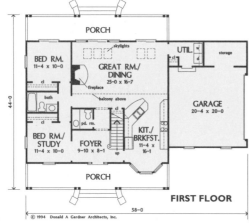

PORCH

BED RM.
11-4 x 10-0

GREAT RM./
DINING
25-0 x 16-7

skylights

UTIL.

storage

fireplace

balcony above

bath

cl

BED RM./
STUDY
11-4 x 10-0

pd. rm.

FOYER
9-10 x 8-1

up

KIT./
BRKFST.
11-4 x 16-1

GARAGE
20-4 x 20-0

PORCH

58-0

44-0

FIRST FLOOR

© 1994 Donald A Gardner Architects, Inc.

attic storage

great room below

railing

MASTER
BED RM.
11-4 x 14-10

down

LOFT/
STUDY
11-4 x 9-4
(optional storage)

cl

master bath

attic storage

SECOND FLOOR

No. 96457

■ **This plan features:**

— Three bedrooms

— Two full and one half baths

■ The large common area combines the Great Room and the Dining Room under a vaulted ceiling that is punctuated with skylights

■ The Kitchen/Breakfast Bay includes a peninsula counter/snackbar

■ From the Great Room extend entertaining outdoors to the covered back Porch

■ The Master Suite has a generous Bath and ample closet space

■ The front Bedroom/Study doubles as a Guest Room

■ On the second floor the Loft/Study makes terrific Office or Play Room

■ This home comes with a crawlspace foundation.

■ Alternate foundation options available at an additional charge, call 1-800-235-5700 for more information.

First floor — 1,234 sq. ft.
Second floor — 609 sq. ft.
Garage — 496 sq. ft.

Relaxed Country Living

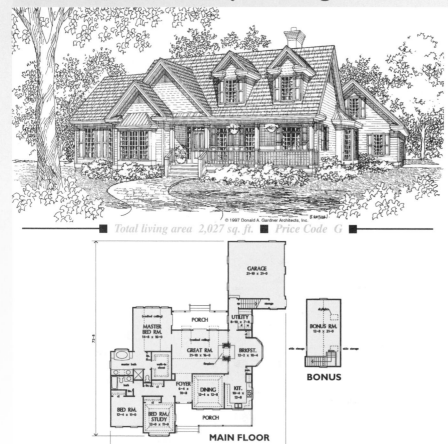

© 1997 Donald A. Gardner Architects, Inc.   B. BATMAN

Total living area 2,027 sq. ft. ■ Price Code G

GARAGE
21-10 x 21-0

storage

PORCH

UTILITY
9-10 x 7-4

MASTER
BED RM.
14-8 x 16-0

vaulted ceiling

vaulted ceiling

GREAT RM.
21-10 x 16-0

master bath

walk-in closet

BRKFST.
12-2 x 10-4

FOYER
6-4 x 8

DINING
12-0 x 12-0

KIT.
10-4 x 12-0

BED RM./
STUDY
12-0 x 11-0

PORCH

68-4

72-0

MAIN FLOOR

© 1997 Donald A Gardner Architects, Inc.

skylights

BONUS RM.
12-8 x 21-0

attic storage

attic storage

BONUS

No. 96402

■ **This plan features:**

— Three bedrooms

— Two full baths

■ Comfortable country home with deluxe Master Suite, front and back Porches and dual-sided fireplace

■ Vaulted Great Room brightened by two clerestory dormers and fireplace shared with Breakfast Bay

■ Dining Room and front Bedroom/Study dressed up with tray ceilings

■ Master Bedroom features vaulted ceiling, back Porch access, and luxurious Bath with over-sized, walk-in closet

■ Skylit Bonus Room over Garage provides extra room for family needs

■ This home comes with a crawlspace foundation.

■ Alternate foundation options available at an additional charge, call 1-800-235-5700 for more information.

Main floor — 2,027 sq. ft.
Bonus room — 340 sq. ft.
Garage & storage — 532 sq. ft.

Traditional Two-Story Home

© Donald A. Gardner Architects, Inc.

B. NATHAN

■ *Total living area 2,250 sq. ft.* ■ *Price Code G* ■

No. 96491

This plan features:

- Three bedrooms

- Two full and two half baths

- Facade handsomely accented by multiple gables, keystone arches and transom windows

- Arched clerestory window lights two-story Foyer for a dramatic entrance

- Two-story Great Room with inviting fireplace, wall of windows and back Porch access

- This home comes with a crawlspace foundation.

- Alternate foundation options available at an additional charge, call 1.800.235.5700 for more information.

- First floor — 1,644 sq. ft.
- Second floor — 606 sq. ft.
- Bonus room — 548 sq. ft.
- Garage & storage — 657 sq. ft.

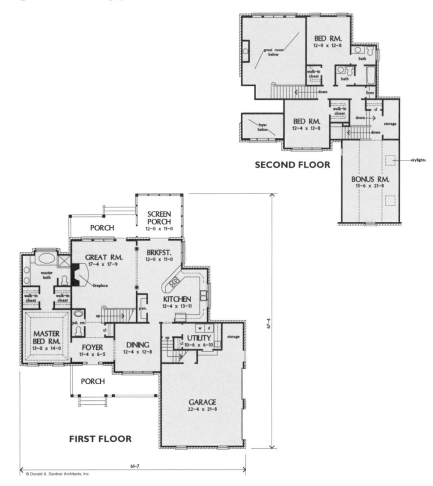

SECOND FLOOR

BED RM. 12-0 x 12-8

BED RM. 12-4 x 12-8

BONUS RM. 15-6 x 21-8

FIRST FLOOR

PORCH

SCREEN PORCH 12-0 x 11-0

GREAT RM. 17-4 x 17-9

BRKFST. 12-0 x 11-0

master bath

KITCHEN 12-4 x 13-11

MASTER BED RM. 13-0 x 14-0

FOYER 11-4 x 6-5

DINING 12-4 x 12-8

UTILITY 10-6 x 6-10

PORCH

GARAGE 22-4 x 21-8

© Donald A. Gardner Architects, Inc.

61-7

Windows Distinguish Design

■ *Total living area 3,525 sq. ft.* ■ *Price Code J* ■

No. 98438

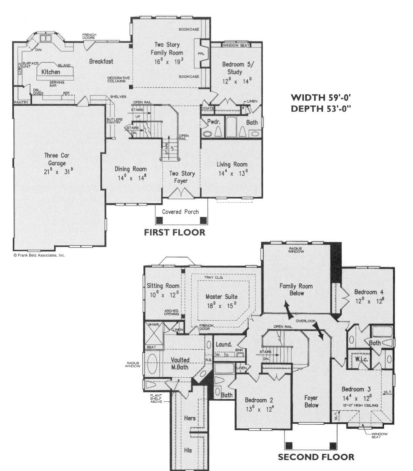

WIDTH 59'-0'
DEPTH 53'-0"

■ **This plan features:**

— Five bedrooms

— Four full and one half baths

■ Light shines into the Dining Room and the Living Room through their respective elegant windows

■ A hall through the Butler's Pantr leads the way into the Breakfast Nook

■ The two-story Family Room has fireplace with built-in bookcases on either side

■ The upstairs Master Suite has a Sitting Room and a French door that leads into the vaulted Maste Bath

■ An optional basement or crawl space foundation — please speci when ordering

First floor — 1,786 sq. ft.
Second floor — 1,739 sq. ft.
Basement — 1,786 sq. ft.
Garage — 704 sq. ft.

No. 98434

■This plan features:

– Three bedrooms

– Two full baths

■Vaulted ceiling crowns spacious Living Room highlighted by a fireplace

■Built-in Pantry and direct access from the Garage adding to the conveniences of the Kitchen

■Walk-in closet and a private five-piece Bath topped by a vaulted ceiling in the Master Bedroom suite

■Proximity to the full Bath in the hall from the secondary Bedrooms

■An optional basement, slab or crawlspace – please specify when ordering

Main floor — 1,346 sq. ft.
Basement — 1,358 sq. ft.
Garage — 395 sq. ft.

Total living area 1,346 sq. ft. ■ Price Code A ■

MAIN FLOOR

© Frank Betz Associates, Inc.

Energy Efficient Air-Lock Entry

No. 24714

This plan features:

- Two bedrooms

- Two full baths

■The attractive covered Porch highlights the curb appeal of this charming home

■A cozy window seat and a vaulted ceiling enhance the private Den

■The sunken Great Room is accented by a fireplace that is nestled between windows

■A screened Porch, accessed from the Dining Room, extends the living space to the outdoors

■The Master Bath features a garden tub, separate shower, his-n-her walk-in closets and a skylight

■An optional slab or combo basement/ crawlspace foundation — please specify when ordering.

Main floor — 1,771 sq. ft.
Basement — 1,194 sq. ft.
Garage — 517 sq. ft.

Total living area 1,771 sq. ft. ■ Price Code C ■

CRAWLSPACE OPTION

MAIN FLOOR

Arches and Gables

No. 93171

■ **This plan features:**

— Three bedrooms

— Two full and one half baths

■ Tiled Entry opens to Living Room with focal point fireplace

■ U-shaped Kitchen with a built-in Pantry, eating bar and nearby Laundry/Garage Entry

■ Comfortable Dining Room with bay window and French doors to Screen Porch expanding Living Area outdoors

■ Corner Master Bedroom offers a great walk-in closet and private Bath

■ Two additional Bedrooms with ample closets and double windows share a full Bath

■ This home comes with a basement foundation.

Main floor — 1,642 sq. ft.
Basement — 1,642 sq. ft.
Porch — 192 sq. ft.

■ *Total living area 1,642 sq. ft.* ■ *Price Code B* ■

MAIN FLOOR

Style and Convenience

No. 92283

■ **This plan features:**

— Three bedrooms

— Two full baths

■ A sheltered Porch leads into an easy-care til Entry

■ Spacious Living Room offers a cozy fireplace, triple window and access to Patio

■ An efficient Kitchen with a skylight, work island, Dining Area, walk-in Pantry and Utility/Garage Entry

■ Secluded Master Bedroom highlighted by a vaulted ceiling, access to Patio and a lavish Bath

■ Two additional Bedrooms, one with a cathedral ceiling, share a full Bath

■ This home comes with a slab foundation.

Main floor — 1,653 sq. ft.
Garage — 420 sq. ft.

■ *Total living area 1,653 sq. ft.* ■ *Price Code B* ■

MAIN FLOOR

An Affordable Floor Plan

■ *Total living area 1,410 sq. ft.* ■ *Price Code A* ■

No. 91807

This plan features:

Three bedrooms

One full and one three-quarter baths

A covered Porch entry

An old-fashioned hearth fireplace in the vaulted ceiling Living Room

An efficient Kitchen with U-shaped counter that is accessible from the Dining Room

A Master Bedroom with a large walk-in closet and private Bath

An optional crawlspace and slab foundation available — please specify when ordering.

Main floor — 1,410 sq. ft.
Garage — 484 sq. ft.

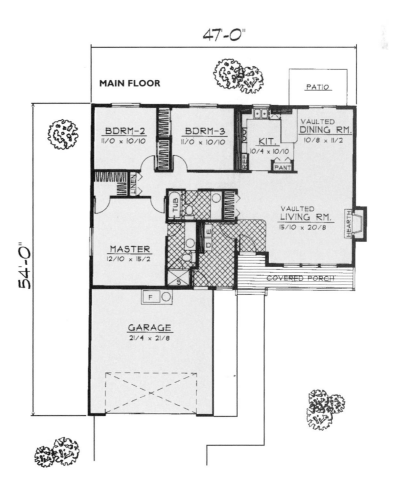

Lattice Trim Adds Nostalgic Charm

■ *Total living area 1,359 sq. ft.* ■ *Price Code A* ■

SECOND FLOOR

MBr
11-8x13

Loft/
Br 3
9x11

Br 2
10x9-8

DN skylight

open to below

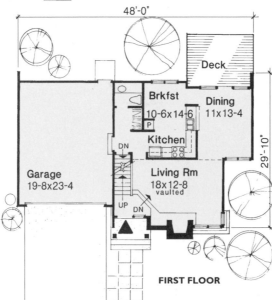

48'-0"

Deck

Brkfst
10-6x14-6

Dining
11x13-4

Kitchen

Garage
19-8x23-4

Living Rm
18x12-8
vaulted

29'-10"

UP DN

FIRST FLOOR

No. 99315

■ **This plan features:**

— Three bedrooms

— Two full and one half baths

■ Wood and fieldstone exterior

■ A vaulted Living Room with balcony view and floor-to-ceiling corner window treatment

■ A Master Suite with private Bath and Dressing Area

■ A two-car Garage with access to Kitchen

■ This home comes with a basemer foundation.

First floor — 668 sq. ft.
Second floor — 691 sq. ft.
Garage — 459 sq. ft.

Livable with a Touch of the Dramatic

No. 92612

This plan features:

Three bedrooms

Two full and one half baths

A dramatic facade created by a natural stone chimney

A two-story, sunken Great Room with a 12' ceiling accenting the stone fireplace

A formal Dining Room stepping from the Great Room

A efficient, U-shaped Kitchen with a built-in Pantry and a bright, glassed Breakfast Area with atrium door to the Deck

A plush Master Suite with a large walk-in closet and a private Bath

This home comes with a basement foundation.

First floor — 1,448 sq. ft.

Second floor — 485 sq. ft.

Basement — 1,322 sq. ft.

Garage — 543 sq. ft.

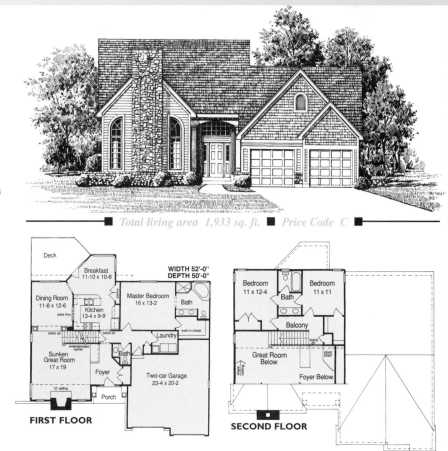

Total living area 1,933 sq. ft. ■ Price Code C

WIDTH 52'-0"
DEPTH 50'-0"

FIRST FLOOR

SECOND FLOOR

Excellent Choice for First Time Buyer

No. 91055

This plan features:

Three bedrooms

Two full and one half baths

A friendly, covered Porch sheltering the front entrance

A formal Living Room with an expansive floor-to-ceiling triple window flowing into a formal Dining Room

A comfortable Family Room with a sliding glass door to the backyard, a Utility Closet with washer and dryer and access to the Kitchen

An efficient Kitchen with a peninsula counter/snackbar on the Family Room side and adjacent to the Dining Room for ease in serving

A cozy Master Bedroom with a recessed dormer window, an oversized, walk-in closet and a private Bath

Two additional Bedrooms, on the second floor, sharing a full hall Bath and a Playroom that could be a fourth Bedroom

This home comes with a crawlspace foundation.

First floor — 805 sq. ft.

Second floor — 961 sq. ft.

Garage — 540 sq. ft.

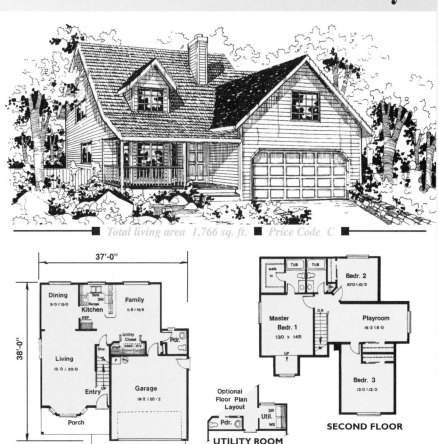

Total living area 1,766 sq. ft. ■ Price Code C

37'-0"
38'-0"

FIRST FLOOR

UTILITY ROOM OPTION

Optional Floor Plan Layout

SECOND FLOOR

Friendly Front Porch

■ Total living area 1,576 sq. ft. ■ Price Code B ■

FIRST FLOOR

FAM RM
17'2 x 11'4

DIN
11'2 x 8'4

KIT
10'6 x 9'6

DIN RM
10'1 x 9'10

Laun

LIV RM
15'6 x 11'6

Lav

FOYER

GARAGE
19'8 x 21'4

SHED 10'T' & EXTRA

WIDTH 58'-0"
DEPTH 34'-0"

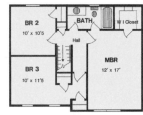

BR 2
10' x 10'5

BATH

W I Closet

Hall

BR 3
10' x 11'5

MBR
12' x 17'

SECOND FLOOR

No. 94138

■ **This plan features:**

– Three bedrooms

– One full and one half baths

■ Country, homey feeling with wrap-around Porch

■ Adjoining Living Room and Dining Room creates spacious feeling

■ Efficient Kitchen easily serves Dining Area with extended counter and a built-in Pantry

■ Spacious Family Room with optional fireplace and access to Laundry/Garage Entry

■ Large Master Bedroom with a walk-in closet and access to a full Bath, offers a private Bath option

■ Two additional Bedrooms with ample closets and full Bath access

■ This home comes with a basement foundation.

First floor — 900 sq. ft.
Second floor — 676 sq. ft.
Basement — 900 sq. ft.
Garage — 448 sq. ft.

Huge Windows Create Cheerful Atmosphere

No. 91040

■ Total living area 1,206 sq. ft. ■ Price Code A ■

■ **This plan features:**

– Three bedrooms

– Two full baths

■ A modern, efficient Kitchen layout flowing into the Nook and Living Room

■ A Living Room, made spacious by an open layout, with a handsome fireplace

■ A Master Suite with ample closet space and a private, full Bath

■ Two additional Bedrooms that share a full hall Bath

■ This home comes with a crawlspace foundation.

Main floor — 1,206 sq. ft.
Garage — 470 sq. ft.

LIVING RM.
18⁶x14⁰

BED-2
10⁸x10⁰

BED-3
10⁰x10⁰

NOOK
10⁰x10⁰

KITCHEN
8⁰x10⁰

B-2

MASTER BDRM.
13⁴x13⁶

GARAGE
19⁴x23⁶

48'-0"

40'-0"

MAIN FLOOR

Charming Southern Traditional

■ *Total living area 1,271 sq. ft.* ■ *Price Code A* ■

No. 92503

■ **This plan features:**

— Three bedrooms

— Two full baths

■ A covered front Porch with striking columns, brick quoins, and dentil molding

■ A spacious Great Room with vaulted ceilings, a fireplace, and built-in cabinets

■ A Utility Room adjacent to the Kitchen which leads to the two-car Garage and Storage Rooms

■ A Master Bedroom including a large walk-in closet and a compartmentalized Bath

■ An optional crawlspace or slab foundation — please specify when ordering.

Main floor — 1,271 sq. ft.
Garage — 506 sq. ft.

garage
21 x 21

kit 12 x 9

ref

rng

dw

b

d
w

cab

shvs

util

sto

dining
11 x 11

living
15⁶ x 16

vault

vault

porch 20¹⁰ x 5

MAIN FLOOR

mbr
14 x 12

shvs

br 2
11 x 11

ra

shvs

br 3
11 x 11

Cabin in the Country

■ *Total living area 928 sq. ft.* ■ *Price Code A* ■

No. 90433

■ **This plan features:**

— Two bedrooms

— One full and one half baths

■ A Screened Porch for enjoyment of your outdoor surroundings

■ A combination Living and Dining Area with cozy fireplace for added warmth

■ An efficiently laid out Kitchen with a built-in Pantry

■ Two large Bedrooms located at the rear of the home

■ An optional slab or crawlspace foundation — please specify when ordering.

Main floor — 928 sq. ft.
Screened porch — 230 sq. ft.
Storage — 14 sq. ft.

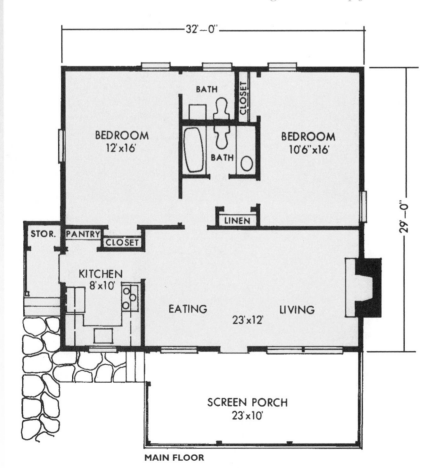

No. 99401

This plan features:

Three bedrooms

Two full and one half baths

A Palladian arch is supported by stylish columns sheltering the Entry stoop

Off the Entry, wide cased openings lead to the bright formal Dining Room

A volume Entry, accented by glass blocks, spotlight a decorative plant shelf above a closet

The Great Room is topped by a 10'8" ceiling, while a fireplace creates a warm atmosphere

The Dinette achieves a light, open sensation with a ten-foot ceiling and large windows

The Master Bedroom with its expansive window area affords maximum privacy

Two secondary Bedrooms on the second floor share a full Bath

This home comes with a basement foundation.

First floor — 1,327 sq. ft.

Second floor — 348 sq. ft.

Basement — 1,327 sq. ft.

Garage — 443 sq. ft.

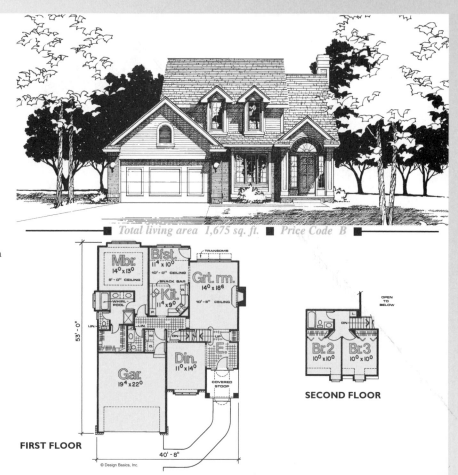

Total living area 1,675 sq. ft. ■ Price Code B

FIRST FLOOR

SECOND FLOOR

No. 98512

This plan features:

Three bedrooms

Two full baths

In the gallery columns separate space into the Great Room and the Dining Room

Access to backyard covered Patio from bayed Breakfast Nook

The large Kitchen is a chef's dream with lots of counter space and a Pantry

The Master Bedroom is removed from traffic areas and contains a luxurious Master Bath

A hall connects the two secondary Bedrooms which share a full skylit Bath

This home comes with a slab foundation.

Main floor — 2,167 sq. ft.

Garage — 690 sq. ft.

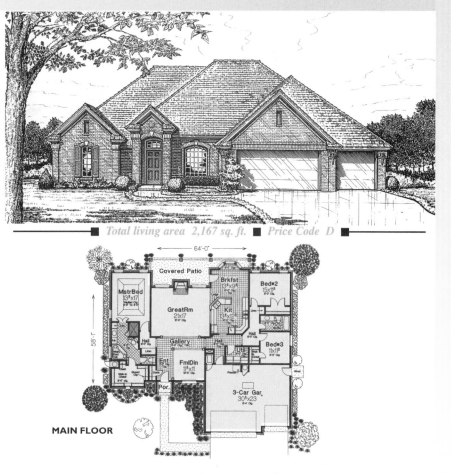

Total living area 2,167 sq. ft. ■ Price Code D

MAIN FLOOR

229

Vaulted Ceilings

Total living area 1,565 sq. ft. ■ Price Code B

MAIN FLOOR

No. 91527

■ **This plan features:**

— Three bedrooms

— Two full baths

■ A formal Living Room with a vaulted ceiling that flows into the formal Dining Room

■ An efficient Kitchen with a built-in Pantry and a peninsula counter that doubles as an eating bar and adjoins the sunny Eating Nook

■ A Family Room with a cozy fireplace and a vaulted ceiling

■ A Master Suite that includes a walk-in closet and a private Bath with a Spa tub and double vanity

■ Two additional Bedrooms that share a full Bath

■ This home comes with a crawlspace foundation.

Main floor — 1,565 sq. ft.
Garage — 440 sq. ft.

One Level Contemporary

Total living area 1,266 sq. ft. ■ Price Code A

No. 24327

■ **This plan features:**

— Three bedrooms

— Two full baths

■ A vaulted ceiling and elegant fireplace in the Living Room

■ An open layout between the Living Room, Dining Room and Kitchen gives a more spacious feeling to these areas

■ A well-equipped Kitchen with a double sink and a peninsula counter that may be used as an eating bar

■ A Master Suite that includes a walk-in closet and a private Bath with a double vanity

■ Two additional Bedrooms that have ample closet space and share a full hall Bath

■ An optional basement, slab or crawlspace foundation — please specify when ordering

Main floor — 1,266 sq. ft.
Garage — 443 sq. ft.
Basement — 1,266 sq. ft.

MAIN FLOOR

Attractive Gables and Arches

■ *Total living area 1,782 sq. ft.* ■ *Price Code C* ■

No. 94917

This plan features:

- Three bedrooms

- Two full baths

- Entry opens to formal Dining Room with arched window

- Angles and transom windows add interest to the Great Room

- Bright Hearth area expands Breakfast/Kitchen area and shares three-sided fireplace

- Kitchen offers an angled snack bar and a large Pantry

- This home comes with a slab foundation.

- Alternate foundation options available at an additional charge, call 1.800.235.5700 for more information.

Main floor — 1,782 sq. ft.
Basement — 1,782 sq. ft.
Garage — 466 sq. ft.

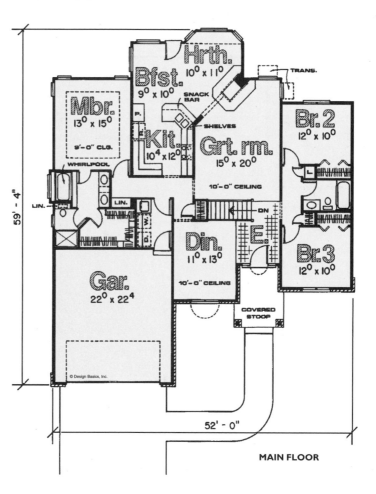

MAIN FLOOR

Letting the Light In

■ *Total living area 1,525 sq. ft.* ■ *Price Code B* ■

No. 91081

■ **This plan features:**

— Four bedrooms

— Two full baths

■ Covered Porch leads into easy-care tile Entry with angled staircase

■ Vaulted ceiling tops corner windows and wood stove in Living Room

■ Kitchen with built-in Pantry, pass through counter and plant shelf window

■ Two first floor Bedrooms share a full Bath and Utility Area

■ French doors lead into Master Bedroom with skylight Bath

■ Loft/Bedroom overlooking Living Room offers many options

■ This home comes with a crawlspace foundation.

First floor — 1076 sq. ft.
Second floor — 449 sq. ft.
Garage — 495 sq. ft.

A Magnificent Manor

No. 98410

This plan features:

- Three bedrooms
- Three full baths
- The two-story Foyer is dominated by a lovely staircase
- The formal Living Room is located directly off the Foyer
- An efficient Kitchen accesses the formal Dining Room for ease in serving
- The Breakfast Area is separated from the Kitchen by an extended counter/serving bar
- The two-story Family Room is highlighted by a fireplace that is framed by windows
- A tray ceiling crowns the Master Bedroom while a vaulted ceiling tops the Master Bath
- Two additional bedrooms share the full double vanity hall Bath
- An optional basement or crawlspace foundation — please specify when ordering

First floor — 1,428 sq. ft.
Second floor — 961 sq. ft.
Bonus room — 472 sq. ft.
Basement — 1,428 sq. ft.
Garage — 507 sq. ft.

■ *Total living area 2,389 sq. ft.* ■ *Price Code E* ■

SECOND FLOOR WITH BONUS

FIRST FLOOR

© Frank Betz Associates, Inc.

SECOND FLOOR

Classic Style and Comfort

No. 94105

This plan features:

- Three bedrooms
- Two full and one half bath
- Covered Entry into two-story Foyer with a dramatic landing staircase brightened by decorative window
- Spacious Living/Dining Room combination with hearth fireplace and decorative windows
- Hub Kitchen with built-in Pantry and informal Dining Area with sliding glass door to rear yard
- First floor Master Bedroom offers a walk-in closet, dressing area and full Bath
- Two additional Bedrooms on second floor share a full Bath
- This home comes with a basement foundation.

First floor — 1,281 sq. ft.
Second floor —511 sq. ft.
Garage — 481 sq. ft.

■ *Total living area 1,792 sq. ft.* ■ *Price Code C* ■

WIDTH 58'
DEPTH 44'

FIRST FLOOR

SECOND FLOOR

Room for a Large Family

■ **Total living area 1,960 sq. ft.** ■ **Price Code C** ■

MAIN FLOOR

SECOND FLOOR

No. 99129

■ **This plan features:**
— Four bedrooms
— Two full and one half baths
■ Gracious Living Room archway leads into a formal Dining Room
■ Family Room with fireplace
■ The L-shaped Kitchen opens into the Nook and has a built-in planning desk
■ The Master Bedroom is located on the second floor and has a private Bath
■ Three more Bedrooms and a full Bath complete the plan
■ This home comes with a basement foundation.

Main floor — 1,000 sq. ft.
Second floor — 960 sq. ft.
Basement — 1,000 sq. ft.

Country Porch Shelters Entry

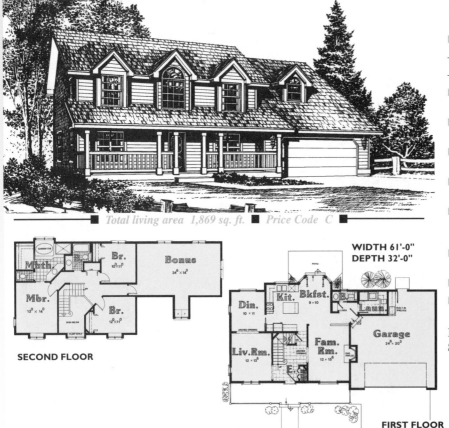

■ **Total living area 1,869 sq. ft.** ■ **Price Code C** ■

SECOND FLOOR

WIDTH 61'-0"
DEPTH 32'-0"

FIRST FLOOR

No. 93904

■ **This plan features:**
— Three bedrooms
— Two full and one half baths
■ A two-story Foyer illuminated by an arched window above
■ A formal Living Room adjoined to the Dining Room by an arched opening
■ A second arched opening into the Family Room highlighted by a gas fireplace
■ An efficient Kitchen equipped with an island and a bayed Breakfast Area
■ A lavish Master Bath with a garden tub and a walk-in closet adding pampering features to the Master Suite
■ Two additional Bedrooms that share the full hall Bath
■ A Bonus Room for future expansion
■ This home comes with a basement foundation.

First floor — 1,121 sq. ft.
Second floor — 748 sq. ft.

Wrapping Front Porch and Gabled Dormers

© Donald A. Gardner Architects, Inc.

■ *Total living area 2,596 sq. ft.* ■ *Price Code H* ■

No. 96411

This plan features:

- Four bedrooms

- Three full baths

■ Generous Great Room with a fireplace, cathedral ceiling and a balcony above

■ Master Suite with a sunny bay window and a private Bath topped by a cathedral ceiling and highlighted by his-n-her vanities, and a separate tub and shower

■ This home comes with a crawlspace foundation.

■ Alternate foundation options available at an additional charge, call 1.800.235.5700 for more information.

First floor — 1,939 sq. ft.
Second floor — 657 sq. ft.
Garage & Storage — 526 sq. ft.
Bonus room — 386 sq. ft.

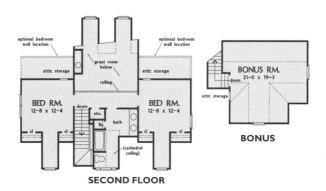

SECOND FLOOR

BONUS

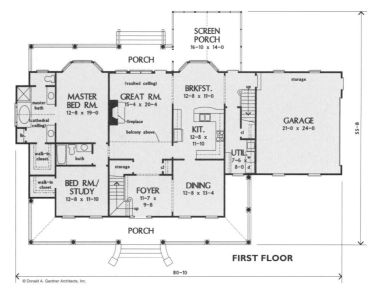

FIRST FLOOR

© Donald A. Gardner Architects, Inc.

Champagne Style on a Soda-Pop Budget

■ *Total living area 988 sq. ft.* ■ *Price Code A* ■

No. 24302

■ **This plan features:**

— Three bedrooms

— One full and one three quarter baths

■ Multiple gables, circle-top windows, and a unique exterior setting this delightful Ranch apar in any neighborhood

■ Living and Dining Rooms flowing together to create a very roomy feeling

■ Sliding doors leading from the Dining Room to a covered Patio

■ A Master Bedroom with a private Bath

■ An optional basement or crawlspace foundation — please specify when ordering.

Main floor — 988 sq. ft.
Basement — 988 sq. ft.
Garage — 280 sq. ft

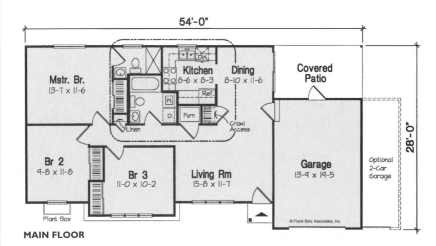

MAIN FLOOR

54'-0"

28'-0"

Mstr. Br.
13-7 x 11-6

Kitchen
8-6 x 8-3

Dining
8-10 x 11-6

Covered Patio

Linen

Crawl Access

Br 2
9-8 x 11-8

Br 3
11-0 x 10-2

Living Rm
15-8 x 11-7

Garage
13-9 x 19-5

Optional 2-Car Garage

Plant Box

© Frank Betz Associates, Inc.

Kitchen
8-6 x 8-3

Ref.

DN

Flue

**OPTIONAL BASEMENT
STAIR LOCATION**

Elegant Elevation

No. 92662

This plan features:

— Three bedrooms

— Two full and one half baths

■ Brick trim, sidelights, and a transom window give a warm welcome to this home

■ High ceilings continue from Foyer into Great Room which counts among its amenities a fireplace and entertainment center

■ The Kitchen serves the formal and informal Dining Areas with ease

■ The Master Suite is positioned for privacy on the first floor

■ The second floor has loads of possibilities with a Bonus Space and a Study

■ Two Bedrooms each with walk in closest share a full Bath

■ This home comes with a basement foundation.

First floor — 1,542 sq. ft.
Second floor — 667 sq. ft.
Bonus — 236 sq. ft.
Basement — 1,367 sq. ft.
Garage — 420 sq. ft.

■ *Total living area 2,209 sq. ft.* ■ *Price Code D* ■

Arches Grace Classic Facade

No. 10677

This plan features:

— Three bedrooms

— Two full and one half baths

■ Built-in planters and half walls define rooms

■ A balcony that connects three upstairs Bedrooms

■ Double sinks and built-in vanities in the Master Bath

■ Ample closet space

■ This home comes with a basement foundation.

First floor — 932 sq. ft.
Second floor — 764 sq. ft.
Garage — 430 sq. ft.
Basement — 920 sq. ft.

■ *Total living area 1,696 sq. ft.* ■ *Price Code B* ■

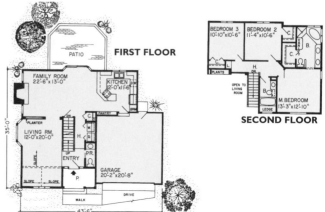

Casual Living Inside and Out

Total living area 1,772 sq. ft. ■ Price Code C

MAIN FLOOR

No. 92703

■ **This plan features:**

– Three bedrooms

– Two full baths

■ A Living Room with a ten-foot ceiling and a cozy corner fireplace

■ An enormous Dining Area that is able to handle even the largest family dinners

■ A large rear Porch that is perfect for outdoor dining

■ A conveniently placed Laundry Room

■ His-n-her walk-in closets and a double vanity in the Master Bath

■ Secondary Bedrooms that share a full hall Bath with a double vanity

■ This home comes with a slab foundation.

Main floor — 1,772 sq. ft.

Modest Tudor with a Massive Look

Total living area 2,209 sq. ft. ■ Price Code D

SECOND FLOOR

FIRST FLOOR

No. 90012

■ **This plan features:**

– Three bedrooms

– Two full and one half baths

■ A large log-burning fireplace centrally located on the far wall of the Living Room

■ A formal Dining Room with access to either the screen Porch, Terrace, or Kitchen

■ A Kitchen with a cooktop island and a built-in Breakfast Nook

■ A Family Room with French door access to another Porch

■ A Master Suite with lounge area, private Master Bath, and a walk-in closet

■ Two additional Bedrooms with access to the full hall Bath

■ This home comes with a basement foundation.

First floor — 1,078 sq. ft.
Second floor — 1,131 sq. ft.
Basement — 785 sq. ft.
Garage — 445 sq. ft.

■ *Total living area 1,715 sq. ft.* ■ *Price Code B* ■

No. 98456

■ This plan features:

- Three bedrooms

- Two full baths

■ A covered Entry gives way to a 14-foot high ceiling in the Foyer

■ An arched opening greets you in the Great Room that also has a vaulted ceiling and a fireplace

■ The Dining Room is brightened by triple windows with transoms above

■ The Kitchen is a gourmet's delight and is open to the Breakfast Nook

■ The Master Suite is sweet with a tray ceiling, vaulted Sitting Area and private Bath

■ Two Bedrooms on the opposite side of the home share a Bath in the hall

■ An optional basement, slab or crawlspace foundation — please specify when ordering

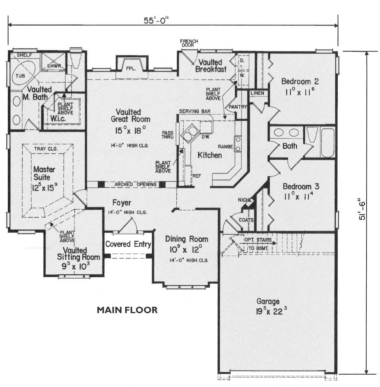

MAIN FLOOR

© Frank Betz Associates, Inc.

Main floor — 1,715 sq. ft.
Basement — 1,715 sq. ft.
Garage — 450 sq. ft.

Gingerbread Charm

■ *Total living area 2,281 sq. ft.* ■ *Price Code E* ■

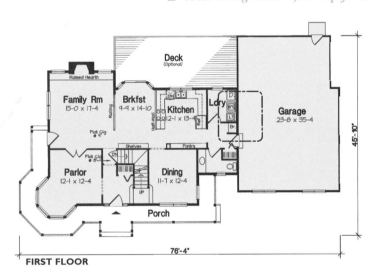

FIRST FLOOR

76'-4"

45'-10"

Deck (Optional)

Raised Hearth

Family Rm
15-0 x 17-4

Brkfst
9-9 x 14-10

Kitchen
12-1 x 13-4

Ldry

Garage
23-8 x 35-4

Flat Clg

Parlor
12-1 x 12-4

Dining
11-7 x 12-4

Shelves

Pantry

UP

Porch

SLAB/CRAWLSPACE OPTION

Attic Space (Optional)

H.P. Tub

Br #3
11-7 x 9-10

MBr #1
12-1 x 15-10
8' Clg

DN   Railing

Plant Shelf

Br #2
11-7 x 11-10

Open to Below

Flat Clg

SECOND FLOOR

No. 10690

■ **This plan features:**

— Three bedrooms

— Two full and one half baths

■ A wrap-around Porch and rear Deck adding lots of outdoor living space

■ A formal Parlor and Dining Room just off the central Entry

■ A Family Room with a fireplace

■ A Master Suite complete with a five-sided Sitting Nook, walk-in closets and a sunken tub

■ An optional basement, slab or crawlspace foundation — please specify when ordering.

First floor — 1,260 sq. ft.
Second floor — 1,021 sq. ft.
Basement — 1,186 sq. ft.
Garage — 851 sq. ft.

Surprisingly Spacious for a Smaller Home

No. 98743

This plan features:

- Three bedrooms

- Two full baths

- A vaulted ceiling in the richly illuminated Foyer, which presents three choices of direction

- An eye-catching Great Room with a vaulted ceiling, a corner fireplace and a bank of windows on the rear wall showering the room with light

- An efficient U-shaped Kitchen with an angled eating bar, built-in Pantry and a double sink that views the Great Room

- A luxurious Master Suite that includes a roomy walk-in closet, access to the rear deck and a private Bath

- A Mini-Master Suite that includes a walk-in closet with a vanity right outside and private access to the hall Bath

- A third Bedroom that shares the use of the hall Bath

- This home comes with a crawlspace foundation.

Main floor — 1,958 sq. ft.

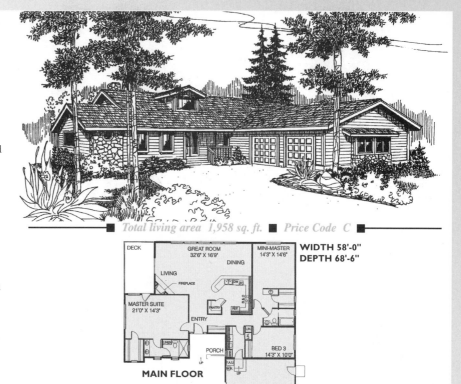

■ Total living area 1,958 sq. ft. ■ Price Code C ■

WIDTH 58'-0"
DEPTH 68'-6"

MAIN FLOOR

Open Air Ranch

No. 84014

This plan features:

- Four bedrooms

- Two full baths

- Stone fireplace, wood storage and bookshelves separate the Living Room from the Family Room

- The Dining Room features doors to the rear Patio

- A convenient U-shaped Kitchen is highlighted by a double sink, a Pantry and ample counter space

- A Laundry/Utility Room is located off of the two-car Garage

- Three Bedrooms share a full Bath

- The Master Bedroom has two closets and a private Bath with dual vanity

- An optional basement, slab or crawlspace foundation — please specify when ordering.

Main floor — 1,901 sq. ft.
Garage — 420 sq. ft.

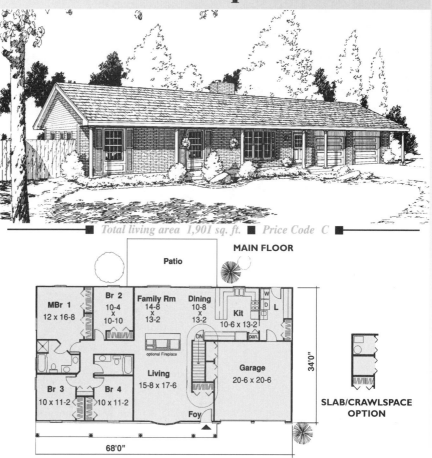

■ Total living area 1,901 sq. ft. ■ Price Code C ■

MAIN FLOOR

SLAB/CRAWLSPACE OPTION

241

Country Elegance

■ Total living area 1,684 sq. ft. ■ Price Code B ■

Fam. Rm. 17⁶, 12⁰

Kit.

Din. 10⁶, 10³

Liv. Rm. 13⁰, 12⁹

Garage 21⁰, 23⁰

E.

PORCH

FIRST FLOOR

40

44

Br. 10⁶, 10⁶

Br. 10⁶, 10⁰

Mb.

B.

Mbr. 13⁰, 13⁶

Bonus 10⁰, 23⁰

SECOND FLOOR

No. 93905

■ **This plan features:**

– Three bedrooms

– Two full and one half baths

■ Welcoming front Porch leads into open Entry with landing staircase

■ Expansive Living Room/Dining Area highlighted by multiple windows front and back

■ Comfortable Family Room with gas fireplace, sliding glass door to Patio and adjoining Kitchen, Laundry and Garage

■ Efficient U-shaped Kitchen with built-in desk and eating bar

■ Private Master Bedroom with an arched window and plush Bath and walk-in closet

■ Two additional Bedrooms with large closet share a full Bath

■ Bonus Room with another arched window and Storage Space offers many options

■ This home comes with a basement foundation.

First floor — 913 sq. ft.
Second floor — 771 sq. ft.
Garage — 483 sq. ft.

Practical Layout

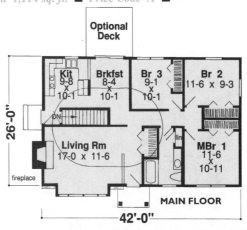

■ Total living area 1,114 sq. ft. ■ Price Code A ■

SLAB/CRAWLSPACE OPTION

D   W

Optional Deck

Kit 9-8 x 10-1

Brkfst 8-4 x 10-1

Br 3 9-1 x 10-1

Br 2 11-6 x 9-3

26'-0"

DN

Living Rm 17-0 x 11-6

fireplace

MBr 1 11-6 x 10-11

MAIN FLOOR

42'-0"

No. 84330

■ **This plan features:**

– Three bedrooms

– One full bath

■ The Living Room is enhanced by a fireplace and bright front window

■ The U-shaped Kitchen has plenty of counter space for ease in meal preparation

■ The Breakfast Nook is adjacent to the Kitchen and has sliding door to the rear Deck

■ All three Bedrooms with large closets

■ An optional basement, slab or crawlspace foundation — please specify when ordering

Main floor — 1,114 sq. ft.

Hip Roof Ranch

■ Total living area 1,540 sq. ft. ■ Price Code B ■

No. 93161

■ This plan features:

– Three bedrooms

– Two full baths

■ Cozy front Porch leads into Entry with vaulted ceiling and sidelights

■ Open Living Room enhanced by a cathedral ceiling, a wall of windows and corner fireplace

■ Large and efficient Kitchen with an extended counter and a bright Dining Area with access to Screened Porch

■ Convenient Utility Area with access to Garage and Storage Area

■ Spacious Master Bedroom with a walk-in closet and private Bath

■ Two additional Bedrooms with ample closets share a full Bath

■ This home comes with a basement foundation.

Main floor — 1,540 sq. ft.
Basement — 1,540 sq. ft.

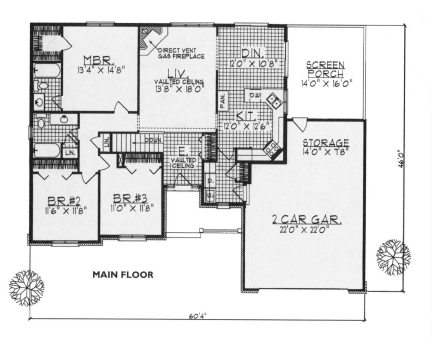

MAIN FLOOR

Backyard Views

■ *Total living area 1,746 sq. ft.* ■ *Price Code B* ■

No. 92655

■ **This plan features:**

— Three bedrooms

— Two full baths

■ Front Porch accesses open Foyer, and spacious Dining Room and Great Room with sloped ceilings

■ Corner fireplace, windows and atrium door to Patio enhance Great Room

■ Convenient Kitchen with a Pantry, peninsula serving counter for bright Breakfast Area and nearby Laundry/Garage entry

■ Luxurious Bath, walk-in closet and back yard view offered in Master Bedroom

■ This home comes with a basement foundation.

Main floor — 1,746 sq. ft.
Garage — 480 sq. ft.
Basement — 1,697 sq. ft.

Modern 'Savior Faire'

No. 99504

This plan features:

— Three bedrooms

— Two full baths

- Spacious country Kitchen has a built-in Pantry, ample storage and workspace

- Great Room crowned in a vaulted ceiling and decorated by a fireplace, has convenient access to the Kitchen

- Master Bedroom highlighted by a private, full Bath and a walk-in closet

- Two additional Bedrooms sharing a full hall Bath

- An optional crawlspace or slab foundation — please specify when ordering

Main floor — 1,127 sq. ft.
Garage — 257 sq. ft.

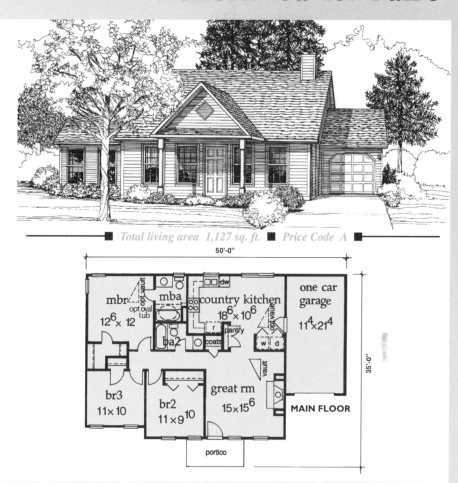

■ *Total living area 1,127 sq. ft.* ■ *Price Code A* ■

Split Bedroom Plan

No. 98427

This plan features:

— Three bedrooms

— Two full baths

- Dining Room is crowned by a tray ceiling

- Living Room/Den privatized by double doors at its entrance, and is enhanced by a bay window

- The Kitchen includes a walk-in Pantry and a corner double sink

- The vaulted Breakfast Room flows naturally from the Kitchen

- The Master Suite is topped by a tray ceiling, and contains a compartmental Bath plus two walk-in closets

- Two roomy additional Bedrooms share a full Bath in the hall

- An optional basement, slab or crawlspace foundation — please specify when ordering

Main floor — 2,051 sq. ft.
Basement — 2,051 sq. ft.
Garage — 441 sq. ft.

■ *Total living area 2,051 sq. ft.* ■ *Price Code D* ■

Amenities Normally Found In Larger Homes

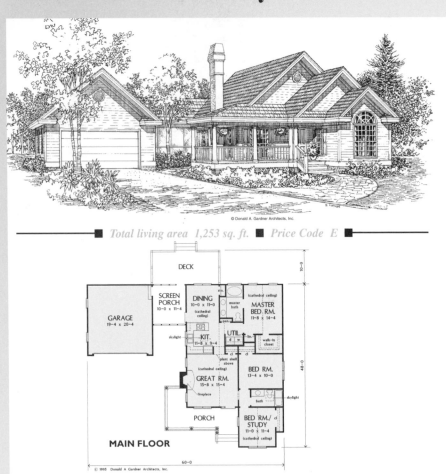

© Donald A. Gardner Architects, Inc.

■ Total living area 1,253 sq. ft. ■ Price Code E ■

MAIN FLOOR

© 1995 Donald A Gardner Architects, Inc.

No. 99858

■ **This plan features:**

— Three bedrooms

— Two full baths

■ A continuous cathedral ceiling in the Great Room, Kitchen, and Dining Room giving a spacious feel to this efficient plan

■ Skylit Kitchen with a seven foot high wall by the Great Room and a popular plant shelf

■ Master Bedroom opens up with a cathedral ceiling and contains walk-in and linen closets and a private Bath with garden tub and dual vanity

■ Cathedral ceiling as the crowning touch to the front Bedroom/Study

■ This home comes with a crawlspace foundation.

■ Alternate foundation options available at an additional charge. Please call 1.800.235.5700 for more information.

Main floor — 1,253 sq. ft.
Garage & Storage — 420 sq. ft.

Family Favorite

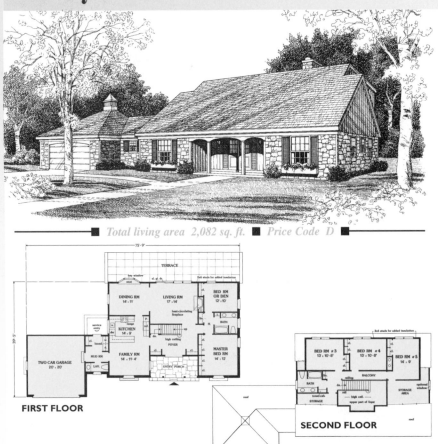

■ Total living area 2,082 sq. ft. ■ Price Code D ■

FIRST FLOOR

SECOND FLOOR

No. 90690

■ **This plan features:**

— Five bedrooms

— Two full and one half baths

■ An efficient Kitchen with a peninsula counter opening into the Family Room

■ A cozy bay window seat in the formal Dining Room

■ A first floor Master Bedroom with an adjoining private Bath including dual vanity

■ A heat-circulating fireplace in the Living Room which has sliding glass doors to the Terrace

■ Three Bedrooms located on the second floor share a full Bath

■ An optional basement or slab foundation — please specify when ordering.

First floor — 1,407 sq. ft.
Second floor — 675 sq. ft.
Basement — 1,304 sq. ft.
Garage — 421 sq. ft.

Colonial with Contemporary Flair

No. 94141

This plan features:

- Four bedrooms
- Two full and one half baths
- The Master Bedroom has a walk-in closet and an attached Bath with a skylight
- Upstairs there are three additional Bedrooms and one full Bath
- The Dining Room and Living Room are traditionally placed
- The Family Room and Dinette are laid out with plenty of open space
- The island Kitchen has a useful snackbar
- This home comes with a basement foundation.

First floor — 1,108 sq. ft.
Second floor — 942 sq. ft.
Basement — 1,108 sq. ft.
Garage — 455 sq. ft.

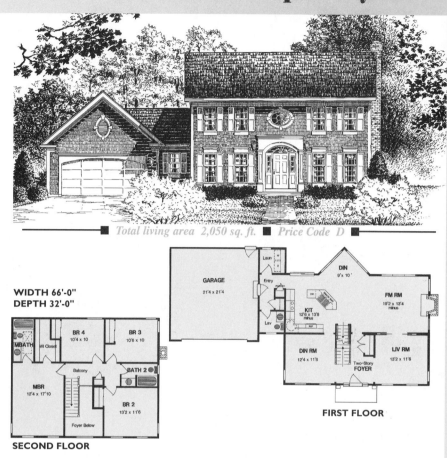

WIDTH 66'-0"
DEPTH 32'-0"

SECOND FLOOR

FIRST FLOOR

Total living area 2,050 sq. ft. ■ *Price Code D*

Wonderful One-Level Living

No. 93193

This plan features:

- Three bedrooms
- Two full and one half baths
- Charming front Porch accesses easy-care Entry with archway to Dining Room
- Central Great Room enhanced by a cathedral ceiling over a cozy fireplace set in a wall of windows
- Large and convenient Kitchen with work island/snackbar, Eating Nook with sliding glass door to backyard, and nearby Laundry/Garage entry
- Corner Master Bedroom features a walk-in closet and plush Bath with a double vanity and Spa tub
- Two additional Bedrooms with ample closets and double windows, share a full Bath
- This home comes with a basement foundation.

Main floor — 1,802 sq. ft.
Basement — 1,802 sq. ft.

Total living area 1,802 sq. ft. ■ *Price Code C* ■

MAIN FLOOR

Secluded Master Suite

■ *Total living area 1,680 sq. ft.* ■ *Price Code B* ■

No. 92527

■ **This plan features:**

— Three bedrooms

— Two full baths

■ A convenient one-level design with an open floor plan between the Kitchen, Breakfast Area and Great Room

■ A vaulted ceiling and a cozy fireplace in the spacious Great Room

■ A well-equipped Kitchen using a peninsula counter as an eating bar

■ A Master Suite with a luxurious Master Bath

■ Two additional Bedrooms having use of a full hall Bath

■ This home comes with a crawlspace foundation.

Main floor — 1,680 sq. ft.
Garage — 538 sq. ft.

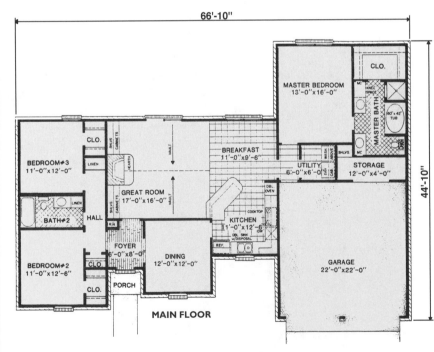

■ *Total living area 1,771 sq. ft.* ■ *Price Code C* ■

No. 99285

This plan features:

- Three bedrooms

- Two full and one half baths

- Inviting atmosphere enhanced by Porch surrounding and shading home

- Two-story Entry Hall graced by a landing staircase and arched window

- Country Kitchen with cooktop island/snackbar, eating alcove and archway to Family Room with cozy fireplace

- First floor Master Suite with bay window, walk-in closet and pampering Bath

- Two double dormer Bedrooms on second floor catch breezes and share a full Bath

- This home comes with a basement foundation.

First floor — 1,171 sq. ft.
Second floor — 600 sq. ft.

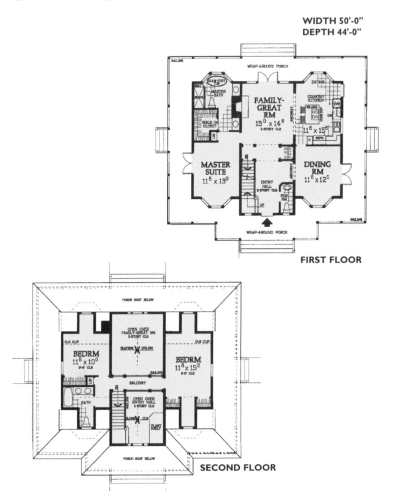

WIDTH 50'-0"
DEPTH 44'-0"

FIRST FLOOR

SECOND FLOOR

Open Plan Accented By Loft and Decks

■ *Total living area 2,015 sq. ft.* ■ *Price Code D* ■

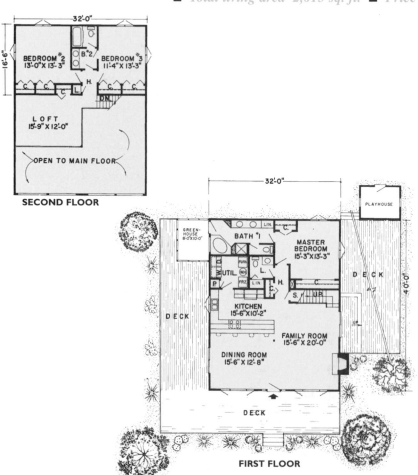

SECOND FLOOR

FIRST FLOOR

No. 10515

■ This plan features:

— Three bedrooms

— Two full and one half baths

■ A fireplaced Family Room and Dining Room

■ A large Kitchen sharing a preparation/eating bar with Dining Room

■ A first floor Master Bedroom featuring two closets and a five-piece Bath

■ An ample Utility Room designed with a Pantry and room for a freezer, a washer and dryer, plus furnace and a hot water heater

■ This home comes with a crawlspace foundation.

First floor — 1,280 sq. ft.
Second floor — 735 sq. ft.
Greenhouse — 80 sq. ft.

Compact Classic

■ *Total living area 1,737 sq. ft.* ■ *Price Code B* ■

No. 91413

This plan features:

- Three bedrooms

- Two full and one half baths

- A spacious Family Room with a cozy fireplace and direct access to the Patio

- A well-appointed Kitchen with an eating bar peninsula, double sink and sunny eating Nook

- A formal Living Room and Dining Room located at the front of the house

- A Master Suite equipped with a walk-in closet, a double vanity and a full Master Bath

- An optional basement, slab or crawlspace foundation — please specify when ordering.

First floor — 963 sq. ft.
Second floor — 774 sq. ft.

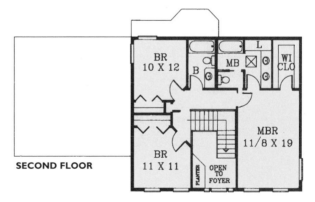

BR 10 X 12
B
MB
L
WI CLO
MBR 11/8 X 19
BR 11 X 11
PLANTER
OPEN TO FOYER

SECOND FLOOR

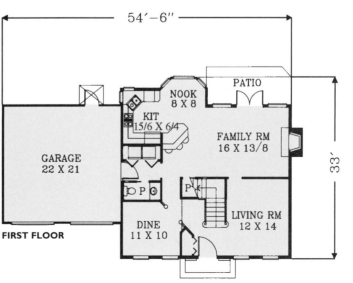

54'—6"

NOOK 8 X 8
PATIO
KIT 15/6 X 6/4
FAMILY RM 16 X 13/8
GARAGE 22 X 21
P
P
LIVING RM 12 X 14
DINE 11 X 10
33'

FIRST FLOOR

Flexibility to Expand

© Donald A. Gardner Architects, Inc.

■ *Total living area 1,831 sq. ft.* ■ *Price Code F* ■

No. 99859

■ **This plan features:**

— Three bedrooms

— Two full and one half baths

■ Two-story Foyer contains palladian window in a clerestory dormer

■ Efficient Kitchen opens to Breakfast Area and Deck for outdoor dining

■ Columns separating the Great Room and Dining Room which have nine-foot ceilings

■ Alternate foundation options available at an additional charge. Please call 1.800.235.5700 for more information.

■ This home comes with a crawlspace foundation.

First floor — 1,289 sq. ft.

Second floor — 542 sq. ft.
Bonus room — 393 sq. ft.
Garage & storage — 521 sq. ft.

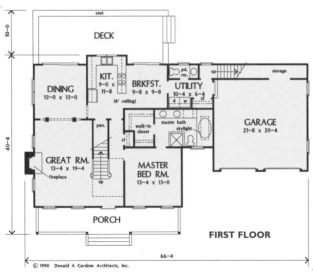

seat

DECK

10–0

KIT.
9–0 x
11–8

BRKFST.
9–8 x 9–8
(8' ceiling)

UTILITY
10–4 x 6–4

pd. rm.

up

storage

DINING
12–0 x 12–0

pan.

walk-in closet

master bath

skylight

GARAGE
21–8 x 20–4

d w

cl

40–4

GREAT RM.
13–4 x 19–4

fireplace

MASTER BED RM.
13–4 x 13–0

up

PORCH

FIRST FLOOR

66–4

© 1990 Donald A Gardner Architects, Inc.

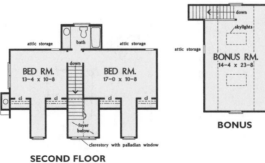

attic storage

bath

attic storage

BED RM.
13–4 x 10–8

down

BED RM.
17–0 x 10–8

cl

cl

d

cl

foyer below

clerestory with palladian window

SECOND FLOOR

down

skylights

attic storage

BONUS RM.
14–4 x 23–8

BONUS

Rustic Exterior; Complete Home

■ *Total living area 1,328 sq. ft.* ■ *Price Code A* ■

No. 34600

This plan features:

Three bedrooms

Two full baths

A two-story, fireplaced Living Room with exposed beams adds to the rustic charm

An efficient, modern Kitchen with ample work and storage space

Two first floor Bedrooms with individual closet space share a full Bath

A Master Bedroom secluded on the second floor with its own full Bath

A welcoming front Porch adding to the living space

An optional basement, slab or crawlspace foundation — please specify when ordering.

First floor — 1,013 sq. ft.
Second floor — 315 sq. ft.
Basement — 1,013 sq. ft.

SLAB/CRAWLSPACE OPTION

Open to Living Room Below

Flat Clg @ 7'-6"

Master Br
12-0 x 13-4

DN

SECOND FLOOR

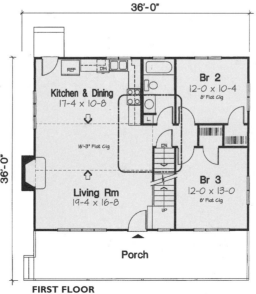

36'-0"

36'-0"

REF   DW

Kitchen & Dining
17-4 x 10-8

16'-3" Flat Clg

Br 2
12-0 x 10-4
8' Flat Clg

DN

Living Rm
19-4 x 16-8

UP

Br 3
12-0 x 13-0
8' Flat Clg

Porch

FIRST FLOOR

Compact and Convenient Colonial

■ *Total living area 1,248 sq. ft.* ■ *Price Code A* ■

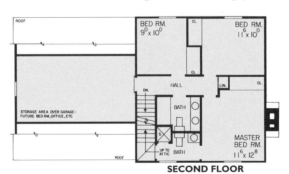

SECOND FLOOR

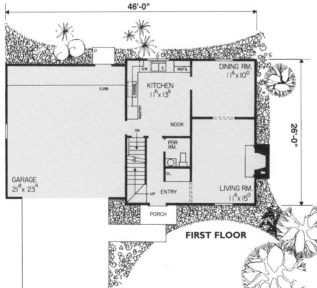

FIRST FLOOR

No. 99255

■ **This plan features:**

— Three bedrooms

— Two full and one half baths

■ Traditional Entry with landing staircase, closet, and Powder Roo▮

■ Living Room with focal point fireplace opens to formal Dining Room for ease in entertaining

■ Efficient, L-shaped Kitchen with built-in Pantry, eating Nook and Garage Entry

■ Corner Master Bedroom with private Bath and attic access

■ Two additional Bedrooms with ample closets share a double vanity Bath

■ This home comes with a baseme▮ foundation.

First floor — 624 sq. ft.
Second floor — 624 sq. ft.
Garage — 510 sq. ft.

Inviting Porch Has Dual Function

■ *Total living area 1,295 sq. ft.* ■ *Price Code A* ■

No. 91021

This plan features:

Three bedrooms

One full and one three-quarter baths

An inviting, wrap-around Porch Entry with sliding glass doors leading right into a bayed Dining Room

A Living Room with a cozy feeling, enhanced by the fireplace

An efficient Kitchen opening to both Dining and Living Rooms

A Master Suite with a walk-in closet and private Master Bath

An optional basement, slab or crawlspace foundation — please specify when ordering.

Main floor — 1,295 sq. ft.
Garage — 400 sq. ft.

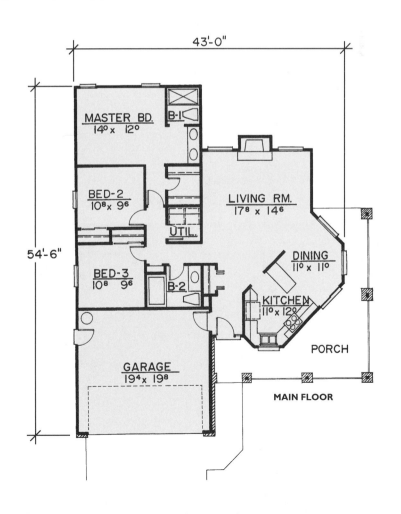

Spacious Family Living

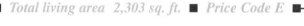
■ *Total living area 2,303 sq. ft.* ■ *Price Code E* ■

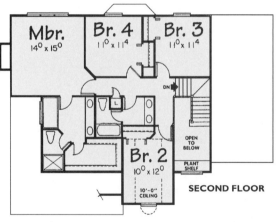

SECOND FLOOR

Mbr. 14⁰ x 15⁰
Br. 4 11⁰ x 11⁴
Br. 3 11⁰ x 11⁴
Br. 2 10⁰ x 12⁰
10'-0" CEILING
DN
OPEN TO BELOW
PLANT SHELF

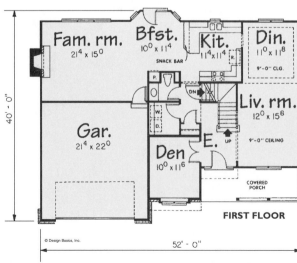

Fam. rm. 21⁴ x 15⁰
Bfst. 10⁰ x 11⁴
SNACK BAR
Kit. 11⁴ x 11⁴
Din. 11⁰ x 11⁸
9'-0" CLG.
Gar. 21⁴ x 22⁰
Den 10⁰ x 11⁶
E.
UP
Liv. rm. 12⁰ x 15⁸
9'-0" CEILING
DN
COVERED PORCH
40'-0"
52'-0"
© Design Basics, Inc.

FIRST FLOOR

No. 94956

■ **This plan features:**

— Four bedrooms

— Two full and one half baths

■ Entry opens to spacious Living Room with a tiered ceiling and Dining Room beyond

■ Hub Kitchen easily serves the Dining Room, the Breakfast Bay and the Family Room

■ Corner Master Bedroom has access to a private Bath

■ This home comes with a slab foundation.

■ Alternate foundation options available at an additional charge call 1.800.235.5700 for more information.

First floor — 1,269 sq. ft.
Second floor — 1,034 sq. ft.
Basement — 1,269 sq. ft.
Garage — 485 sq. ft.

Fireplace-Equipped Family Room

■ *Total living area 1,505 sq. ft.* ■ *Price Code B* ■

No. 24326

This plan features:

Four bedrooms

One full, one three-quarter and one half baths

A spacious Living Room that opens into the Dining Area which flows into the efficient Kitchen

A Family Room equipped with a cozy fireplace and sliding glass doors to a patio

A Master Suite with a large walk-in closet and a private Bath

Three additional Bedrooms that share a full hall Bath

An optional basement, slab or crawlspace foundation — please specify when ordering.

First floor — 692 sq. ft.
Second floor — 813 sq. ft.
Basement — 699 sq. ft.
Garage — 484 sq. ft.

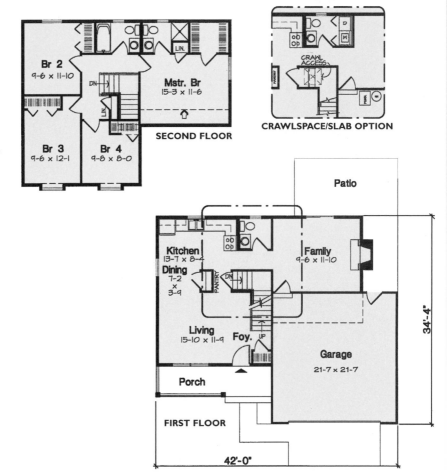

Four Bedroom Country Classic

© Donald A. Gardner Architects, Inc.

B. NATHAN

■ *Total living area 2,164 sq. ft.* ■ *Price Code G* ■

SECOND FLOOR

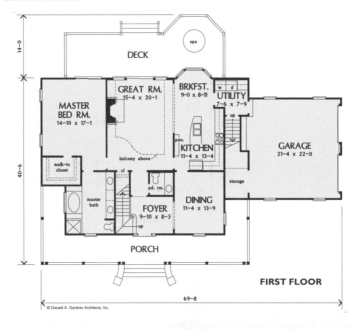

FIRST FLOOR

© Donald A. Gardner Architects, Inc.

No. 96408

■ **This plan features:**

— Four bedrooms

— Two full and one half baths

■ Foyer open to the Dining Room creating a hall with a balcony ov the vaulted Great Room

■ Great Room opens to the Deck and to the island Kitchen with convenient Pantry

■ Master Suite pampered by a whirlpool tub, double vanity, separate shower, and Deck access

■ This home comes with a crawlspace foundation.

■ Alternate foundation options available at an additional charge call 1.800.235.5700 for more information.

First floor — 1,499 sq. ft.
Second floor — 665 sq. ft.
Garage & storage — 567 sq. ft
Bonus room — 380 sq. ft.

Comfortable Design Encourages Relaxation

© Donald A. Gardner Architects, Inc.

B. NATHAN

■ *Total living area 2,349 sq. ft.* ■ *Price Code G* ■

No. 96413

This plan features:

Four bedrooms

Three full baths

Center dormer lights Foyer, as columns punctuate the Entry to the Dining Room and Great Room

Spacious Kitchen with angled countertop and open to the Breakfast Bay

Tray ceilings add elegance to the Dining Room and the Master Suite

Alternate foundation options available at an additional charge, call 1.800.235.5700 for more information.

This home comes with a crawlspace foundation.

Main floor — 2,349 sq. ft.

Bonus — 435 sq. ft.

Garage — 615 sq. ft.

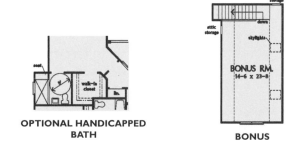

OPTIONAL HANDICAPPED BATH

BONUS

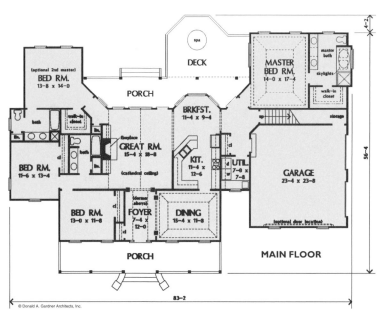

MAIN FLOOR

© Donald A. Gardner Architects, Inc.

Amenity-Packed Affordability

■ *Total living area 1,484 sq. ft.* ■ *Price Code A* ■

No. 92525

■ **This plan features:**

— Three bedrooms

— Two full baths

■ A sheltered entrance inviting you guests onward

■ A fireplace in the Den offering a focal point, while the decorative ceiling adds definition to the room

■ A well-equipped Kitchen flowing with ease into the Breakfast Bay or Dining Room

■ A Master Bedroom, having two closets and a private Master Bath

■ An optional crawlspace or slab foundation — please specify when ordering.

Main floor — 1,484 sq. ft.
Garage — 544 sq. ft.

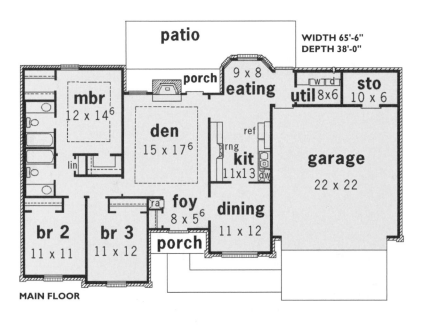

WIDTH 65'-6"
DEPTH 38'-0"

patio

porch

mbr
12 x 14⁶

den
15 x 17⁶

eating

9 x 8

util 8x6   sto
10 x 6

lin

kit
11x13

ref
rng

garage
22 x 22

br 2
11 x 11

br 3
11 x 12

foy
8 x 5⁶

dining
11 x 12

porch

MAIN FLOOR

Surrounded with Sunshine

■ *Total living area 1,731 sq. ft.* ■ *Price Code B* ■

No. 90986

This plan features:

Three bedrooms

Two full and one half baths

An Italianate style, featuring columns and tile originally designed to sit on the edge of a golf course

An open design with pananoramic vistas in every direction

A whirlpool tub in the elaborate and spacious Master Bedroom suite

A Great Room with a corner gas fireplace

A turreted Breakfast Nook and an efficient Kitchen with peninsula counter

Two family Bedrooms that share a full hall Bath

An optional basement or crawlspace foundation – please specify when ordering.

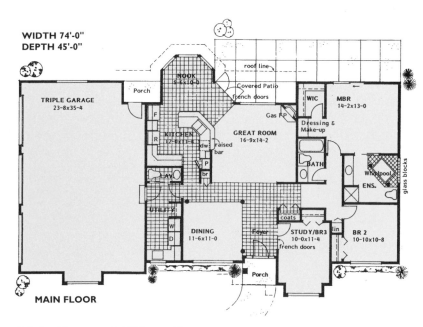

Main floor — 1,731 sq. ft.
Garage — 888 sq. ft.
Basement — 1,715 sq. ft.

Inviting Porch Adorns Affordable Home

■ *Total living area 1,243 sq. ft.* ■ *Price Code A* ■

No. 90682

■ **This plan features:**

— Three bedrooms

— Two full baths

■ A large and spacious Living Roo[m] that adjoins the Dining Room fo[r] ease in entertaining

■ A private Bedroom wing offerin[g] a quiet atmosphere

■ A Master Bedroom with his-n-he[r] closets and a private Bath

■ An efficient Kitchen with a walk[-] in Pantry

■ An optional basement or slab foundation — please specify whe[n] ordering.

Main floor — 1,243 sq. ft.

MAIN FLOOR

66'-4"

30'-4"

PATIO

BED RM
11'-0" x 11'-0"

BED RM
10'-0" x 10'-0"

DINING RM
12'-4" x 10'-0"

KITCHEN
11'-0" x 10'-0"

service

sl. gl. dr.

dw   s.

range

pantry

cl

MUD RM
laundry

w.

d.

STORAGE

cl

ref

dn

HALL

htr.
flue

cl

BATH

lin

cl

cl

cl

MASTER
BED RM
14'-0" x 11'-4"

space
divider

LIVING RM
21'-4" x 12'-10"

stor.

TWO CAR GARAGE
20'-0" x 19'-0"

BATH

PORTICO

■ *Total living area 2,162 sq. ft.* ■ *Price Code D* ■

No. 91343

This plan features:

Three bedrooms

Two full and one half baths

A stone-faced fireplace and vaulted ceiling in the Living Room

An island food preparation center with a sink and a breakfast bar in the Kitchen

Sliding glass doors leading from the Dining Room to the adjacent Deck

A Master Suite with a vaulted ceiling, a Sitting Room, and a lavish Master Bath with a whirlpool tub, skylights, double vanity and a walk-in closet

This home comes with a combo basement/crawlspace foundation.

First floor — 1,338 sq. ft.

Second floor — 763 sq. ft.

Lower floor — 61 sq. ft.

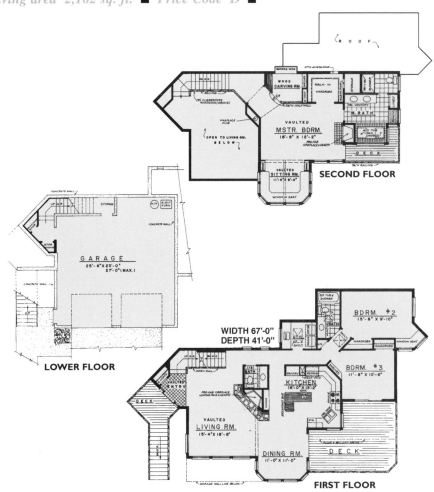

Quaint and Cozy

© Donald A. Gardner Architects, Inc.

B. NATHAN

■ *Total living area 1,864 sq. ft.* ■ *Price Code F* ■

No. 99878

■ **This plan features:**

— Three bedrooms

— Two full and one half baths

■ Spacious floor plan with large Great Room crowned by cathedral ceiling

■ Central Kitchen with angled counter opens to the Breakfast Area and Great Room

■ Privately located Master Bedroom has a cathedral ceiling

■ Alternate foundation options available at an additional charge. Please call 1.800.235.5700 for more information.

■ This home comes with a crawlspace foundation.

Main floor — 1,864 sq. ft.
Garage — 614 sq. ft.
Bonus — 420 sq. ft.

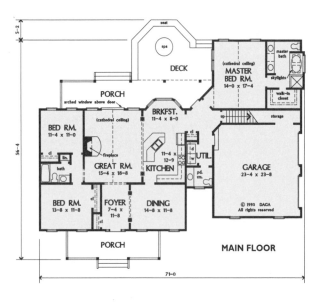

MAIN FLOOR

BONUS

Country Living in Any Neighborhood

■ *Total living area 2,181 sq. ft.* ■ *Price Code D* ■

No. 90436

This plan features:

Three bedrooms

Two full and two half baths

An expansive Family Room with fireplace

A Dining Room and Breakfast Nook lit by flowing natural light from bay windows

A first floor Master Suite with a double vanity Bath that wraps around his and her closets

An optional basement, slab or crawlspace foundation — please specify when ordering.

First floor — 1,477 sq. ft.
Second floor — 704 sq. ft.
Basement — 1,374 sq. ft.

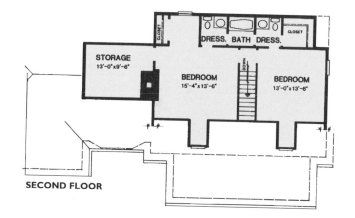

SECOND FLOOR

STORAGE
13'-0"x9'-6"

DRESS. BATH DRESS.

BEDROOM
15'-4"x13'-6"

BEDROOM
13'-0"x13'-6"

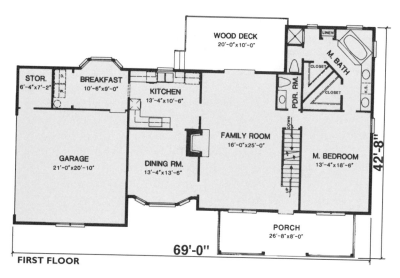

FIRST FLOOR

WOOD DECK
20'-0"x10'-0"

M. BATH

STOR.
6'-4"x7'-2"

BREAKFAST
10'-6"x9'-0"

KITCHEN
13'-4"x10'-6"

PDR. RM.

LINEN

CLOSET

CLOSET

GARAGE
21'-0"x20'-10"

DINING RM.
13'-4"x13'-6"

FAMILY ROOM
16'-0"x25'-0"

M. BEDROOM
13'-4"x18'-6"

PORCH
26'-8"x8'-0"

69'-0"

42'-8"

Traditional Brick with Detailing

■ *Total living area 1,869 sq. ft.* ■ *Price Code C* ■

No. 92536

■ **This plan features:**

— Three bedrooms

— Two full baths

■ Covered Entry leads into the Foyer, the formal Dining Room and the Den

■ Expansive Den with a decorative ceiling over a hearth fireplace an sliding glass doors to the rear yar

■ Country Kitchen with a built-in Pantry, double ovens and a cooktop island easily serves the Breakfast Area and Dining Room

■ Private Master Bedroom suite with a decorative ceiling, a walk-in closet, a double vanity and a whirlpool tub

■ Two additional Bedrooms share full Bath

■ An optional slab or crawlspace foundation — please specify whe ordering.

Main floor — 1,869 sq. ft.
Garage — 561 sq. ft.

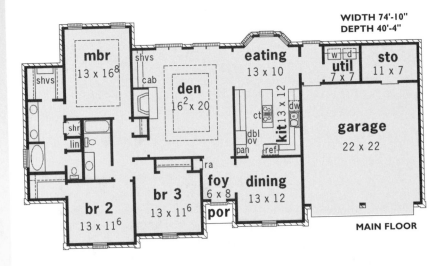

WIDTH 74'-10"
DEPTH 40'-4"

MAIN FLOOR

Three Porches Offer Outdoor Charm

■ *Total living area 1,274 sq. ft.* ■ *Price Code A* ■

o. 90048

his plan features:

hree bedrooms

wo full baths

n oversized log burning fireplace
 the spacious Living/Dining
rea which is two stories high
ith sliding glass doors

hree Porches offering the
aximum in outdoor living space

 private Bedroom located on the
econd floor

n efficient Kitchen including an
ating bar and access to the
overed Dining Porch

his home comes with a basement
undation.

st floor — 974 sq. ft.
ond floor — 300 sq. ft.

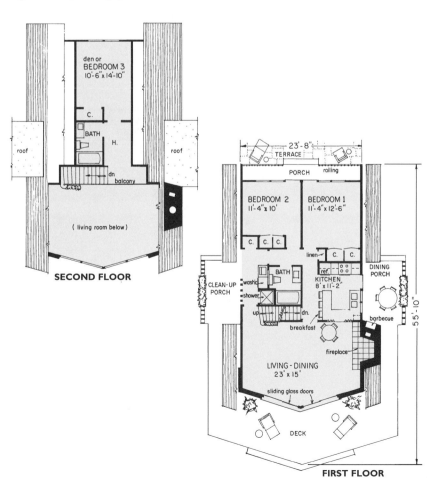

SECOND FLOOR

FIRST FLOOR

Designed for Today's Family

© Donald A. Gardner Architects, Inc.

■ *Total living area 2,192 sq. ft.* ■ *Price Code G* ■

No. 99838

■ **This plan features:**

— Three bedrooms

— Two full and one half baths

■ Volume and 9' ceilings add elega
to a comfortable, open floor plan

■ Airy Foyer topped by a vaulted
dormer allows natural light to
stream in

■ Formal Dining Room delineated
from the Foyer by columns toppe
with a tray ceiling

■ Extra flexibility in the front
Bedroom which could double
as a Study

■ Alternate foundation options
available at an additional charge.
Please call 1.800.235.5700 for mo
information.

■ This home comes with a crawlspa
foundation.

Main floor — 2,192 sq. ft.
Garage & Storage — 582 sq. ft.
Bonus — 390 sq. ft.

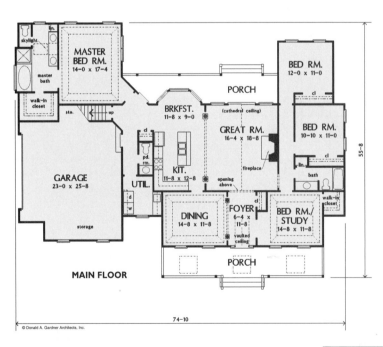

MAIN FLOOR

74–10

© Donald A. Gardner Architects, Inc.

BONUS

Tremendous Curb Appeal

© Donald A. Gardner Architects, Inc.

■ *Total living area 1,246 sq. ft.* ■ *Price Code E* ■

o. 99806

his plan features:

hree bedrooms

wo full baths

reat Room topped by a cathedral eiling and enhanced by a replace

antry, skylight and peninsula ounter add to the comfort and fficiency of the Kitchen

athedral ceiling crowns the Master Suite and has these menities; walk-in and linen loset, a luxurious private Bath

wing Room, Bedroom or Study, opped by a cathedral ceiling

lternate foundation options vailable at an additional charge. lease call 1.800.235.5700 for nore information.

his home comes with a rawlspace foundation.

in floor — 1,246 sq. ft.

rage — 420 sq. ft.

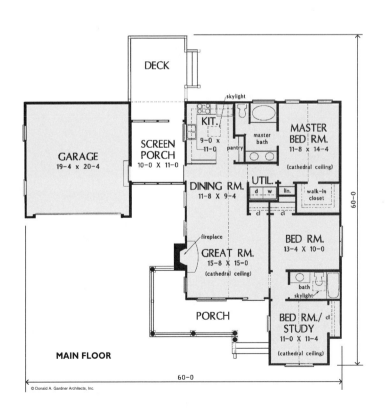

DECK

GARAGE
19-4 x 20-4

SCREEN PORCH
10-0 X 11-0

KIT.
9-0 x
11-0
skylight
pantry

master bath

MASTER BED RM.
11-8 x 14-4
(cathedral ceiling)

DINING RM.
11-8 X 9-4

UTIL.
d w lin.

walk-in closet

GREAT RM.
15-8 X 15-0
(cathedral ceiling)
fireplace

BED RM.
13-4 x 10-0

PORCH

bath
skylight

BED RM./ STUDY
11-0 x 11-4
(cathedral ceiling)

60-0

60-0

MAIN FLOOR

© Donald A. Gardner Architects, Inc.

271

Maximum Privacy

■ *Total living area 2,201 sq. ft.* ■ *Price Code D* ■

No. 24726

■ **This plan features:**

— Three bedrooms

— Two full and one half baths

■ The Master Suite encompasses the entire second floor

■ The Great Room is enhanced by skylights and a cozy fireplace

■ The efficient Kitchen is equipped with a work island

■ The formal Dining Room is directly across from the Foyer

■ A screened Porch off the Great Room adds to the living space

■ An optional basement, slab or crawlspace foundation — please specify when ordering.

First floor — 1,525 sq. ft.
Second floor — 676 sq. ft.
Bonus — 288 sq. ft.
Basement — 1,510 sq. ft.
Garage — 614 sq. ft.

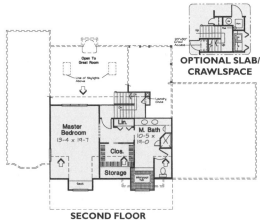

SECOND FLOOR

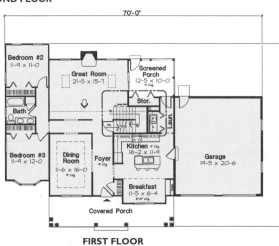

FIRST FLOOR

■ *Total living area 1,950 sq. ft.* ■ *Price Code C* ■

No. 99757

This plan features:

- Three bedrooms

- Two full and one half baths

- Front Porch invites visiting and leads into an open Entry with an angled staircase

- Living Room with a wall of windows and an island fireplace

- Kitchen with a work island, walk-in Pantry, garden window over sink, skylit Nook and nearby Deck

- Corner Master Suite enhanced by Deck access, vaulted ceiling, a large walk-in closet and Spa Bath

- Guest/Utility Room offers a pullman bed and Laundry

- Two second floor Bedrooms with large closets share a full Bath

- This home comes with a crawlspace foundation.

First floor — 1,472 sq. ft.
Second floor — 478 sq. ft.
Garage — 558 sq. ft.

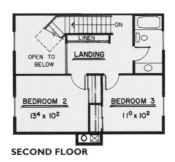

SECOND FLOOR

WIDTH 62'-0"
DEPTH 51'-0"

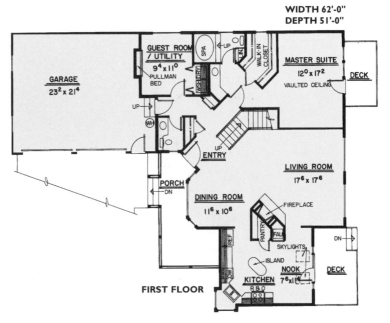

FIRST FLOOR

Mixture of Traditional and Country Charm

© Donald A. Gardner Architects, Inc.

■ *Total living area 1,954 sq. ft.* ■ *Price Code F* ■

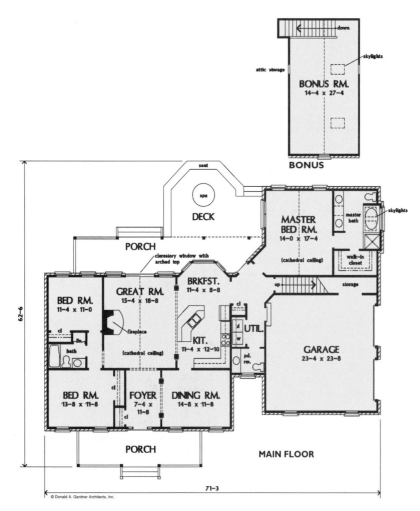

BONUS

MAIN FLOOR

© Donald A. Gardner Architects, Inc.

No. 99845

■ **This plan features:**

— Three bedrooms

— Two full and one half baths

■ Stairs to the skylit Bonus Room located near the Kitchen and Master Suite

■ Master Suite crowned in cathedral ceilings has a skylit Bath that contains a whirlpool tub and dual vanity

■ Great Room, topped by a cathedral ceiling and highlighted by a fireplace

■ Alternate foundation options available at an additional charge. Please call 1.800.235.5700 for more information.

■ This home comes with a crawlspace foundation.

Main floor — 1,954 sq. ft.
Bonus area — 436 sq. ft.
Garage — 649 sq. ft.

Brick Opulence and Grandeur

■ *Total living area 3,921 sq. ft.* ■ *Price Code K* ■

No. 92248

■ This plan features:

- Four bedrooms

- Three full and one half baths

- Dramatic two-story glass Entry with a curved staircase

- Both Living and Family rooms offer high ceilings, decorative windows and large fireplaces

- Large, efficient Kitchen with a cooktop serving island, walk-in Pantry, bright Breakfast Area and Patio access

- Lavish Master Bedroom with a cathedral ceiling, two walk-in closets and large Bath

- Two additional Bedrooms with ample closets share a double vanity Bath

- An optional basement or slab foundation — please specify when ordering.

First floor — 2,506 sq. ft.
Second floor — 1,415 sq. ft.
Basement — 2,400 sq. ft.
Garage — 660 sq. ft.

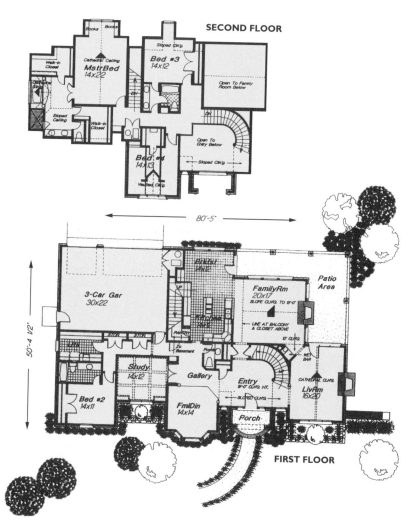

Perfect for Family Gatherings

© Donald A. Gardner Architects, Inc.

Total living area 1,346 sq. ft. ■ Price Code E

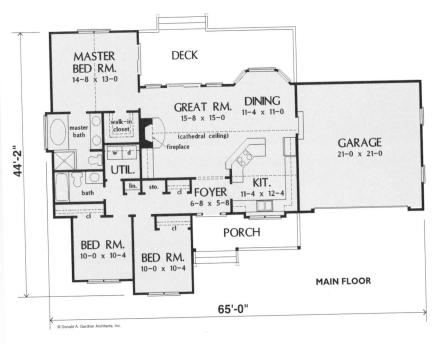

© Donald A. Gardner Architects, Inc.

No. 99826

■ **This plan features:**

— Three bedrooms

— Two full baths

■ An open layout between the Great Room, Kitchen, and Dining Area sharing a cathedral ceiling and a fireplace

■ Master Bedroom with a soaring cathedral ceiling, direct access to the Deck and a well appointed Bath with a large walk-in closet

■ Additional Bedrooms sharing a full Bath in the hall

■ Alternate foundation options available at an additional charge Please call 1.800.235.5700 for more information.

■ This home comes with a crawlspace foundation.

Main floor — 1,346 sq. ft.
Garage & storage — 462 sq. ft

Country Cottage Charm

■ *Total living area 3,423 sq. ft.* ■ *Price Code I* ■

No. 98536

This plan features:

Four bedrooms

Two full and one half baths

Vaulted Master Bedroom has a private skylit Bath

Three more Bedrooms have walk-in closets and share a full Bath

A loft and Bonus Room above the Living Room

Family Room has built-in book shelves, a fireplace, and overlooks the covered Verandah

The huge three-car Garage has a separate Shop Area

An optional slab or a crawl space foundation — please specify when ordering

First floor — 2,787 sq. ft.
Second floor — 636 sq. ft.
Garage — 832 sq. ft.

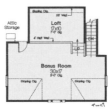

SECOND FLOOR

FIRST FLOOR

Charming Country Style

■ *Total living area 1,596 sq. ft.* ■ *Price Code B* ■

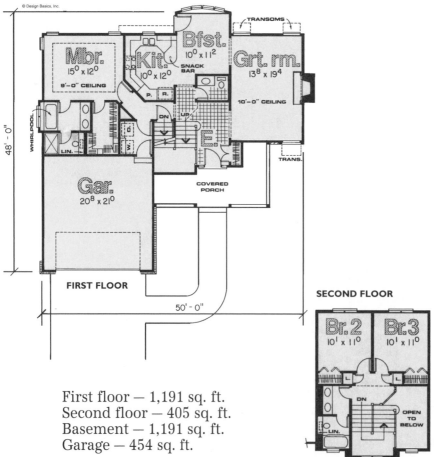

© Design Basics, Inc.

FIRST FLOOR

Mbr.
15⁰ x 12⁰
9'-0" CEILING

Kit.
10⁰ x 12⁰

Bfst.
10⁰ x 11²

SNACK BAR

Grt. rm.
13⁸ x 19⁴
10'-0" CEILING

TRANSOMS

P. R.

DN UP

W d

LIN.

WHIRLPOOL

48' - 0"

Gar.
20⁸ x 21⁰

COVERED PORCH

TRANS.

50' - 0"

SECOND FLOOR

Br. 2
10¹ x 11⁰

Br. 3
10¹ x 11⁰

L   L

DN

LIN.

OPEN TO BELOW

First floor — 1,191 sq. ft.
Second floor — 405 sq. ft.
Basement — 1,191 sq. ft.
Garage — 454 sq. ft.

No. 99404

■ **This plan features:**

— Three bedrooms

— Two full and one half baths

■ Spacious Great Room enhanced by a fireplace and transom windows

■ Breakfast Room with a bay window and direct access to the Kitchen

■ Snack bar extending work space in the Kitchen

■ Master Suite enhanced by a crowning in a boxed nine-foot ceiling, a compartmental whirlpool Bath and a large walk-in closet

■ Second floor balcony overlooking the U-shaped stairs and Entry

■ This home comes with a basement foundation.

278

■ *Total living area 1,575 sq. ft.* ■ *Price Code B* ■

No. 20083

This plan features:

- Three bedrooms

- Two full baths

- Wide-open active areas that are centrally-located

- A spacious Dining, Living, and Kitchen Area

- A Master Suite at the rear of the house with a full Bath

- Two additional Bedrooms that share a full hall Bath and the quiet atmosphere that results from an intelligent design

- This home comes with a basement foundation.

Main floor — 1,575 sq. ft.
Basement — 1,575 sq. ft.
Garage — 475 sq. ft.

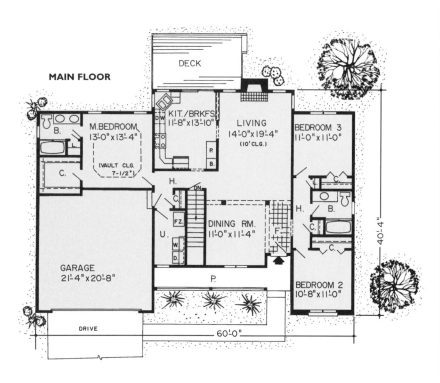

MAIN FLOOR

DECK

KIT./BRKFS
11'-8"x13'-10"

LIVING
14'-0"x19'-4"
(10' CLG.)

BEDROOM 3
11'-0"x11'-0"

M.BEDROOM
13'-0"x13'-4"

(VAULT CLG.
7-1/2')

DINING RM.
11'-0"x11'-4"

GARAGE
21'-4"x20'-8"

BEDROOM 2
10'-8"x11'-0"

DRIVE

60'-0"

40'-4"

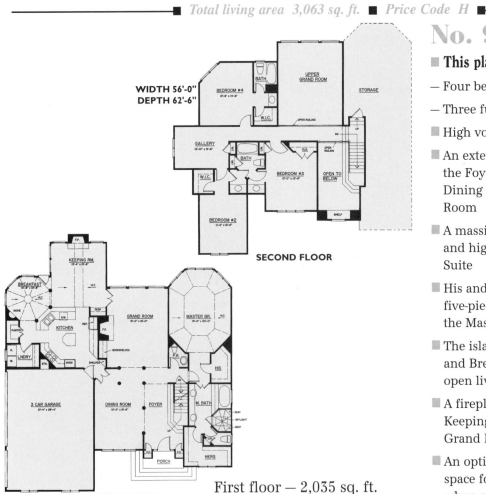

Total living area 3,063 sq. ft. ■ *Price Code H* ■

WIDTH 56'-0"
DEPTH 62'-6"

SECOND FLOOR

FIRST FLOOR

No. 98211

■ This plan features:

— Four bedrooms

— Three full and one half baths

■ High volume ceilings

■ An extended staircase highlights the Foyer as columns define the Dining Room and the Grand Room

■ A massive glass exterior rear wall and high ceiling in the Master Suite

■ His and her walk-in closets and a five-piece lavish Bath highlight the Master Bath

■ The island Kitchen, Keeping Room and Breakfast Room create an open living space

■ A fireplace accents both the Keeping Room and the two-story Grand Room

■ An optional basement or crawl space foundation — please specify when ordering

First floor — 2,035 sq. ft.
Second floor — 1,028 sq. ft.
Basement — 2,035 sq. ft.
Garage — 530 sq. ft.

■ *Total living area 1,665 sq. ft.* ■ *Price Code B* ■

No. 91418

■ **This plan features:**

— Three bedrooms

— Two full baths

— A dramatic vaulted Foyer

— A range-top island Kitchen with a sunny eating Nook surrounded by a built-in planter

— A vaulted ceiling in the Great Room with a built-in bar and corner fireplace

— A bayed Dining Room that combines with the Great Room for a spacious feeling

— A Master Bedroom with a private reading nook, vaulted ceiling, walk-in closet and a well-appointed private Bath

— Two additional Bedrooms sharing a full hall Bath

— An optional basement, crawlspace or slab foundation — please specify when ordering

Main floor — 1,665 sq. ft.

BASEMENT OPTION

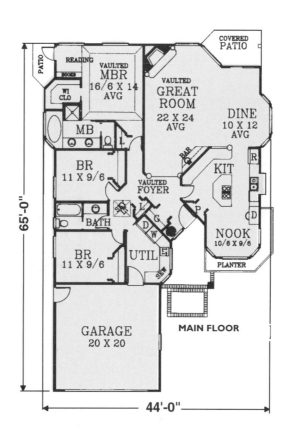

MAIN FLOOR

For First Time Buyers

■ *Total living area 1,310 sq. ft.* ■ *Price Code A* ■

No. 93048

■ **This plan features:**

— Three bedrooms

— Two full baths

■ A sunny Breakfast Room with a convenient hide-away Laundry center

■ An expansive Family Room that includes a corner fireplace and direct access to the Patio

■ A private Master Suite with a walk-in closet and a double vanity Bath

■ Two additional Bedrooms, both with walk-in closets, that share a full hall Bath

■ An optional crawlspace or slab foundation — please specify when ordering.

Main floor — 1,310 sq. ft.
Garage — 449 sq. ft.

WIDTH 49–10

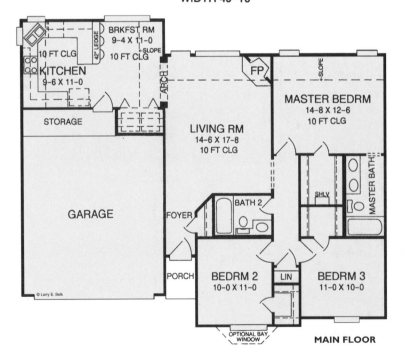

BRKFST RM
9-4 X 11-0
10 FT CLG

10 FT CLG

KITCHEN
9-6 X 11-0

STORAGE

GARAGE

FOYER

PORCH

LIVING RM
14-6 X 17-8
10 FT CLG

FP

MASTER BEDRM
14-8 X 12-6
10 FT CLG

MASTER BATH

SHLV

BATH 2

DEPTH 40–6

BEDRM 2
10-0 X 11-0

LIN

BEDRM 3
11-0 X 10-0

OPTIONAL BAY WINDOW

MAIN FLOOR

© Larry E. Belk

■ Total living area 1,568 sq. ft. ■ Price Code B ■

No. 20220

■ This plan features:

— Three bedrooms

— Two full baths

■ A large front palladian window provides great curb appeal, and allows a view of the front yard from the Living Room

■ A vaulted ceiling in the Living Room, adding to the architectural interest and the spacious feel of the room

■ Sliding glass doors in the Dining Room that lead to a wood Deck

■ A Master Suite that includes a walk-in closet and a private Bath with a double vanity

■ An optional basement, slab or crawlspace foundation — please specify when ordering.

Main floor — 1,568 sq. ft.
Basement — 1,568 sq. ft.
Garage — 509 sq. ft.

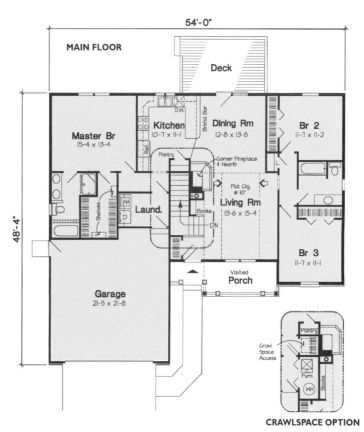

MAIN FLOOR

54'-0"

48'-4"

Deck

Master Br
15-4 x 13-4

Kitchen
10-7 x 11-1

Dining Rm
12-8 x 13-8

Br 2
11-7 x 11-2

Pantry

Corner Fireplace & Hearth

Flat Clg. @ 10"

Living Rm
13-6 x 15-4

Br 3
11-7 x 11-1

Laund.

Books

DN

Shelves

Garage
21-5 x 21-8

Vaulted Porch

CRAWLSPACE OPTION

Crawl Space Access

Pantry

Furn

WH

Books

Easy, Economical Building

© Donald A. Gardner Architects, Inc.

■ Total living area 1,959 sq. ft. ■ Price Code F ■

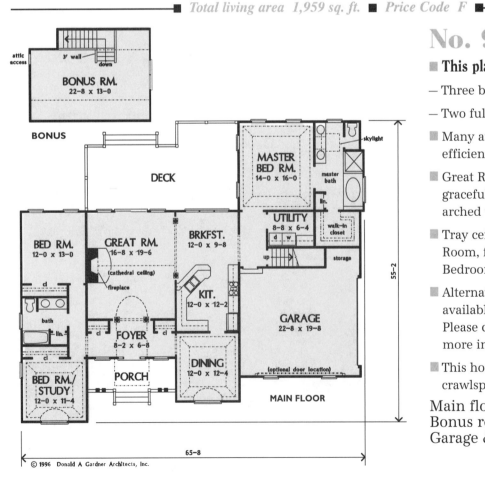

attic access

3' wall

down

BONUS RM.
22-8 x 13-0

BONUS

DECK

BED RM.
12-0 x 13-0

GREAT RM.
16-8 x 19-6
(cathedral ceiling)
fireplace

BRKFST.
12-0 x 9-8

MASTER BED RM.
14-0 x 16-0

master bath

skylight

lin.

UTILITY
8-8 x 6-4

walk-in closet

d w

up

storage

bath

lin.

cl

KIT.
12-0 x 12-2

GARAGE
22-8 x 19-8

FOYER
8-2 x 6-8

cl

cl

BED RM./ STUDY
12-0 x 11-4

PORCH

DINING
12-0 x 12-4

(optional door location)

MAIN FLOOR

55-2

65-8

© 1996 Donald A Gardner Architects, Inc.

No. 99813

■ **This plan features:**

— Three bedrooms

— Two full baths

■ Many architectural elements offer efficient and economical design

■ Great Room vaulted ceiling gracefully arches to include arched window dormer

■ Tray ceilings enhance Dining Room, front Bedroom and Master Bedroom

■ Alternate foundation options available at an additional charge. Please call 1.800.235.5700 for more information.

■ This home comes with a crawlspace foundation.

Main floor — 1,959 sq. ft.
Bonus room — 385 sq. ft.
Garage & storage — 484 sq. ft.

■ *Total living area 1,303 sq. ft.* ■ *Price Code A* ■

No. 99339

■ **This plan features:**

— Three bedrooms

— Two full baths

■ A vaulted ceiling in the Living Room with a half-round transom window and a fireplace

■ A Dining Area flowing into either the Kitchen or the Living Room with sliders to the Deck

■ A main floor Master Suite with corner windows, walk-in closet and private access to a full Bath

■ Two additional Bedrooms on the second floor, one with a walk-in closet, having use of a full Bath

■ This home comes with a basement foundation.

First floor — 857 sq. ft.
Second floor — 446 sq. ft.
Garage — 400 sq. ft.

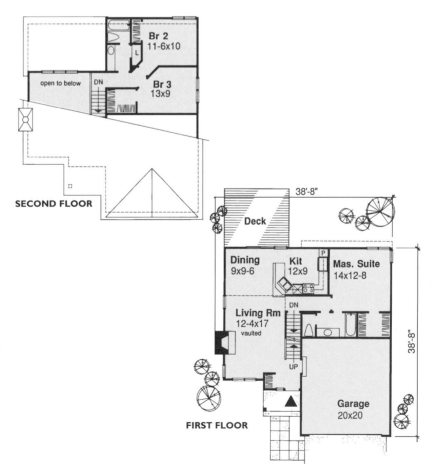

SECOND FLOOR

Br 2
11-6x10

Br 3
13x9

open to below   DN

FIRST FLOOR

38'-8"

Deck

Dining
9x9-6

Kit
12x9

Mas. Suite
14x12-8

Living Rm
12-4x17
vaulted

DN

UP

Garage
20x20

38'-8"

Covered Porch with Columns

■ *Total living area 1,856 sq. ft.* ■ *Price Code C* ■

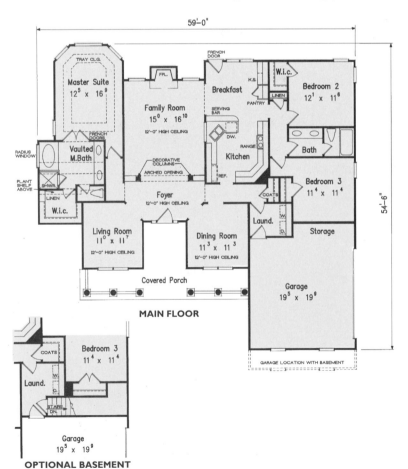

MAIN FLOOR

OPTIONAL BASEMENT STAIR LOCATION

No. 98408

■ **This plan features:**

— Three bedrooms

— Two full baths

■ The foyer with 12' ceiling leads past decorative columns into the Family Room with a center fireplace

■ The Living and Dining rooms are linked by Foyer and have windows overlooking the front Porch

■ The Kitchen has a serving bar and is adjacent to the Breakfast Nook which has a French door that opens to the backyard

■ The private Master Suite has a tray ceiling and a vaulted Bath with a double vanity

■ An optional basement, slab or a crawl space foundation — please specify when ordering

Main floor — 1,856 sq. ft.
Basement — 1,856 sq. ft.
Garage — 429 sq. ft.

© Donald A. Gardner Architects, Inc.

■ *Total living area* *1,879 sq. ft.* ■ *Price Code* *F* ■

No. 99807

This plan features:

Three bedrooms

Two full baths

Great Room crowned with a cathedral ceiling and accented by columns and a fireplace

Secluded Master Suite highlighted by a tray ceiling and contains a Bath with skylight, a garden tub and spacious walk-in closet

Two additional Bedrooms share a full Bath

Alternate foundation options available at an additional charge. Please call 1.800.235.5700 for more information.

This home comes with a crawlspace foundation.

Main floor — 1,879 sq. ft.
Bonus — 360 sq. ft.
Garage — 485 sq. ft.

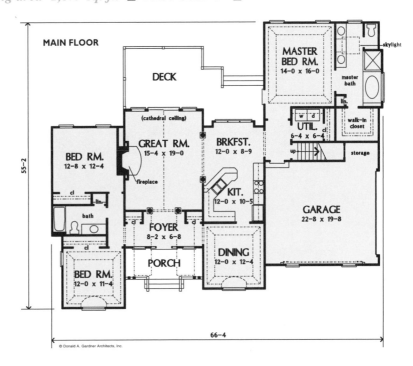

MAIN FLOOR

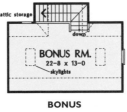

BONUS

Exciting Arched Accents Give Impact

Total living area 2,209 sq. ft. ▪ *Price Code D*

Great Room Below

walk-in closet

skylight

Study 10'3" x 13'6"

Bedroom 13'10" x 10'8"

wood rail

stairs dn

Hall

linen

Bath

slope ceiling

Bedroom 11'0" x 13'0"

walk-in closet

Bonus Room 11'1" x 20'

slope ceiling

slope ceiling

SECOND FLOOR

entertainment center

Great Room 15'6" x 18'1"

high ceiling

Breakfast 11'7" x 12'0"

Laun.

hanging space

walk-in closet

Bath

wood rail

stair dn

Kitchen 11'9" x 11'

Hall

walk-in pantry

Bath

Foyer

Dining Room 11' x 13'

Master Bedroom 13' x 13'11"

Porch

Two-car Garage 20' x 21'

49'

FIRST FLOOR

58'6"

No. 92643

▪ **This plan features:**

– Three bedrooms

– Two full and one half baths

▪ Keystone arch accents entrance

▪ Great Room enhanced by an entertainment center, a hearth fireplace and a wall of windows

▪ Efficient, angled Kitchen offers work island/snackbar, Breakfast Area with access to backyard, Laundry, a Bath and Garage

▪ Master Bedroom wing features a lavish Bath with two vanities and corner window tub

▪ This home comes with a basement foundation.

First floor — 1,542 sq. ft.
Second floor — 667 sq. ft.
Bonus — 236 sq. ft.
Basement — 1,470 sq. ft.
Garage — 420 sq. ft.

■ *Total living area 1,203 sq. ft.* ■ *Price Code A* ■

No. 99365

■ This plan features:

— Three bedrooms

— Two full baths and opt. half bath

■ 10-foot high ceilings in the Living Room, Family Room and Dinette Area

■ A heat-circulating fireplace in Living Room

■ A Master Bath with separate stall shower and whirlpool tub

■ A two-car Garage with access through the Mudroom

■ This home comes with a basement foundation.

Main floor — 1,203 sq. ft.
Lower floor — 676 sq. ft.
Garage — 509 sq. ft.

Regal Residence

■ *Total living area 3,039 sq. ft.* ■ *Price Code H* ■

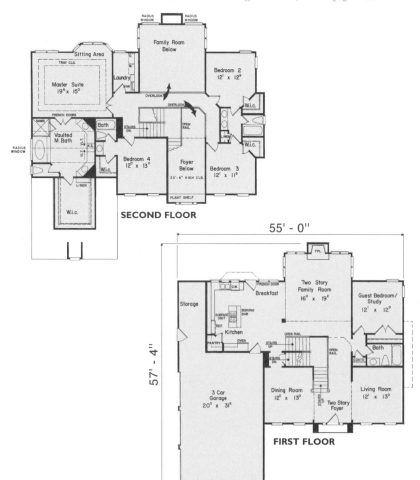

SECOND FLOOR

Sitting Area
TRAY CLG.
Master Suite
19⁶ x 15⁰
Family Room Below
Laundry
Bedroom 2
12¹ x 12⁸
Vaulted M. Bath
Bath
Bedroom 4
12² x 13⁰
Foyer Below
20'-6" HIGH CLG.
Bedroom 3
12¹ x 11⁰
W.i.c.
LINEN
PLANT SHELF
RADIUS WINDOW
FRENCH DOORS
OVERLOOK
OPEN RAIL

FIRST FLOOR

55' - 0"

57' - 4"

Storage
Breakfast
D.W.
FRENCH DOOR
Two Story Family Room
16⁰ x 19²
Guest Bedroom/Study
12¹ x 12⁰
SURFACE UNIT
SERVING BAR
REF.
Kitchen
PANTRY
OVEN
STAIRS UP
OPEN RAIL
OPEN RAIL
Bath
3 Car Garage
20⁵ x 31⁶
STAIRS DN.
Dining Room
12⁰ x 13⁰
COATS
Living Room
12¹ x 13⁰
Two Story Foyer
FPL

© Frank Betz Associates, Inc.

No. 98405

■ This plan features:

— Five bedrooms

— Four full baths

■ Keystone, arched windows accent entrance into two-story Foyer

■ Spacious two-story Family Room enhanced by a fireplace

■ Kitchen with a cooktop island/serving bar and a walk-in Pantry

■ First floor Guest Room/Study with roomy closet and adjoining full Bath

■ Luxurious Master Suite offers a tray ceiling, Sitting Area, a huge walk-in closet and a vaulted Bath

■ Optional basement or crawl space foundation — please specify when ordering

First floor — 1,488 sq. ft.
Second floor — 1,551 sq. ft.
Basement — 1,488 sq. ft.
Garage — 667 sq. ft.

Two-Story Foyer Adds to Elegance

■ *Total living area 2,454 sq. ft.* ■ *Price Code E* ■

No. 93240

■ **This plan features:**

- Four bedrooms

- Two full and one half baths

- Two-story entrance with lovely, curved staircase

- Family Room enhanced by fireplace and access to Sundeck

- Country-sized Kitchen with bright Breakfast Area, adjoins Dining Room and Utility/Garage Entry

French doors lead into plush Master Bedroom with decorative ceiling and large Master Bath

Three additional bedrooms with ample closets share a full Bath and Bonus Room

An optional basement, crawlspace or slab foundation — please specify when ordering.

rst floor — 1,277 sq. ft.
econd floor — 1,177 sq. ft.
onus room — 392 sq. ft.
asement — 1,261 sq. ft.
arage — 572 sq. ft.

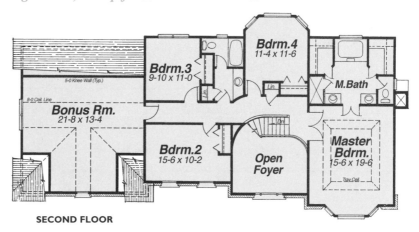

SECOND FLOOR

- Bdrm.3 9-10 x 11-0
- Bdrm.4 11-4 x 11-6
- M.Bath
- Bonus Rm. 21-8 x 13-4
- Bdrm.2 15-6 x 10-2
- Open Foyer
- Master Bdrm. 15-6 x 19-6

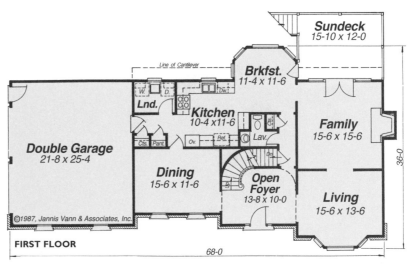

FIRST FLOOR

- Sundeck 15-10 x 12-0
- Brkfst. 11-4 x 11-6
- Lnd.
- Kitchen 10-4 x11-6
- Family 15-6 x 15-6
- Double Garage 21-8 x 25-4
- Dining 15-6 x 11-6
- Open Foyer 13-8 x 10-0
- Living 15-6 x 13-6

©1987, Jannis Vann & Associates, Inc.

68-0

Easy Maintenance

■ *Total living area 786 sq. ft.* ■ *Price Code A* ■

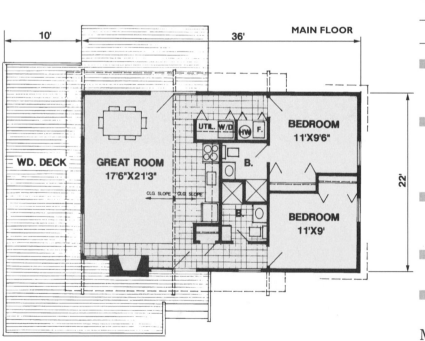

No. 94307

■ **This plan features:**

— Two bedrooms

— Two three-quarter baths

■ Abundant glass and a wrap-around Deck to enjoy the outdoors

■ A tiled entrance into a large Great Room with a fieldstone fireplace and dining area below a sloped ceiling

■ A compact tiled Kitchen open to a Great Room and adjacent to the Utility Area

■ Two Bedrooms, one with a private Bath, offer ample closet space

■ This home comes with a crawlspace foundation.

Main floor — 786 sq. ft.

■ *Total living area 1,354 sq. ft.* ■ *Price Code A* ■

No. 91026

■ **This plan features:**

- Two bedrooms

- One full and one three-quarter baths

- Sweeping panels of glass and a wood stove, creating atmosphere for the Great Room

- An open plan that draws the Kitchen into the warmth of the Great Room's wood stove

- A sleeping Loft that has a full Bath all to itself

- This home comes with a basement foundation.

First floor — 988 sq. ft.
Second floor — 366 sq. ft.
Basement — 742 sq. ft.
Garage — 283 sq. ft.

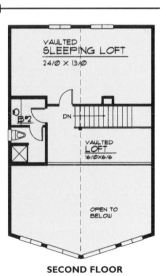

SECOND FLOOR

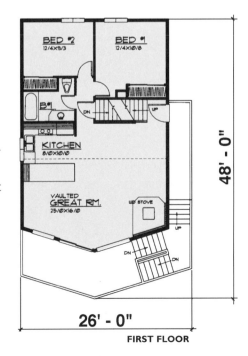

FIRST FLOOR

Distinctive Design

■ *Total living area 1,998 sq. ft.* ■ *Price Code C* ■

No. 94904

■ **This plan features:**

— Three bedrooms

— Two full and one half baths

■ Living Room is distinguished by warmth of bayed window and French doors leading to Family Room

■ Built-in curio cabinet adds interest to formal Dining Room

■ Well-appointed Kitchen with island cooktop and Breakfast Area

■ Family Room with focal point fireplace for informal gatherings

■ Spacious Master Suite with vaulted ceiling over decorative window and plush Dressing Area

■ This home comes with a basement foundation.

First floor — 1,093 sq. ft.
Second floor — 905 sq. ft.
Basement — 1,093 sq. ft.
Garage — 527 sq. ft.

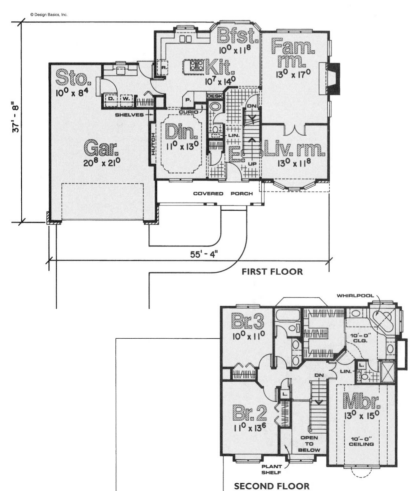

© Design Basics, Inc.

Sto.
10⁰ x 8⁴

Gar.
20⁸ x 21⁰

Bfst.
10⁰ x 11⁸

Kit.
10⁷ x 14⁰

Fam. rm.
13⁰ x 17⁰

Din.
11⁰ x 13⁰

Liv. rm.
13⁰ x 11⁸

SHELVES

HUTCH

CURIO

DESK

LIN.

DN

UP

37' - 8"

55' - 4"

COVERED PORCH

FIRST FLOOR

WHIRLPOOL

Br. 3
10⁰ x 11⁰

Br. 2
11⁰ x 13⁶

Mbr.
13⁰ x 15⁰

10'-0" CLG.

10'-0" CEILING

LIN.

DN

OPEN TO BELOW

PLANT SHELF

SECOND FLOOR

■ *Total living area 2,263 sq. ft.* ■ *Price Code E* ■

No. 90458

■ **This plan features:**

- Three bedrooms

- Two full and one half baths

■ The wrap-around Porch gives a nostalgic appeal to this home

■ The Great Room with fireplace is accessed directly from the Foyer

■ The formal Dining Room has direct access to the efficient Kitchen

■ An island, double sink, plenty of counter/cabinet space and a built-in Pantry complete the Kitchen

The second floor Master Suite has a five-piece, private Bath and a walk-in closet

Two other Bedrooms have walk-in closets and share a full Bath

An optional basement or crawlspace foundation — please specify when ordering.

First floor — 1,125 sq. ft.
Second floor — 1,138 sq. ft.
Basement — 1,125 sq. ft.

SECOND FLOOR

FIRST FLOOR

Great Room Heart of Home

■ *Total living area 1,087 sq. ft.* ■ *Price Code A* ■

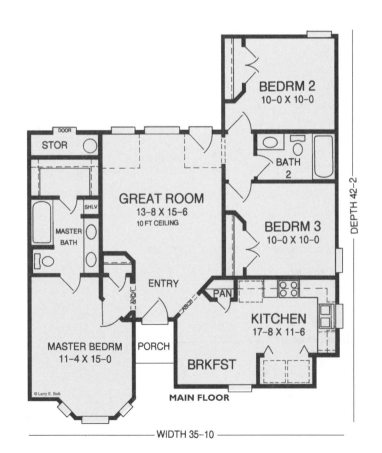

STOR

DOOR

GREAT ROOM
13-8 X 15-6
10 FT CEILING

SHLV

MASTER
BATH

ENTRY

MASTER BEDRM
11-4 X 15-0

© Larry E. Belk

PORCH

BRKFST

KITCHEN
17-8 X 11-6

PAN

BEDRM 2
10-0 X 10-0

BATH
2

BEDRM 3
10-0 X 10-0

DEPTH 42-2

MAIN FLOOR

WIDTH 35-10

No. 93015

■ **This plan features:**

— Three bedrooms

— Two full baths

■ Sheltered Porch leads into the Entry with arches and a Great Room

■ Spacious Great Room with a ten- foot ceiling above a wall of windows and rear yard access

■ Efficient Kitchen with a built-in Pantry, a Laundry closet and a Breakfast Area accented by a decorative window

■ Bay of windows enhances the Master Bedroom suite with a double vanity Bath and a walk-in closet

■ Two additional Bedrooms with ample closets, share a full Bath

■ This home comes with a slab foundation.

Main floor — 1,087 sq. ft.

Traditional Two-Story with Special Details

■ *Total living area 2,157 sq. ft.* ■ *Price Code D* ■

No. 92631

This plan features:

Four bedrooms

Two full and one half baths

Front entrance into two-story Foyer with a plant shelf and lovely railing staircase

Expansive Great Room with corner fireplace and access to rear yard is topped by two-story ceiling

Efficient Kitchen with peninsula counter, walk-in Pantry, Breakfast bay and access to Deck, Laundry, Garage and formal Dining Room

Secluded Master Bedroom offers a sloped ceiling and lavish Bath with walk-in closet

This home comes with a basement foundation.

First floor — 1,511 sq. ft.
Second floor — 646 sq. ft.
Basement — 1,479 sq. ft.
Garage — 475 sq. ft.

Columns Punctuate the Interior Space

S. NATHAN

■ *Total living area 2,188 sq. ft.* ■ *Price Code G* ■

No. 99801

■ **This plan features:**

— Three bedrooms

— Two full and one half baths

■ A two-story Great Room and Foyer, both with dormer window

■ Columns punctuate interior spaces

■ Master Bedroom Suite, privately situated on the first floor, has a double vanity, garden tub and separate shower

■ Alternate foundation options available at an additional charge. Please call 1.800.235.5700 for more information.

■ This home comes with a crawlspace foundation.

First floor — 1,618 sq. ft.
Second floor — 570 sq. ft.
Bonus room — 495 sq. ft.
Garage & storage — 649 sq. ft.

FIRST FLOOR

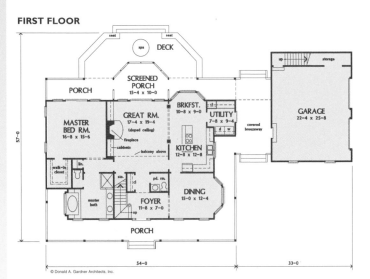

© Donald A. Gardner Architects, Inc.

SECOND FLOOR

BONUS

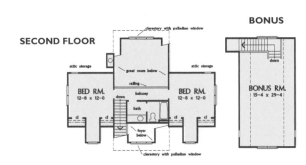

Economical Vacation Home With Viewing Deck

■ *Total living area 1,288 sq. ft.* ■ *Price Code A* ■

No. 99238

This plan features:

Three bedrooms

Two full baths

A large rectangular Living Room with a fireplace at one end and plenty of room for separate activities at the other end

A galley-style Kitchen with adjoining Dining Area

A second-floor Master Bedroom with a children's Dormitory across the hall

A second-floor Deck outside the Master Bedroom

This home comes with a basement foundation.

First floor — 784 sq. ft.

Second floor — 504 sq. ft.

SECOND FLOOR

FIRST FLOOR

Charming Brick Ranch

■ *Total living area 1,782 sq. ft.* ■ *Price Code C* ■

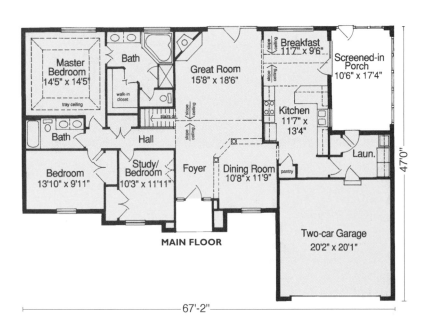

MAIN FLOOR

67'-2"

Main floor — 1,782 sq. ft.
Garage — 407 sq. ft.
Basement — 1,735 sq. ft.

No. 92630

■ **This plan features:**

— Three bedrooms

— Two full baths

■ Sheltered entrance leads into open Foyer and Dining Room defined by columns

■ Vaulted ceiling spans Foyer, Dining Room and Great Room with corner fireplace and atrium door to rear yard

■ Central Kitchen with separate Laundry and Pantry easily serves Dining Room, Breakfast Area and Screened Porch

■ Luxurious Master Bedroom offer tray ceiling and French doors to double vanity, walk-in closet and whirlpool tub

■ Two additional Bedrooms, one which easily converts to a Study, share a full Bath

■ This home comes with a baseme foundation.

■ *Total living area 3,783 sq. ft.* ■ *Price Code K* ■

No. 92237

This plan features:

Four bedrooms

Three full and one half baths

A stone hearth fireplace and built-in book shelves enhance the Living Room

Family Room with a huge fireplace, cathedral ceiling and access to Covered Veranda

Spacious Kitchen with cooktop island/snackbar, built-in Pantry and Breakfast Room

Master Bedroom with a pullman ceiling, Sitting Area, private Covered Patio, two walk-in closets and a whirlpool tub

An optional basement or slab foundation — please specify when ordering.

First floor — 2,804 sq. ft.
Second floor — 979 sq. ft.
Basement — 2,804 sq. ft.
Garage — 802 sq. ft.

SECOND FLOOR

FIRST FLOOR

Three Bedroom Ranch

■ *Total living area 1,575 sq. ft.* ■ *Price Code B* ■

No. 98414

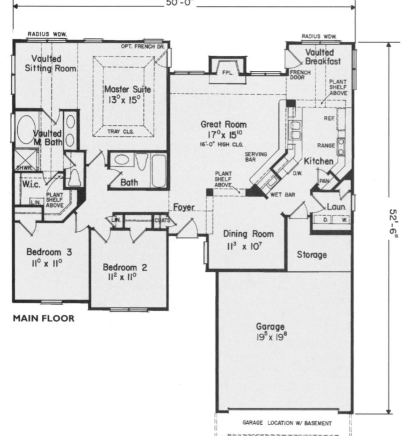

MAIN FLOOR

- 50'-0"
- 52'-6"

RADIUS WDW.

Vaulted Sitting Room

OPT. FRENCH DR.

Master Suite
13⁰ x 15⁰

TRAY CLG.

Vaulted M. Bath

SHWR.

W.i.c.

PLANT SHELF ABOVE

LIN.

Bath

Foyer

LIN.

COATS

Bedroom 3
11⁰ x 11⁰

Bedroom 2
11² x 11⁰

FPL

RADIUS WDW.

Vaulted Breakfast

FRENCH DOOR

PLANT SHELF ABOVE

Great Room
17⁰ x 15¹⁰
16'-0" HIGH CLG.

REF.

RANGE

SERVING BAR

Kitchen

D.W.

PAN.

WET BAR

PLANT SHELF ABOVE

Laun.

D W

Dining Room
11³ x 10⁷

Storage

Garage
19⁵ x 19⁶

GARAGE LOCATION W/ BASEMENT

■ This plan features:

— Three bedrooms

— Two full baths

■ Formal Dining Room enhanced by a plant shelf and a side window

■ Wetbar located between the Kitchen and the Dining Room

■ Built-in Pantry, a double sink and a snack bar highlight the Kitchen

■ Breakfast Room containing a radius window and a French door to the rear yard

■ Large cozy fireplace framed by windows in the Great Room

■ Master Suite with a vaulted ceiling over the sitting area, a Master Bath and a walk-in closet

■ An optional basement or crawlspace foundation available – please specify when ordering

Main floor — 1,575 sq. ft.
Garage — 459 sq. ft.
Basement — 1,658 sq. ft.

High Ceilings and Arched Windows

■ *Total living area 1,502 sq. ft.* ■ *Price Code B* ■

No. 98441

This plan features:

Three bedrooms

Two full baths

Natural illumination streaming into the Dining Room and Sitting Area of the Master Suite

Kitchen with convenient pass-through to the Great Room and a serving bar for the Breakfast Room

Great Room topped by a vaulted ceiling accented by a fireplace and a French door

Decorative columns accenting the entrance of the Dining Room

Tray ceiling over the Master Suite and a vaulted ceiling over the Sitting Room and the Master Bath

An optional basement or crawl space foundation — please specify when ordering

Main floor — 1,502 sq. ft.
Basement — 1,555 sq. ft.
Garage — 448 sq. ft.

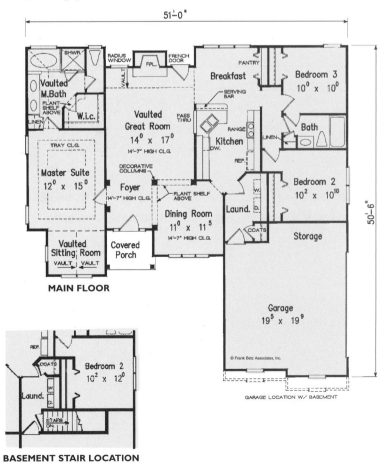

MAIN FLOOR

**BASEMENT STAIR LOCATION
OPTION**

© Frank Betz Associates, Inc.

GARAGE LOCATION W/ BASEMENT

An Estate of Epic Proportion

■ *Total living area 3,936 sq. ft.* ■ *Price Code K* ■

No. 98539

■ **This plan features**

— Four bedrooms

— Two full one three quarter and one half baths

■ Front door opening into a grand Entry way with a 20' ceiling and spiral staircase

■ Living Room with cathedral ceiling and fireplace

■ Walk down the Gallery to the Study with a full wall, built-in bookcase

■ The enormous Master Bedroom has a walk-in closet, sumptuous Bath and a bayed Sitting Area

■ Family Room has a wetbar and a fireplace

■ An optional basement or slab foundation — please specify when ordering

First floor — 2,751 sq. ft.
Second floor — 1,185 sq. ft.
Bonus — 343 sq. ft.
Garage — 790 sq. ft.

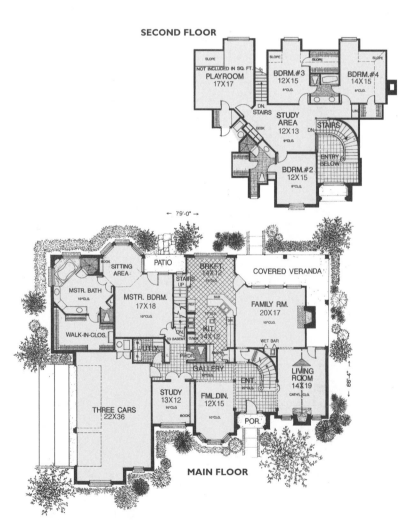

Towering Windows Enhance Elegance

■ *Total living area 2,838 sq. ft.* ■ *Price Code G* ■

No. 93034

This plan features:

- Four bedrooms

- Three full baths

- Designed for a corner or pie-shaped lot

- Spectacular split staircase highlights Foyer

- Expansive Great Room with hearth fireplace opens to formal Dining Room and Patio

- Quiet Study can easily convert to another Bedroom or Home Office

- Secluded Master Suite offers private Porch, two walk-in closets two vanities and a corner whirlpool tub

- Three second floor Bedrooms with walk-in closets, share a balcony and double vanity Bath

An optional basement, slab or crawlspace foundation — please specify when ordering.

First floor — 1,966 sq. ft.
Second floor — 872 sq. ft.
Garage — 569 sq. ft.

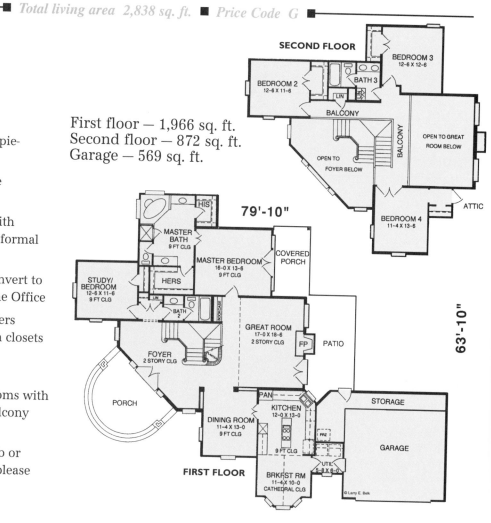

305

Second Floor Balcony Overlooks Great Room

■ *Total living area 1,785 sq. ft.* ■ *Price Code C* ■

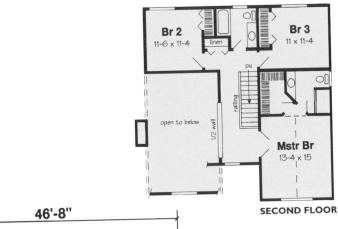

SECOND FLOOR

No. 24610

■ **This plan features:**

— Three bedrooms

— Two full and one half baths

■ A Great Room with a focal point fireplace and a two-story ceiling

■ An efficient Kitchen with an island, double sinks, built-in Pantry and ample storage and counter space

■ A convenient first floor Laundry Room

■ A Master Suite with a private Master Bath and a walk-in closet

■ Two additional Bedrooms with ample closet space that share a full hall Bath

■ An optional basement, slab or crawlspace foundation — please specify when ordering.

FIRST FLOOR

First floor — 891 sq. ft.
Second floor — 894 sq. ft.
Basement — 891 sq. ft.
Garage — 534 sq. ft.

Stone and Siding

■ *Total living area 2,690 sq. ft.* ■ *Price Code F* ■

No. 94810

This plan features:

Four bedrooms

Three full and one half baths

Attractive styling using a combination of stone and siding and a covered Porch add to the curb appeal

Former foyer giving access to the bedroom wing, Library or Activity Room

Activity Room showcasing a focal point fireplace and including direct access to the rear Deck and the Breakfast Room

A secluded Guest Suite is located off the Kitchen Area

Master Suite topped by a tray ceiling and pampered by five-piece Bath

This home comes with a basement foundation.

Main floor — 2,690 sq. ft.
Basement — 2,690 sq. ft.
Garage — 660 sq. ft.

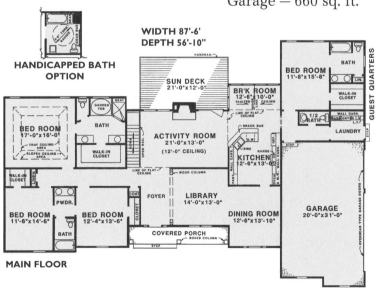

Exciting Ceilings Add Appeal

■ *Total living area 1,475 sq. ft.* ■ *Price Code E* ■

DECK

spa

GARAGE
20-4 x 22-5

storage

fireplace
(cathedral ceiling)

KIT.
10-4 x 13-6

UTIL.

w
d

walk-in
closet

BED RM.
11-4 x 10-0

cl

lin.

bath

GREAT RM.
15-4 x 16-0

cl

MASTER
BED RM.
13-4 x 14-4

54-7

cl

FOYER
15-4 x 3-8

master
bath

BED RM./
STUDY
11-4 x 10-4

PORCH

DINING
10-4 x 12-0

MAIN FLOOR

59-6

© Donald A. Gardner Architects, Inc.

No. 96452

■ **This plan features:**

— Three bedrooms

— Two full baths

■ Open design enhanced by cathedral and tray ceilings above arched windows

■ Foyer with columns defining Great Room with central fireplace and Deck access

■ Ultimate Master Bedroom suite offers walk-in closet, tray ceiling, and whirlpool Bath

■ Alternate foundation options available at an additional charge. call 1.800.235.5700 for more information.

■ This home comes with a crawlspace foundation.

Main floor — 1,475 sq. ft.
Garage & storage — 478 sq. ft.

■ *Total living area 2,647 sq. ft.* ■ *Price Code F* ■

No. 24403

■ **This plan features:**

– Three or four bedrooms

– Two full and one three-quarter baths

■ A large Foyer with an attractive staircase

■ Study/Guest Room with convenient access to a full, hall Bath

■ Expansive Family Room equipped with a massive fireplace with built-in bookshelves

■ Peninsula counter/eating bar, a built-in Pantry, double sink, and ample counter space in the Kitchen

■ A cathedral ceiling crowning the Master Suite

■ An optional basement, slab or crawlspace foundation — please specify when ordering.

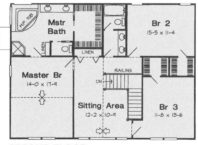

SECOND FLOOR

OPTIONAL CRAWLSPACE/SLAB

First floor — 1,378 sq. ft.
Second floor — 1,269 sq. ft.
Basement — 1,378 sq. ft.
Garage — 717 sq. ft.

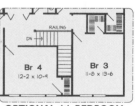

OPTIONAL 4th BEDROOM

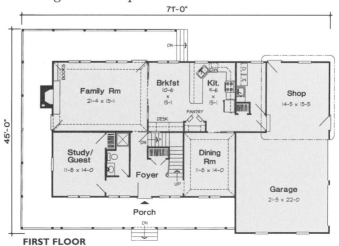

FIRST FLOOR

Luxurious Yet Cozy

■ *Total living area 3,395 sq. ft.* ■ *Price Code I* ■

No. 98403

■ This plan features:

— Four bedrooms

— Three full and one half baths

■ Living Room is enhanced by a fieldstone fireplace and vaulted ceiling

■ Inviting fireplace between windows, and a vaulted ceiling enhance Great Room

■ Kitchen with a work island, serving bar, bright Breakfast Area and walk-in Pantry

■ Corner Master Suite includes a cozy fireplace, a vaulted Sitting Room and a lavish Dressing Area

■ Optional basement, crawlspace or slab foundation — please specify when ordering

First floor — 2,467 sq. ft.
Second floor — 928 sq. ft.
Bonus — 296 sq. ft.
Basement — 2,467 sq. ft.
Garage — 566 sq. ft.

SECOND FLOOR

FIRST FLOOR

European Styling with a Georgian Flair

■ *Total living area 1,873 sq. ft.* ■ *Price Code C* ■

No. 92552

This plan features:

- Four bedrooms

- Two full baths

- Elegant European styling spiced with Georgian Styling

- Arched windows, quoins and shutters on the exterior, a columned covered front and a rear Porch

- Formal foyer gives access to the Dining Room to the left and spacious Den straight ahead

- Kitchen flows into the informal eating area and is separated from the Den by an angled extended counter eating bar

- An optional crawlspace or slab foundation — please specify when ordering.

Main floor — 1,873 sq. ft.
Bonus — 145 sq. ft.
Garage — 613 sq. ft.

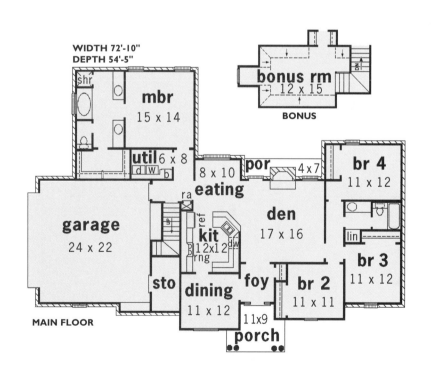

WIDTH 72'-10"
DEPTH 54'-5"

shr

mbr
15 x 14

bonus rm
12 x 15

BONUS

util 6 x 8
d w b

8 x 10

por
4 x 7

br 4
11 x 12

garage
24 x 22

ra
eating

ref
kit
12x12
rng
dw

den
17 x 16

lin

br 3
11 x 12

sto

dining
11 x 12

foy

br 2
11 x 11

11x9
porch

MAIN FLOOR

A Modern Slant On A Country Theme

■ Total living area 1,648 sq. ft. ■ Price Code B ■

No. 96513

■ **This plan features:**

— Three bedrooms

— Two full and one half baths

■ Country styled front Porch highlighting exterior which is enhanced by dormer windows

■ Modern open floor plan for a more spacious feeling

■ Great Room accented by a quaint corner fireplace and a ceiling fan

■ Dining Room flowing from the Great Room for easy entertaining

■ Kitchen graced by natural light from attractive bay window and convenient snack bar for meals on the go

■ An optional slab or crawlspace foundation — please specify when ordering.

Main floor — 1,648 sq. ft.
Garage — 479 sq. ft.

■ *Total living area 2,218 sq. ft.* ■ *Price Code D* ■

No. 90454

■ This plan features:

— Three bedrooms

— Two full baths

■ Large Foyer set between the formal Living and Dining rooms

■ Spacious Great Room adjacent to the open Kitchen/Breakfast Area

■ Secluded Master Bedroom highlighted by the Master Bath with a garden tub, separate shower and his and her vanities

■ Bay window allows bountiful natural light into the Breakfast Area

■ Two additional Bedrooms sharing a full Bath

■ An optional basement or crawlspace foundation — please specify when ordering.

Main floor — 2,218 sq. ft.
Basement — 1,658 sq. ft.
Garage — 528 sq. ft.

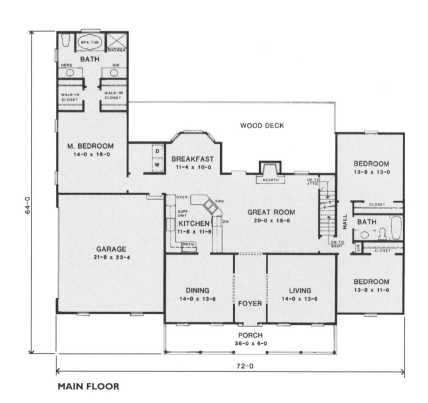

MAIN FLOOR

Farmhouse Flavor

■ *Total living area 1,907 sq. ft.* ■ *Price Code C* ■

No. 10785

■ This plan features:

— Three bedrooms

— Two full and one half baths

■ A inviting wrap-around Porch with old-fashioned charm

■ Two-story Foyer

■ A wood stove in the Living Room that warms the entire house

■ A modern Kitchen flowing easily into the bayed Dining Room

■ A first floor Master Bedroom with private Master Bath

■ Two additional Bedrooms with walk-in closets and cozy gable sitting nooks

■ An optional basement, slab or crawlspace foundation — please specify when ordering.

First floor — 1,269 sq. ft.
Second floor — 638 sq. ft.
Basement — 1,269 sq. ft.

SLAB/CRAWLSPACE OPTION

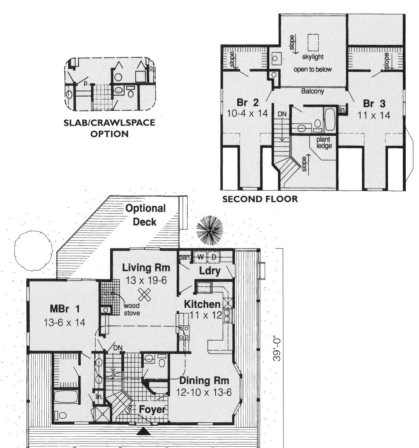

Br 2
10-4 x 14

Br 3
11 x 14

skylight

open to below

Balcony

plant ledge

SECOND FLOOR

Optional Deck

Living Rm
13 x 19-6

Ldr

MBr 1
13-6 x 14

wood stove

Kitchen
11 x 12

Dining Rm
12-10 x 13-6

Foyer

39'-0"

47'-0"

FIRST FLOOR

■ *Total living area 2,091 sq. ft.* ■ *Price Code D* ■

No. 93212

■ This plan features:

— Three bedrooms

— Two full and one half baths

■ Living Room with a cozy fireplace

■ A formal Dining Room with a bay window and direct access to the Sun Deck

■ U-shaped Kitchen efficiently arranged with ample work space

■ Master Suite with an elegant private Bath complete with jacuzzi and a step-in shower

■ A future Bonus Room to finish, tailored to your needs

■ An optional basement, crawlspace or slab foundation — please specify when ordering

First floor — 1,362 sq. ft.
Second floor — 729 sq. ft.
Bonus room — 384 sq. ft.
Basement — 988 sq. ft.
Garage — 559 sq. ft.

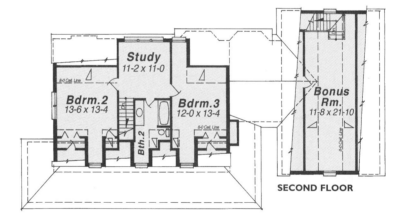

SECOND FLOOR

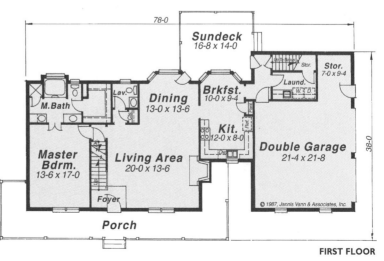

FIRST FLOOR

Country-Style Home for Quality Living

■ Total living area 2,466 sq. ft. ■ Price Code E ■

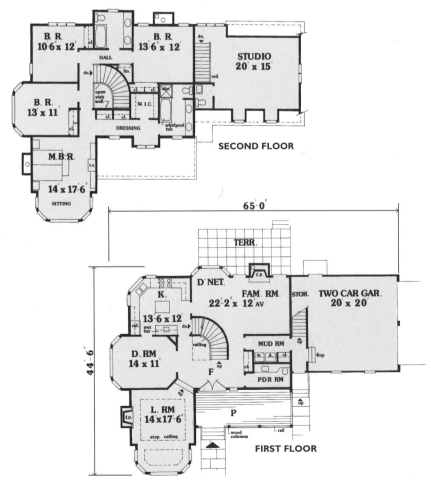

SECOND FLOOR

- B. R. 10-6 x 12
- B. R. 13-6 x 12
- STUDIO 20' x 15'
- HALL
- B. R. 13' x 11'
- W. I. C.
- whirlpool tub
- DRESSING
- open stair well
- M.B.R.
- 14' x 17-6
- SITTING

FIRST FLOOR

- 65'-0"
- 44'-6'
- TERR.
- D'NET.
- K.
- 13-6 x 12
- FAM. RM. 22'-2 x 12' AV
- STOR.
- TWO CAR GAR. 20' x 20'
- D. RM 14 x 11'
- railing
- MUD RM
- PDR RM
- L. RM 14 x 17'-6'
- step ceiling
- P
- wood columns
- rail

No. 99640

■ **This plan features:**

— Four bedrooms

— Two full and two half baths

■ A spacious central Foyer leads to all rooms

■ A sunken Living Room, enhanced by a focal point fireplace and a large windowed bay

■ An elegant formal Dining Room with interior corners angled to form an octagon

■ A luxurious Master Bedroom includes a Dressing Area, a walk-in closet and a deluxe Bath

■ A Studio area above the Garage that includes a half Bath

■ An optional basement or slab foundation — please specify when ordering.

First floor — 1,217 sq. ft.
Second floor — 1,249 sq. ft.
Basement — 1,217 sq. ft.
Garage — 431 sq. ft.

Easy Living Plan

■ *Total living area 1,600 sq. ft.* ■ *Price Code B* ■

No. 98406

This plan features:

Three bedrooms

Two full and one half baths

Kitchen, Breakfast Bay, and Family Room blend into a spacious open Living Area

Convenient Laundry Center is tucked into the rear of the Kitchen

Luxurious Master Suite is topped by a tray ceiling while a vaulted ceiling is in the Bath

Two roomy secondary Bedrooms share the full Bath in the hall

An optional basement, crawlspace or slab foundation — please specify when ordering

First floor — 828 sq. ft.
Second floor — 772 sq. ft.
Basement — 828 sq. ft.
Garage — 473 sq. ft.

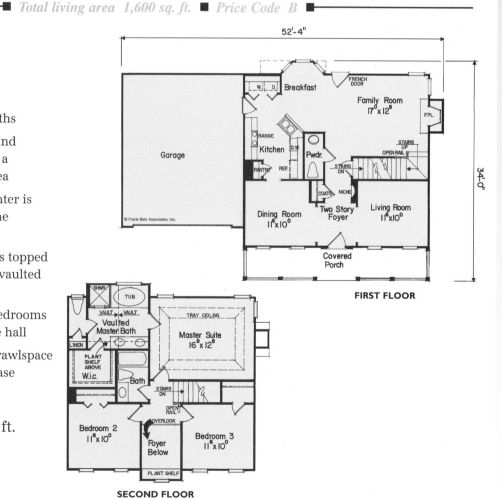

FIRST FLOOR

SECOND FLOOR

Family Favorite

■ Total living area 1,359 sq. ft. ■ Price Code A ■

No. 20156

■ **This plan features:**

— Three bedrooms

— Two full baths

■ An open arrangement with the Dining Room that combines with ten foot ceilings to make the Living Room seem more spacious

■ An efficient, compact Kitchen with a built-in Pantry and peninsula counter

■ A Master Suite with a romantic window seat, a compartmentalized private Bath and a walk-in closet

■ Two additional Bedrooms that share a full hall Bath

■ An optional basement, slab or crawlspace foundation — please specify when ordering.

Main floor — 1,359 sq. ft.
Basement — 1,359 sq. ft.
Garage — 501 sq. ft.

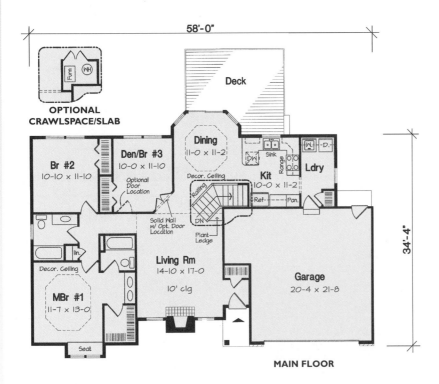

OPTIONAL CRAWLSPACE/SLAB

58'-0"

34'-4"

Deck

Dining
11-0 x 11-2
Decor. Ceiling

Br #2
10-10 x 11-10

Den/Br #3
10-0 x 11-10

Optional Door Location

Kit
10-0 x 11-2

Ldry

Sink

Range

Ret.

Pan.

Railing

DN

Plant Ledge

Solid Wall w/ Opt. Door Location

Decor. Ceiling

MBr #1
11-7 x 13-0

Living Rm
14-10 x 17-0

10' clg

Garage
20-4 x 21-8

Seat

MAIN FLOOR

Bathed in Natural Light

■ *Total living area 1,619 sq. ft.* ■ *Price Code B* ■

No. 98416

This plan features:

Three bedrooms

Two full and one half baths

A high arched window illuminates the Foyer and adds style to the exterior of the home

Vaulted ceilings in the formal Dining Room, Breakfast Room and Great Room create volume

The Master Suite is crowned with a decorative tray ceiling

The Master Bath has a double vanity, oval tub, separate shower and a walk-in closet

The Loft, with the option of becoming a fourth Bedroom, highlights the second floor

An optional basement or crawl space foundation — please specify when ordering

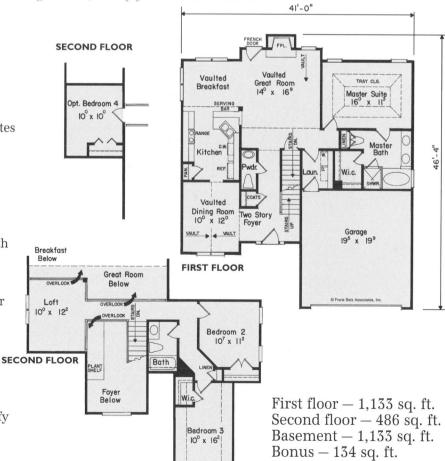

SECOND FLOOR

Opt. Bedroom 4
10⁰ x 10⁰

FIRST FLOOR

41'-0"

46'-4"

FRENCH DOOR   FPL.

Vaulted Breakfast

Vaulted Great Room
14⁰ x 16⁹

VAULT

TRAY CLG.
Master Suite
16⁰ x 11⁰

SERVING BAR

RANGE

Kitchen

D.W.

REF.

PAN.

Pwdr.

STAIRS DN.

LINEN

W.

Master Bath

Laun.

W.i.c.

SHWR

Vaulted Dining Room
10⁰ x 12⁰

COATS

Two Story Foyer

STAIRS UP

Garage
19⁰ x 19⁹

VAULT   VAULT

© Frank Betz Associates, Inc.

Breakfast Below

OVERLOOK

Great Room Below

OVERLOOK

Loft
10⁰ x 12²

STAIRS DN.

OVERLOOK

Bedroom 2
10⁷ x 11²

SECOND FLOOR

PLANT SHELF

Foyer Below

Bath

LINEN

W.i.c.

Bedroom 3
10⁰ x 16²

First floor — 1,133 sq. ft.
Second floor — 486 sq. ft.
Basement — 1,133 sq. ft.
Bonus — 134 sq. ft.
Garage — 406 sq. ft.

Easy Everyday Living and Entertaining

■ *Total living area 1,664 sq. ft.* ■ *Price Code B* ■

No. 92238

■ This plan features:

— Three bedrooms

— Two full baths

■ Front entrance accented by segmented arches, sidelight and transom windows

■ Open Living Room with focal point fireplace, wetbar and access to Patio

■ Efficient Kitchen with a cooktop island, walk-in Pantry and Utility Area with a Garage entry

■ Large walk-in closet, double vanity Bath and access to Patio featured in the Master Bedroom suite

■ An optional basement, slab or crawlspace foundation — please specify when ordering.

Main floor — 1,664 sq. ft.
Basement — 1,600 sq. ft.
Garage — 440 sq. ft.

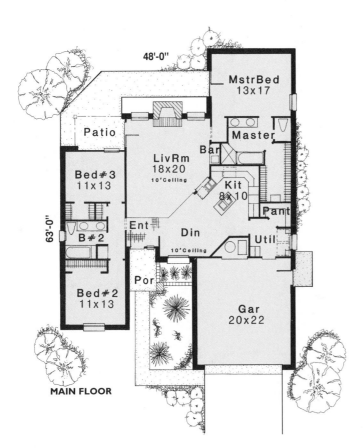

MAIN FLOOR

Open Plan is Full of Air & Light

■ Total living area 1,505 sq. ft. ■ Price Code B ■

No. 98463

■ This plan features:

— Three bedrooms

— Two full and one half baths

■ Foyer open to the Family Room and highlighted by a fireplace

■ Dining Room with a sliding glass door to rear yard adjoins Family Room

■ Second floor Master Suite topped by tray ceiling over the Bedroom and a vaulted ceiling over the lavish Bath

■ Two additional Bedrooms sharing a full Bath in the hall

■ An optional basement or crawlspace foundation — please specify when ordering

First floor — 767 sq. ft.
Second floor — 738 sq. ft.
Bonus room — 240 sq. ft.
Basement — 767 sq. ft.
Garage — 480 sq. ft.

SECOND FLOOR

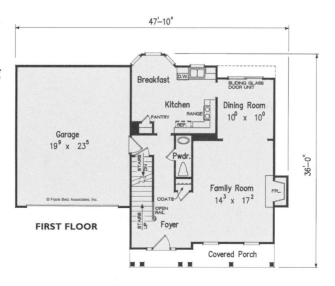

FIRST FLOOR

Small But Room To Grow

■ *Total living area 1,607 sq. ft.* ■ *Price Code B* ■

No. 20205

■ **This plan features:**

— Three bedrooms

— Two full baths

■ A Master Suite with a vaulted ceiling and private skylit Bath

■ A fireplaced Living Room with a sloped ceiling

■ Efficient Kitchen with a Breakfast Nook

■ Options for growth on the lower level

■ This home comes with a basemen foundation.

Main floor — 1,321 sq. ft.
Lower floor — 286 sq. ft.
Garage — 655 sq. ft.

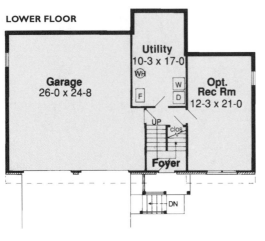

LOWER FLOOR

Garage
26-0 x 24-8

Utility
10-3 x 17-0

Opt.
Rec Rm
12-3 x 21-0

Foyer

48'-0"

32'-0"

MBr
13 x 13-5
vaulted clg

Brkfst

patio

Kitchen
10-4
x
9-10

w.i. cl
shelf

Hall

Living Rm
12-8 x 23-4

Br 2
11-10 x 10

Br 1
11-10 x 10

Foyer

MAIN FLOOR

Inviting Wrap-Around Porch

■ *Total living area 1,716 sq. ft.* ■ *Price Code B* ■

No. 93909

■ **This plan features:**

— Three bedrooms

— Two full baths

■ A warm and inviting welcome, achieved by a wrap-around Porch

■ A corner gas fireplace and two skylights highlighted in the Great Room

■ Flowing from the Great Room, the Dining Room naturally lighted by the sliding glass doors leads to a rear Deck and a skylight above

■ A well-appointed, U-shaped Kitchen separated from the Dining Room by a breakfast bar contains another skylight

■ A luxurious Master Bedroom equipped with a plush Bath

■ Two additional Bedrooms sharing the full Bath in the hall and receiving light from the dormers

■ This home comes with a basement foundation.

Main floor — 1,716 sq. ft.

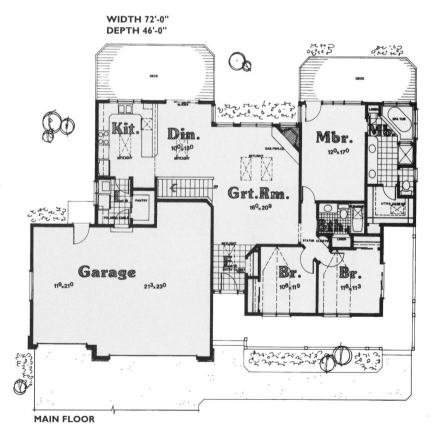

WIDTH 72'-0"
DEPTH 46'-0"

MAIN FLOOR

Stately Colonial Home

■ *Total living area 2,959 sq. ft.* ■ *Price Code G* ■

SECOND FLOOR

- BDRM.#2 13X11 8" CLG.
- BDRM.#3 13X12 8" CLG.
- BATH
- LINENS
- BALCONY
- STAIRS DOWN
- STOR.
- RAIL'G.
- DBL. BATH
- LIN.
- CLO.
- ENTRY BELOW
- RAIL'G.
- BDRM.#4 13X12 8" CLG.
- LOFT AREA 13X14 8" CLG.
- PLANT LEDGE
- PORCH BELOW

WIDTH 73'-4"
DEPTH 44'-1"

- PATIO AREA
- COVERED AREA
- PATIO
- THREE CAR TANDEM GARAGE 22X40 9" CLG.
- BREAKFAST 13X12 9" CLG.
- ISLAND
- GREAT ROOM 19X16 9" CLG.
- MSTR. BDRM. 18X14 VAULTED CLG. 8" TO 11"
- KITCHEN 13X13 9" CLG.
- DW
- W. D.
- UTLY.
- PANT.
- HALL
- NICHE
- PWDR.
- MSTR. BATH
- LIN.
- WALK-IN CLOSET
- SHOP AREA
- FORMAL DINING 13X13 9" CLG.
- ENT. 13' CLG.
- UP STAIRS
- FORMAL LIVING 13X13 9" CLG.
- PORCH

FIRST FLOOR

324

No. 98534

■ This plan features:

— Four bedrooms

— Three full and one half baths

■ Stately columns and lovely arched windows

■ The Entry is highlighted by a palladian window, a plant shelf and an angled staircase

■ The formal Living and Dining Rooms located off the Entry for ease in entertaining

■ Great Room has a fireplace and opens to Kitchen/Breakfast Area and the Patio

■ The Master Bedroom wing offers Patio access, a luxurious Bath and a walk-in closet

■ An optional slab or combo basement/crawlspace foundation — please specify when ordering.

First floor — 1,848 sq. ft.
Second floor — 1,111 sq. ft.
Garage & shop — 722 sq. ft.

Attractive Ceiling Treatments and Open Layout

■ *Total living area   1,654 sq. ft.* ■ *Price Code B* ■

No. 96506

■ **This plan features:**

— Three bedrooms

— Two full and one half baths

■ Great Room and Master Suite with step-up ceiling treatments

■ A cozy fireplace providing warm focal point in the Great Room

■ Open layout between Kitchen, Dining and Great Room lending a more spacious feeling

■ Five-piece, private Bath and walk-in closet pampering Master Suite

■ Two additional Bedrooms located at opposite end of home from Master Suite

■ An optional slab or crawlspace foundation — please specify when ordering.

Main floor — 1,654 sq. ft.
Garage — 480 sq. ft.

MAIN FLOOR

Old-Fashioned Country Porch

■ *Total living area 1,668 sq. ft.* ■ *Price Code B* ■

No. 93219

■ This plan features:

— Three bedrooms

— Two full and one half baths

■ A Traditional front Porch, with matching dormers above and a Garage hidden below, leading into an open, contemporary layout

■ A Living Area with a cozy fireplace visible from the Dining Room for warm entertaining

■ An efficient U-shaped Kitchen featuring a corner, double sink and pass-thru to the Dining Room

■ A convenient half Bath with a laundry center on the first floor

■ A spacious, first floor Master Suite with a lavish Bath including a double vanity, walk-in closet and an oval, corner window tub

■ This home comes with a basement foundation.

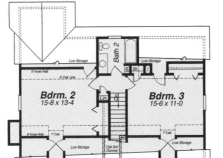

SECOND FLOOR

Bdrm. 2
15-8 x 13-4

Bdrm. 3
15-6 x 11-0

Bath 2

Sundeck
16-0 x 12-0

Brkfst.
9-0 x 8-0

Kit.
9-0 x 9-6

Dining
9-10 x 11-4

Lav.

M.Bath

Living Area
18-0 x 13-6

Master
Bdrm.
15-6 x 13-6

©1983, Jannis Vann & Associates, Inc.

Porch

38-0

40-4

FIRST FLOOR

First floor — 1,057 sq. ft.
Second floor — 611 sq. ft.
Basement — 511 sq. ft.
Garage — 546 sq. ft.

■ *Total living area 1,808 sq. ft.* ■ *Price Code C* ■

No. 93413

■ This plan features:

- Three bedrooms

- Two full and one half baths

- The Foyer is naturally lit by a dormer window above

- Family Room is highlighted by two front windows and a fireplace

- Kitchen includes an angled extended counter/snack bar and an abundance of counter/cabinet space

- Dining Area opens to the Kitchen, for a more spacious feeling

- The roomy Master Suite is located on the first floor and has a private five-piece Bath plus a walk-in closet

- Laundry Room doubles as a mudroom from the side entrance

- This home comes with a basement foundation.

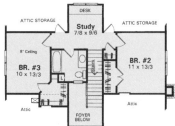

SECOND FLOOR

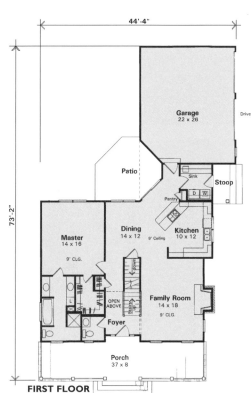

FIRST FLOOR

First floor — 1,271 sq. ft.
Second floor — 537 sq. ft.
Basement — 1,271 sq. ft.
Garage — 555 sq. ft.

Total living area 2,411 sq. ft. ■ Price Code E

ALTERNATE KITCHEN

SECOND FLOOR

OPTIONAL RETREAT

FIRST FLOOR

No. 24262

■ **This plan features:**

— Four bedrooms

— Two full and one half baths

■ A see-through fireplace between the Living Room and the Family Room

■ A Master Bedroom with a vaulted ceiling

■ A Master Bath with large double vanity, linen closet, corner tub, separate shower, compartmented toilet and huge walk-in closet

■ Three additional Bedrooms, one with walk-in closet, share full hall Bath

■ An optional basement, slab or crawlspace foundation — please specify when ordering.

First floor — 1,241 sq. ft.
Second floor — 1,170 sq. ft.
Garage — 500 sq. ft.

L-Shaped Front Porch

■ *Total living area 1,280 sq. ft.* ■ • *Price Code A* ■ ■

No. 98747

■ **This plan features:**

- Three bedrooms

- Two full baths

■ Attractive wood siding and a large L-shaped covered Porch

■ Front Entry leading to generous Living Room with a vaulted ceiling

■ Large two-car Garage with access through Utility Room

■ Roomy secondary Bedrooms share the full Bath in the hall

■ Vaulted ceiling adds volume to the Dining Room

■ Master Suite in an isolated location enhanced by abundant closet space, separate vanity, and linen storage

■ This home comes with a crawlspace foundation.

ain floor — 1,280 sq. ft.

Family-Sized Accommodations

■ *Total living area 1,874 sq. ft.* ■ *Price Code C* ■

SECOND FLOOR

- Family Room Below
- VAULT
- Bedroom 3/ Opt. Loft 10⁰ x 10¹
- Bedroom 4 10⁰ x 10¹
- OPEN RAIL W/LOFT
- STAIRS DN.
- LINEN
- Bath
- Foyer Below
- VAULT
- Bedroom 2 11⁰ x 10⁰
- Opt. Bonus Room 10⁹ x 13⁶

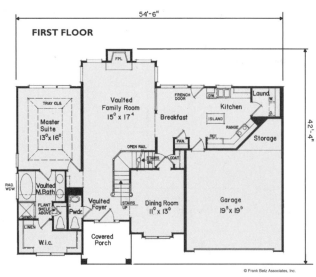

FIRST FLOOR

54'-6"

42'-4"

- TRAY CLG.
- Master Suite 13⁰ x 16⁰
- Vaulted Family Room 15⁰ x 17⁴
- Breakfast
- FPL
- FRENCH DOOR
- DW
- Kitchen
- Laund. W
- ISLAND
- RANGE
- REF.
- Storage
- OPEN RAIL
- STAIRS DN.
- PAN.
- COAT
- RAD. WDW.
- Vaulted M.Bath
- PLANT SHELF ABOVE
- Pwdr.
- Vaulted Foyer
- STAIRS UP
- Dining Room 11⁰ x 13⁰
- Garage 19⁸ x 19⁹
- LINEN
- W.i.c.
- Covered Porch

© Frank Betz Associates, Inc.

No. 98454

■ This plan features:

— Four bedrooms

— Two full and one half baths

■ A spacious feeling provided by a vaulted ceiling in Foyer

■ A fireplace is nestled by an alcove of windows in the Family Room

■ An angled Kitchen, with a work island and a Pantry, easily serves the Breakfast Area and the Dining Room

■ The Master Bedroom is accented by a tray ceiling, a lavish Bath, and a walk-in closet

■ An optional basement or crawlspace foundation — please specify when ordering.

First floor — 1,320 sq. ft.
Second floor — 554 sq. ft.
Bonus room — 155 sq. ft.
Basement — 1,320 sq. ft.
Garage — 406 sq. ft.

One-Story Country Home

■ *Total living area 1,367 sq. ft.* ■ *Price Code A* ■

No. 99639

■ **This plan features:**

- Three bedrooms

- Two full baths

- A Living Room with an imposing high ceiling that slopes down to a normal height of eight feet, focusing on the decorative heat-circulating fireplace at the rear wall

- A Dinette Area for informal eating in the Kitchen that can comfortably seat six people

- A Master Suite arranged with a large Dressing Area that has a walk-in closet plus two linear closets and space for a vanity

- An optional basement or slab foundation — please specify when ordering.

- Main floor — 1,367 sq. ft.
- Basement — 1,267 sq. ft.
- Garage — 431 sq. ft.

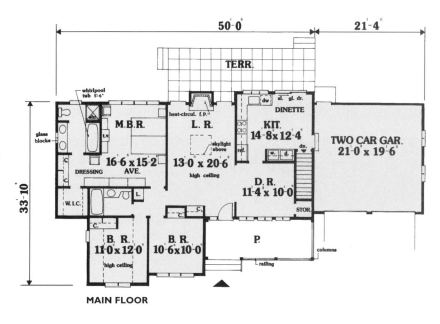

MAIN FLOOR

Everything You Need...
...to Make Your Dream Come True!

You pay only a fraction of the original cost for home designs by respected professionals.

You've Picked Your Dream Home!

You can imagine your new home situated on your lot in the morning sunlight. You can visualize living there, enjoying your family, entertaining friends and celebrating holidays. All that remains are the details. That's where we can help. Whether you plan to build it yourself, act as your own general contractor or hire a professional builder, your Garlinghouse Co. home plans will provide the perfect design and specifications to help make your dream home a reality.

We can offer you an array of additional products and services to help you with your planning needs. We can supply materials lists, construction cost estimates based on your local material and labor costs and modifications to your selected plan if you would like.

For over 90 years, homeowners and builders have relied on us for accurate, complete, professional blueprints. Our plans help you get results fast... and save money, too! These pages will give you all the information you need to order. So get started now... We know you'll love your new Garlinghouse home!

Sincerely,

James D. McNair III

Chief Executive Officer

EXTERIOR ELEVATIONS

Elevations are scaled drawings of the front, rear, left, and right sides of a home. All of the necessary information pertaining to the exterior finish materials, roof pitches, and exterior height dimensions of your home are defined.

CABINET PLANS

These plans, or in some cases elevations, will detail the layout of the kitchen and bathroom cabinets at a larger scale. This gives you an accurate layout for your cabinets or an ideal starting point for a modified custom cabinet design. Available for most plans. You may also show the floor plan without a cabinet layout. This will allow you to start from scratch and design your own dream kitchen.

TYPICAL WALL SECTION

This section is provided to help your builder understand the structural components and materials used to construct the exterior walls of your home. This section will address insulation, roof components, and interior and exterior wall finishes. Your plans will be designed with either 2x4 or 2x6 exterior walls, but most professional contractors can easily adapt the plans to the wall thickness you require.

FIREPLACE DETAILS

If the home you have chosen includes a fireplace, the fireplace detail will show typical methods to construct the firebox, hearth and flue chase for masonry units, or a wood frame chase for a zero-clearance unit. Available for most plans.

FOUNDATION PLAN

These plans will accurately dimension the footprint of your home including load bearing points and beam placement if applicable. The foundation style will vary from plan to plan. Your local climatic conditions will dictate whether a basement, slab or crawlspace is best suited for your area. In most cases, if your plan comes with one foundation style, a professional contractor can easily adapt the foundation plan to an alternate style.

ROOF PLAN

The information necessary to construct the roof will be included with your home plans. Some plans will reference roof trusses, while many others contain schematic framing plans. These framing plans will indicate the lumber sizes necessary for the rafters and ridgeboards based on the designated roof loads.

TYPICAL CROSS SECTION

A cut-away cross-section through the entire home shows your building contractor the exact correlation of construction components at all levels of the house. It will help to clarify the load bearing points from the roof all the way down to the basement. Available for most plans.

DETAILED FLOOR PLANS

The floor plans of your home accurately dimension the positioning of all walls, doors, windows, stairs and permanent fixtures. They will show you the relationship and dimensions of rooms, closets and traffic patterns. The schematic of the electrical layout may be included in the plan. This layout is clearly represented and does not hinder the clarity of other pertinent information shown. All these details will help your builder properly construct your new home.

STAIR DETAILS

If stairs are an element of the design you have chosen, the plans will show the necessary information to build these, either through a stair cross section, or on the floor plans. Either way, the information provides your builders the essential reference points that they need to build the stairs.

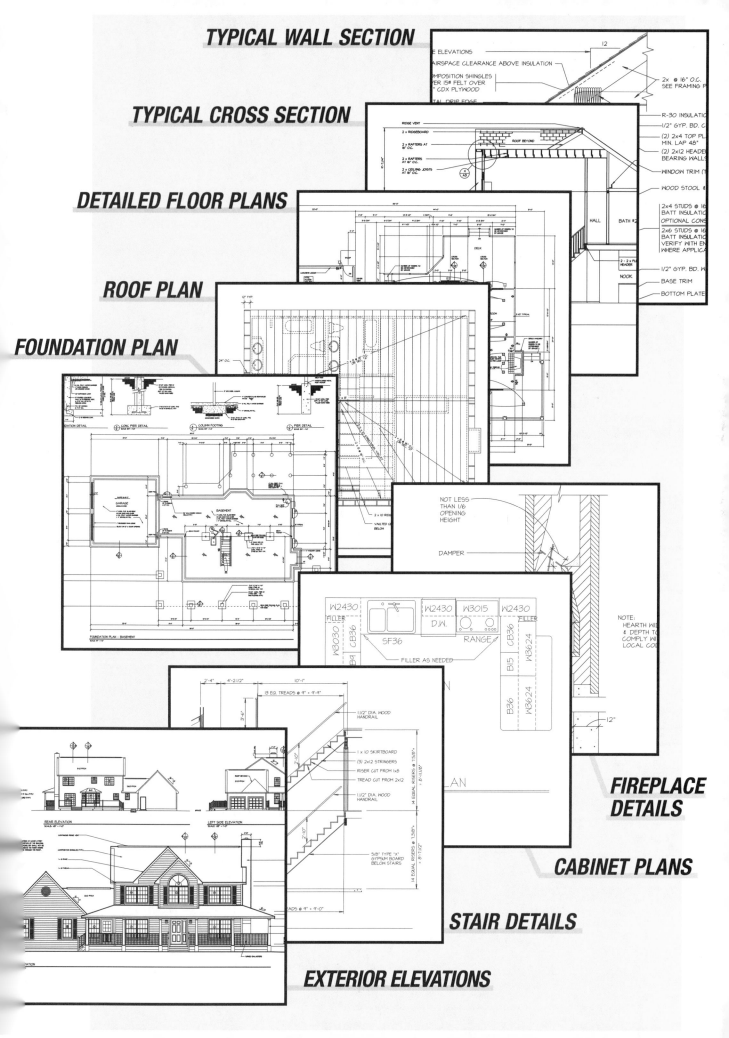

TYPICAL WALL SECTION

TYPICAL CROSS SECTION

DETAILED FLOOR PLANS

ROOF PLAN

FOUNDATION PLAN

FIREPLACE DETAILS

CABINET PLANS

STAIR DETAILS

EXTERIOR ELEVATIONS

Garlinghouse Options & Extras ...Make Your Dream A Home

Reversed Plans Can Make Your Dream Home Just Right!

"That's our dream home...if only the garage were on the other side!"

You could have exactly the home you want by flipping it end-for-end. Check it out by holding your dream home page of this book up to a mirror. Then simply order your plans "reversed." We'll send you one full set of mirror-image plans (with the writing backwards) as a master guide for you and your builder.

The remaining sets of your order will come as shown in this book so the dimensions and specifications are easily read on the job site...but most plans in our collection come stamped "REVERSED" so there is no construction confusion.

As Shown   Reversed

We can only send reversed plans with multiple-set orders. There is a $50 charge for this service.

Some plans in our collection are available in Right Reading Reverse. Right Reading Reverse plans will show your home in reverse, with the writing on the plan being readable. This easy-to-read format will save you valuable time and money. Please contact our Customer Service Department at (860) 659-5667 to check for Right Reading Reverse availability. (There is a $135 charge for this service.)

Specifications & Contract Form

We send this form to you free of charge with your home plan order. The form is designed to be filled in by you or your contractor with the exact materials to use in the construction of your new home. Once signed by you and your contractor it will provide you with peace of mind throughout the construction process.

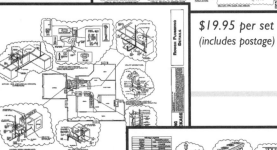

$19.95 per set
(includes postage)

Remember To Order Your Materials List

It'll help you save money. Available at a modest additional charge, the Materials List gives the quantity, dimensions, and specifications for the major materials needed to build your home. You will get faster, more accurate bids from your contractors and building suppliers — and avoid paying for unused materials and waste. Materials Lists are available for all home plans except as otherwise indicated, but can only be ordered with a set of home plans. Due to differences in regional requirements and homeowner or builder preferences... electrical, plumbing and heating/air conditioning equipment specifications are not designed specifically for each plan. However, non-plan specific detailed typical prints of residential electrical, plumbing and construction guidelines can be provided. Please see below for additional information.

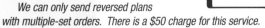

Detail Plans Provide Valuable Information About Construction Techniques

Because local codes and requirements vary greatly, we recommend that you obtain drawings and bids from licensed contractors to do your mechanical plans. However, if you want to know more about techniques — and deal more confidently with subcontractors — we offer these remarkably useful detail sheets. These detail sheets will aid in your understanding of these technical subjects. **The detail sheets are not specific to any one home plan and should be used only as a general reference guide.**

RESIDENTIAL CONSTRUCTION DETAILS

Ten sheets that cover the essentials of stick-built residential home construction. Details foundation options — poured concrete basement, concrete block, or monolithic concrete slab. Shows all aspects of floor, wall and roof framing. Provides details for roof dormers, overhangs, chimneys and skylights. Conforms to requirements of Uniform Building code or BOCA code. Includes a quick index and a glossary of terms.

RESIDENTIAL PLUMBING DETAILS

Eight sheets packed with information detailing pipe installation methods, fittings, and sized. Details plumbing hook-ups for toilets, sinks, washers, sump pumps, and septic system construction. Conforms to requirements of National Plumbing code. Color coded with a glossary of terms and quick index.

RESIDENTIAL ELECTRICAL DETAILS

Eight sheets that cover all aspects of residential wiring, from simple switch wiring to service entrance connections. Details distribution panel layout with outlet and switch schematics, circuit breaker and wiring installation methods, and ground fault interrupter specifications. Conforms to requirements of National Electrical Code. Color coded with a glossary of terms.

Modifying Your Favorite Design, Made *EASY!*

OPTION #1

Modifying Your Garlinghouse Home Plan

Simple modifications to your dream home, including minor non-structural changes and material substitutions, can be made between you and your builder by marking the changes directly on your blueprints. However, if you are considering making significant changes to your chosen design, we recommend that you use the services of The Garlinghouse Design Staff. We will help take your ideas and turn them into a reality, just the way you want. Here's our procedure!

When you place your Vellum order, you may also request a free Garlinghouse Modification Kit. In this kit, you will receive a red marking pencil, furniture cut-out sheet, ruler, a self addressed mailing label and a form for specifying any additional notes or drawings that will help us understand your design ideas. Mark your desired changes directly on the Vellum drawings. NOTE: Please use only a **red pencil** to mark your desired changes on the Vellum. Then, return the redlined Vellum set in the original box to us. **IMPORTANT**: Please **roll** the Vellums for shipping, **do not fold** the Vellums for shipping.

We also offer modification estimates. We will provide you with an estimate to draft your changes based on your specific modifications before you purchase the vellums, for a $50 fee. After you receive your estimate, if you decide to have us do the changes, the $50 estimate fee will be deducted from the cost of your modifications. If, however, you choose to use a different service, the $50 estimate fee is non-refundable. (Note: Personal checks cannot be accepted for the estimate.)

Within 5 days of receipt of your plans, you will be contacted by the Design Staff with an estimate for the design services to draw those changes. A 50% deposit is required before we begin making the actual modifications to your plans.

Once the design changes have been completed to your vellum plan, a representative will call to inform you that your modified Vellum plan is complete and will be shipped as soon as the final payment has been made. For additional information call us at 1-860-659-5667. Please refer to the Modification Pricing Guide for estimated modification costs.

OPTION #2

Reproducible Vellums for Local Modification Ease

If you decide not to use Garlinghouse for your modifications, we recommend that you follow our same procedure of purchasing our Vellums. You then have the option of using the services of the original designer of the plan, a local professional designer, or architect to make the modifications to your plan.

With a Vellum copy of our plans, a design professional can alter the drawings just the way you want, then can print as many copies of the modified plans as you need to build your house. And, since you have already started with our complete detailed plans, the cost of those expensive professional services will be significantly less than starting from scratch. Refer to the price schedule for Vellum costs.

IMPORTANT RETURN POLICY: Upon receipt of your Vellums, if for some reason you decide you do not want modified plan, then simply return the Kit and the unopened Vellums. Reproducible Vellum copies of our home plans are copyright protected and only sold under the terms of a license agreement that you will receive with your order. Should you not agree to the terms, then the Vellums may be exchanged, less the shipping and handling charges, and a 20% exchange fee. For any additional information, please call us at 1-860-659-5667.

CATEGORIES	ESTIMATED COST
KITCHEN LAYOUT — PLAN AND ELEVATION	$175.00
BATHROOM LAYOUT — PLAN AND ELEVATION	$175.00
FIREPLACE PLAN AND DETAILS	$200.00
INTERIOR ELEVATION	$125.00
EXTERIOR ELEVATION — MATERIAL CHANGE	$140.00
EXTERIOR ELEVATION — ADD BRICK OR STONE	$400.00
EXTERIOR ELEVATION — STYLE CHANGE	$450.00
NON BEARING WALLS (INTERIOR)	$200.00
BEARING AND/OR EXTERIOR WALLS	$325.00
WALL FRAMING CHANGE — 2X4 TO 2X6 OR 2X6 TO 2X4	$240.00
ADD/REDUCE LIVING SPACE — SQUARE FOOTAGE	QUOTE REQUIRED
NEW MATERIALS LIST	QUOTE REQUIRED
CHANGE TRUSSES TO RAFTERS OR CHANGE ROOF PITCH	$300.00
FRAMING PLAN CHANGES	$325.00
GARAGE CHANGES	$325.00
ADD A FOUNDATION OPTION	$300.00
FOUNDATION CHANGES	$250.00
RIGHT READING PLAN REVERSE	$575.00
ARCHITECTS SEAL (Available for most states.)	$300.00
ENERGY CERTIFICATE	$150.00
LIGHT AND VENTILATION SCHEDULE	$150.00

Questions?

Call our customer service department at *1-860-659 5667*

"How to obtain a construction cost calculation based on labor rates and building material costs in <u>your</u> Zip Code area!"

ZIP-QUOTE!
HOME COST CALCULATOR

ZIP QUOTE
HOME COST CALCULATOR

WHY?

Do you wish you could quickly find out the building cost for your new home without waiting for a contractor to compile hundreds of bids? Would you like to have a benchmark to compare your contractor(s) bids against? **Well, Now You Can!!,** with **Zip-Quote** Home Cost Calculator. Zip-Quote is only available for zip code areas within the United States.

HOW?

Our new **Zip-Quote** Home Cost Calculator will enable you to obtain the calculated building cost to construct your new home, based on labor rates and building material costs within your zip code area, without the normal delays or hassles usually associated with the bidding process. Zip-Quote can be purchased in two separate formats, an itemized or a bottom line format.

"How does **Zip-Quote** actually work?" When you call to order, you must choose from the options available, for your specific home, in order for us to process your order. Once we receive your **Zip-Quote** order, we process your specific home plan building materials list through our Home Cost Calculator which contains up-to-date rates for all residential labor trades and building material costs in your zip code area. "The result?" A calculated cost to build your dream home in your zip code area. This calculation will help you (as a consumer or a builder) evaluate your building budget. This is a valuable tool for anyone considering building a new home.

All database information for our calculations is furnished by Marshall & Swift, L.P. For over 60 years, Marshall & Swift L.P. has been a leading provider of cost data to professionals in all aspects of the construction and remodeling industries.

OPTION 1

The **Itemized Zip-Quote** is a detailed building material list. Each building material list line item will separately state the labor cost, material cost and equipment cost (if applicable) for the use of that building material in the construction process. Each category within the building material list will be subtotaled and the entire Itemized cost calculation totaled at the end. This building materials list will be summarized by the individual building categories and will have additional columns where you can enter data from your contractor's estimates for a cost comparison between the different suppliers and contractors who will actually quote you their products and services.

OPTION 2

The **Bottom Line Zip-Quote** is a one line summarized total cost for the home plan of your choice. This cost calculation is also based on the labor cost, material cost and equipment cost (if applicable) within your local zip code area.

COST

The price of your **Itemized Zip-Quote** is based upon the pricing schedule of the plan you have selected, in addition to the price of the materials list. Please refer to the pricing schedule on our order form. The price of your initial **Bottom Line Zip-Quote** is $29.95. Each additional **Bottom Line Zip-Quote** ordered in conjunction with the initial order is only $14.95. **Bottom Line Zip-Quote** may be purchased separately and does NOT have to be purchased in conjunction with a home plan order.

FYI

An **Itemized Zip-Quote** Home Cost Calculation can ONLY be purchased in conjunction with a Home Plan order. The **Itemized Zip-Quote** can not be purchased separately. The **Bottom Line Zip-Quote** can be purchased separately and doesn't have to be purchased in conjunction with a home plan order. Please consult with a sales representative for current availability. If you find within 60 days of your order date that you will be unable to build this home, then you may exchange the plans and the materials list towards the price of a new set of plans (see order info pages for plan exchange policy). The **Itemized Zip-Quote** and the **Bottom Line Zip-Quote** are NOT returnable. The price of the initial **Bottom Line Zip-Quote** order can be credited towards the purchase of an **Itemized Zip-Quote** order only. Additional **Bottom Line Zip-Quote** orders, within the same order can not be credited. Please call our Customer Service Department for more information.

Itemized Zip-Quote is available for plans where you see this symbol.

Bottom Line Zip-Quote is available for all plans under 4,000 square feet. **BL**

SOME MORE INFORMATION

Itemized and Bottom Line Zip-Quotes give you approximated costs for constructing the particular house in your area. These costs are not exact and are only intended to be used as a preliminary estimate to help determine the affordability of a new home and/or as a guide to evaluate the general competitiveness of actual price quotes obtained through local suppliers and contractors. However, Zip-Quote cost figures should never be relied upon as the only source of information in either case. Land, sewer systems, site work, landscaping and other expenses are not included in our building cost figures. Garlinghouse and Marshall & Swift L.P. can not guarantee any level of data accuracy or correctness in a Zip-Quote and disclaim all liability for loss with respect to the same, in excess of the original purchase price of the Zip-Quote product. All Zip-Quote calculations are based upon the actual blueprints and do not reflect any differences or options that may be shown on the published house renderings, floor plans, or photographs.

IMPORTANT INFORMATION TO READ BEFORE YOU PLACE YOUR ORDER

How Many Sets Of Plans Will You Need?

The Standard 8-Set Construction Package

Our experience shows that you'll speed every step of construction and avoid costly building errors by ordering enough sets to go around. Each tradesperson wants a set — the general contractor and all subcontractors; foundation, electrical, plumbing, heating/air conditioning and framers. Don't forget your lending institution, building department and, of course, a set for yourself. * Recommended For Construction *

The Minimum 4-Set Construction Package

If you're comfortable with arduous follow-up, this package can save you a few dollars by giving you the option of passing down plan sets as work progresses. You might have enough copies to go around if work goes exactly as scheduled and no plans are lost or damaged by subcontractors. But for only $60 more, the 8-set package eliminates these worries. * Recommended For Bidding *

The Single Study Set

We offer this set so you can study the blueprints to plan your dream home in detail. They are stamped "study set only-not for construction", and you cannot build a home from them. In pursuant to copyright laws, it is _illegal_ to reproduce any blueprint.

An Important Note About Building Code Requirements:

All plans are drawn to conform to one or more of the industry's major national building standards. However, due to the variety of local building regulations, your plan may need to be modified to comply with local requirements — snow loads, energy loads, seismic zones, etc. Do check them fully and consult your local building officials.

A few states require that all building plans used be drawn by an architect registered in that state. While having your plans reviewed and stamped by such an architect may be prudent, laws requiring non-conforming plans like ours to be completely redrawn forces you to unnecessarily pay very large fees. If your state has such a law, we strongly recommend you contact your state representative to protest.

The rendering, floor plans, and technical information contained within publication are not guaranteed to be totally accurate. Consequently, no information from this publication should be used either as a guide to construct a home or for estimating the cost of building a home. Complete blueprints must be purchased for such purposes.

the Garlinghouse company

ORDER TOLL FREE — 1-800-235-5700
Monday-Friday 8:00 a.m. to 8:00 p.m. Eastern Time
or FAX your Credit Card order to 1-860-659-5692
All foreign residents call 1-800-659-5667

Please have ready: 1. Your credit card number   2. The plan number   3. The order code number ⇨ *CHP26*

Garlinghouse 2002 Blueprint Price Code Schedule   *Additional sets with original order $50*

	1 Set	4 Sets	8 Sets	Vellums	ML	Itemized ZIP Quote
A	$345	$385	$435	$525	$60	$50
B	$375	$415	$465	$555	$60	$50
C	$410	$450	$500	$590	$60	$50
D	$450	$490	$540	$630	$60	$50
E	$495	$535	$585	$675	$70	$60
F	$545	$585	$635	$725	$70	$60
G	$595	$635	$685	$775	$70	$60
H	$640	$680	$730	$820	$70	$60
I	$685	$725	$775	$865	$80	$70
J	$725	$765	$815	$905	$80	$70
K	$765	$805	$855	$945	$80	$70
L	$800	$840	$890	$980	$80	$70

BEST PLAN VALUE IN THE INDUSTRY!

Shipping — (Plans 1-59999)

	1-3 Sets	4-6 Sets	7+ & Vellums
Standard Delivery (UPS 2-Day)	$25.00	$30.00	$35.00
Overnight Delivery	$35.00	$40.00	$45.00

Shipping — (Plans 60000-99999)

	1-3 Sets	4-6 Sets	7+ & Vellums
Ground Delivery (7-10 Days)	$15.00	$20.00	$25.00
Express Delivery (3-5 Days)	$20.00	$25.00	$30.00

International Shipping & Handling

	1-3 Sets	4-6 Sets	7+ & Vellums
Regular Delivery Canada (7-10 Days)	$25.00	$30.00	$35.00
Express Delivery Canada (5-6 Days)	$40.00	$45.00	$50.00
Overseas Delivery Airmail (2-3 Weeks)	$50.00	$60.00	$65.00

ur Reorder and Exchange Policies:

If you find after your initial purchase that you require additional sets of plans you may purchase them from us at special reorder ces (please call for pricing details) provided that you reorder within 6 months of your original order date. There is a $28 reorder pro- ssing fee that is charged on all reorders. For more information on reordering plans please contact our Customer Service Department.

Your plans are custom printed especially for you once you place your order. For that reason we cannot accept any returns.

f for some reason you find that the plan you have purchased from us does not meet your needs, then you may exchange that plan for other plan in our collection. We allow you sixty days from your original invoice date to make an exchange. At the time of the exchange will be charged a processing fee of 20% of the total amount of your original order plus the difference in price between the plans (if licable) plus the cost to ship the new plans to you. Call our Customer Service Department for more information. Please Note: roducible vellums can only be exchanged if they are unopened.

portant Shipping Information

Please refer to the shipping charts on the order form for service availability for your specific plan number. Our delivery service must e a street address or Rural Route Box number — never a post office box. (PLEASE NOTE: Supplying a P.O. Box number *only* will y the shipping of your order.) Use a work address if no one is home during the day.

Orders being shipped to APO or FPO must go via First Class Mail.

For our International Customers, only Certified bank checks and money orders are accepted and must be payable in U.S. currency. speed, we ship international orders Air Parcel Post. Please refer to the chart for the correct shipping cost.

Thank you.

INDEXINDEXINDEX

CRE▲TIVE HOMEOWNER®

How-To Books for...

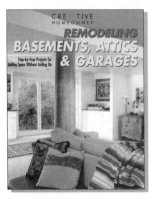

REMODELING BASEMENTS, ATTICS & GARAGES

Cramped for space? This book shows you how to find space you may not know you had and convert it into useful living areas. 40 colorful photographs and 530 full-color drawings.

BOOK #: 277680   192pp.   8½"x10⅞"

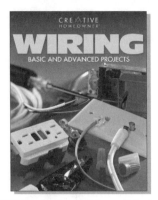

WIRING: Basic and Advanced Projects
(Conforms to latest National Electrical Code)

Included are 350 large, clear, full-color illustrations and no-nonsense step-by-step instructions. Shows how to replace receptacles and switches; repair a lamp; install ceiling and attic fans; and more.

BOOK #: 277049   256pp.   8½"x10⅞"

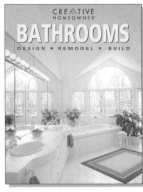

BATHROOMS: Design, Remodel, Build

Shows how to plan, construct, and finish a bathroom. Remodel floors; rebuild walls and ceilings; and install windows, skylights, and plumbing fixtures. Specific tools and materials are given for each project. Includes 90 color photos and 470 color illustrations.

BOOK #: 277053   192pp.   8½"x10⅞"

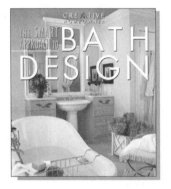

The Smart Approach to BATH DESIGN

Everything you need to know about designing a bathroom like a professional is explained in *this book*. Creative solutions and practical advice about space, the latest in fixtures and fittings, and safety features accompany over 150 photographs.

BOOK #: 287225   176pp.   9"x10"

BUILD A KIDS' PLAY YARD

Here are detailed plans and step-by-step instructions for building the play structures that kids love most: swing set, monkey bars, balance beam, playhouse, teeter-totter, sandboxes, kid-sized picnic table, and a play tower that supports a slide. 200 color photographs and illustrations.

BOOK #: 277662   144 pp.   8½"x10⅞"

CABINETS & BUILT-INS

26 custom cabinetry projects are included for every room in the house, from kitchen cabinets to a bedroom wall unit, a bunk bed, computer workstation, and more. Also included are chapters on tools, techniques, finishing, and materials.

BOOK #: 277079   160 pp.   8½"x10⅞"

DECKS: Planning, Designing, Building

With this book, even the novice builder can build a deck that perfectly fits his yard. The step-by-step instructions lead the reader from laying out footings to adding railings. Includes three deck projects, 500 color drawings, and photographs.

BOOK #: 277162   192pp.   8½"x10⅞"

FURNITURE REPAIR & REFINISHING

From structural repairs to restoring older finishes or entirely refinishing furniture: a hands-on step-by-step approach to furniture repair and restoration. More than 430 color photographs and 60 full-color drawings.

BOOK #: 277335   240pp.   8½"x10⅞"

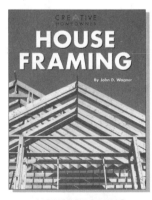

HOUSE FRAMING

Written for those with beginning to intermediate building skills, this book is designed to walk you through the framing basics, from assembling simple partitions to cutting compound angles on dormer rafters. More than 400 full-color drawings.

BOOK #: 277655   240pp.   8½"x10⅞"